THE Family Tree Problem Solver

Proven methods for scaling the inevitable brick wall

Marsha Hoffman Rising

FAMILY TREE BOOKS
CINCINNATI, OHIO
www.familytreemagazine.com/store

 Published by Family Tree Books, an imprint of F+W Publications, Inc., 4700 East Galbraith Road, Cincinnati, Ohio 45236. (800) 289-0963. First edition.

Other fine Family Tree Books are available from your local bookstore or on our Web site at www.familytreemagazine.com.

10 09 08 07 7 6 5 4

Library of Congress Cataloging-in-Publication Data

Rising, Marsha Hoffman
Family tree problem solver / Marsha Hoffman Rising—1st ed.
p. cm.
Includes bibliographical references and index.
ISBN 13: 978-1-55870-685-9 (pbk. : alk. paper)
ISBN 10: 1-55870-685-2 (pbk. : alk. paper)
1. Genealogy. 2. United States—Genealogy—Handbooks, manuals, etc. I. Title.
CS14.R57 2005
929'.1'072073—dc22 2004058108
CIP

Editor: Sharon DeBartolo Carmack, CG
Associate editor: Erin Nevius
Production coordinator: Robin Richie
Assistant production coordinator: Logan Cummins
Interior designer: Sandy Conopeotis Kent
Cover design: Nick Gliebe, Design Matters
Icon designer: Cindy Beckmeyer

DEDICATED TO
Elizabeth Shown Mills, teacher par excellence
and Sandra Hargreaves Luebking,
who encouraged me to teach genealogy

About the Author

Marsha Hoffman Rising CG, FASG, is a professional genealogist who specializes in problem-solving in the nineteenth century, especially in the upper South. She has been a certified genealogist since 1992 and is currently serving as vice president of the American Society of Genealogists. She is the vice president of the National Genealogical Society and has served on the boards of the Association of Professional Genealogists, the Board for Certification of Genealogists, the New England Historic Genealogical Society, and as president of the Federation of Genealogical Societies and the Genealogical Speaker's Guild.

Known for her problem-solving lectures, she began teaching practical and effective methods for solving genealogical problems in 1981. She has lectured at most national conferences of the National Genealogical Society and the Federation of Genealogical Societies. She taught the Advanced Methodology class at the Institute of Historical Genealogical Research at Samford University in Birmingham, Alabama, from 1987–1995.

During her twenty-five year professional career in genealogy, she has received the National Genealogical Society Award of Merit (1989), been elected a Fellow of the Utah Genealogical Society (1990), received the FGS George E. Williams Award (1991), the National Genealogical Society Award of Excellence (1992), and the FGS Malcolm H. Stern Humanitarian Award (1999).

She is the author of numerous articles published in *The American Genealogist, Ozar'kin,* and the *National Genealogical Society Quarterly.*

Foreword

In 1980, when the concept of major annual genealogical conferences emerged, virtually all genealogical instruction, whether disseminated through lectures, classes, or printed form, concentrated on the description of source material and how to find it. Virtually nothing existed in the area that we now refer to as genealogical methodology.

A movement began soon after 1980 among genealogical educators to alter that state of affairs. Marsha Hoffman Rising has been one of the leaders in that movement, and this volume represents the distillation of more than twenty years of her experience in genealogical research and the teaching of genealogical methodology.

Marsha approaches her task with a blend of topical chapters. In the first variety, she examines a particular class of records, such as deeds, probates, censuses, and vital records. She does not, however, take the traditional path of telling us where and how to find these records. Rather, she explains how these records, once collected, may be employed in the solution of our genealogical problems. She does this by investigating the meaning of the documents, and, of particular importance, the relative reliability or unreliability of the records.

The author's second type of chapter explores a number of broad themes in problem-solving. She takes up such topics as distinguishing people of the same name and the study of the context within which a given ancestor lived, from the immediate family to the extended family to the larger community. She concludes with a chapter on the analysis of evidence, in which she ties together all the lessons of the preceding chapters and promulgates "Rising's Reminders" as an encapsulation of her approach to genealogy.

Marsha has broader interests and experience than most genealogists, beginning first with her own ancestry, which includes heavy doses of New England and German. For the last fifteen years she has concentrated on her Ozarks Migration Project, which has required that she spend thousands of hours researching not only in the early records of Missouri, but in the many states of origin of the early Ozarks settlers, with special emphasis on Kentucky, Tennessee, and North Carolina.

One of the strongest features of this book is the high density of specific examples that amply and accurately demonstrate the broader points the author is making. Because of her research background, these examples are heavily weighted toward discoveries made and lessons learned in her Ozarks work, with a liberal seasoning of New England and German examples.

This emphasis on examples garnered from a limited time and place should not deter those with research interests in other states or other centuries from delving deeply into Marsha's exposition. She has carefully chosen the examples she presents so that they will demonstrate the more general principles that she wishes to pass on to the reader. Social customs, legal procedures, and the details of record keeping may vary from time to time and place to place, but the principles of interpretation and analysis presented by the author are applicable to all types of genealogical problems. Any researcher interested in improving his or her genealogical skills will benefit greatly from studying the examples included here and determining how they apply to any problem of interest. This volume is an important and welcome addition to the short shelf of books dedicated to the subject of genealogical methodology.

—Robert Charles Anderson, FASG

Table of Contents

Introduction

I remember as if it were yesterday the day I became hooked on genealogy twenty-five years ago. My husband and I were visiting my maternal relatives in Kansas, and he urged me to seize the opportunity and learn something about my family history. We took my Aunt Margaret to the family cemetery and asked her to point out various tombstones and to tell us how the people buried there were related to one another. She told me that Christian Deschner, my maternal great-grandfather, had been an only child. When we returned to the farmhouse for the colossal old-fashioned meal that awaited us, I tried to confirm what Aunt Margaret had told me. The family agreed: Chris Deschner had been an only child.

The next day my husband and I visited the office of the local newspaper. The staff kindly admitted me to the "morgue" where the old bound newspapers were kept. The dim light and the dust that rose as we opened each volume only made the search more intriguing. We found several obituaries that I dictated into my tape recorder, and at last we came upon the one for Christian Deschner. "His funeral was attended by many friends and relatives, including his sister from Denver, Colorado." A sister! Who was she? Why did none of my family know about her? I was hooked, and have been addicted to solving genealogical problems ever since.

I gave my first lecture on problem-solving in 1984 at the Federation of Genealogical Societies Conference in Denver, Colorado. I continue to be challenged by the fun, frustrations, and rewards of genealogy. During this quarter-century I have discovered many techniques, tools, and methods for solving problems. I have lectured to thousands over that time period, and now the time has come to put my strategies in print. I hope this book will reach the large number of genealogists who encounter genealogical riddles, love the search, and are eager to solve the dilemmas. It is not always easy—genealogy is time-consuming, and solving difficult problems is even more so.

This book is not intended for those who are just beginning their genealogical research. If you find too many words, phrases, or acronyms with which you are not familiar, you may want to read one of the many genealogical reference books that are readily available, such as *The Genealogist's*

Companion & Sourcebook by Emily Anne Croom (Cincinnati: Betterway Books, 2003). Relatively few genealogy books are intended for the advanced researcher, as this one is.

Instead, this book is intended to give each reader new ideas for tackling those knotty problems that have been sitting on the backburner of the research schedule for months or even years. I have solved dozens of problems using these techniques and hope you will find them useful as well.

The First Step: Analyzing the Problem and Planning a Strategy for Success

We are not afraid to follow truth wherever it may lead, nor to tolerate any error so long as reason is left free to combat it.
—Thomas Jefferson

Family researchers have caught "genealogy fever" and are serious about their work to seek the truth, not legends, about family origins and their ancestor's lives. They want to do their research properly, solve the dead ends, and overcome the brick walls that have blocked others while tracing family lines. They know that the search for the truth could reveal skeletons, destroy beloved family traditions, or call into question the research of others. Nevertheless, they seek the truth. This chapter will help those who want to begin that quest.

There are two basic ways of conducting your family history quest: searching and researching. **All successful genealogists use a combination of search and research as they pursue their studies.** However, rarely do they distinguish between the two and a vast difference exists. We are all aware of the enormous array of new sources becoming available for genealogists. The multitude of census and other public records on the Internet, the online family trees made available by myriad researchers, data on CD-ROMs, and publications that offer extensive query assistance provide many avenues for research. All of these make the task of searching an easier one. Many of these may indeed provide an easy solution to finding your ancestors.

Reminder

Searching can be a quick and painless path to a wealth of information. I once responded to a query in my local genealogical journal, *Ozar'kin*, thinking it might lead to answers regarding Daniel Hance, a man I was researching for whom I had little information. A fellow researcher answered with the proof of Daniel Hance's parentage and his marriage in Jefferson County, Tennessee. In finding this bit of information, I had conducted no *research*. Someone else had done the work—I had only *searched*.

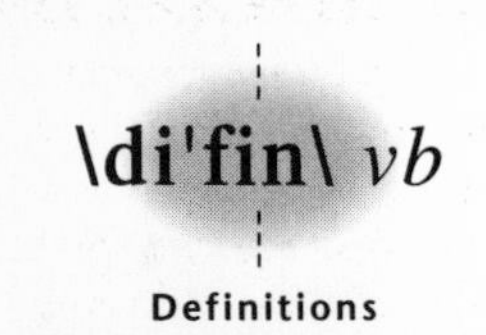

Definitions

The International Genealogical Index is a product of the Family History Library in Salt Lake City, Utah, that includes both extractions from vital records and patron submissions from all over the world. It includes baptisms, marriages, and deaths. It can be accessed on the Web through FamilySearch.com, at the Family History Library, or one of the many Family History Centers throughout the country.

On the other hand, a search can also sometimes get answers that research can't. I did research for the origins of Littleberry Hendrick. I tried all the methods I learned at conferences and seminars, followed many of the techniques I will discuss later in this chapter, and spent many hours creating and testing theories. Nothing worked. I knew a lot about Littleberry from 1833 until his death in 1862, but not where he came from. Then, the Family History Library updated the International Genealogical Index (known as the IGI). On a whim I decided to try searching for Littleberry again, and lo and behold, up popped his marriage record in Allen County, Kentucky! It was difficult to suppress a shout of triumph. The long-sought answer to my question was finally revealed through a *search*—not *research*. If we are serious researchers, we must become more precise in defining the difference between a search and research.

RESEARCH STEPS

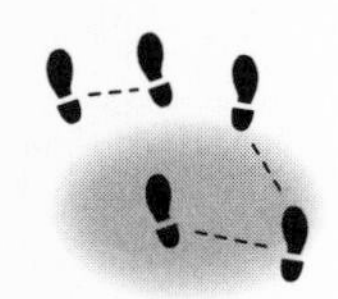

Step By Step

Research is a diligent and systematic inquiry into a problem. It includes the following prescribed methods: developing a hypothesis, surveying the existing literature and information, gathering evidence, evaluating the evidence, and reaching a conclusion. Here are steps you need to take in problem-solving research.

1. Define the problem.
2. Survey existing material, including published genealogies, the Periodical Source Index, online family trees, genealogical forums, and message boards.
3. Analyze the information you obtain for reliability, citations, and credibility. If there is no documentation for the data presented, contact the individual who submitted it. If that individual is not able to supply evidence, consider the material hearsay and essentially worthless. When reviewing the material you have gathered and what you have obtained from family members and correspondents, consider what is known, what is not known, and what information has been assumed but not verified.
4. Develop a strategy. One of the most successful strategies is the "neighborhood concept" or "cluster genealogy," a research tactic in which you study your ancestor's siblings, friends, and neighbors in order to learn more about your ancestor. This strategy will be discussed in detail in this chapter and throughout the book.

5. Gather data. You will need a thorough knowledge of the sources of the time period, the exact geographical location of the individuals (have you ever noticed how often this vital information is lacking among the various lineages published online?), the laws of the local, state, and federal government in power at the time, and the various public and private records that may have been created during the period you are researching. A good researcher always ventures beyond the standard genealogical publications and sources to using such nontraditional records as manuscripts and historical records.
6. Evaluate the information obtained. This crucial step deserves significant thought and attention. The value of the data contained in the record will be lost if the data is analyzed superficially or incorrectly. Inadequate analysis may result in overlooking or misinterpreting important information, leading to inaccurate conclusions or dead ends. This step is so important that I have devoted chapter eleven to it.
7. Draw conclusions and form subsequent plans. Continue to implement these steps until the evidence is either conclusive or provides a strong enough argument that no other conceivable conclusion can be reached with the information that exists (see Figure 1-1 on page 6).

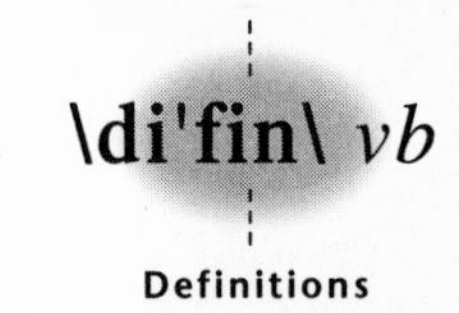

The Periodical Source Index, produced by the Allen County Public Library in Ft. Wayne, Indiana, indexes family information from a wide variety of genealogical magazines and journals that have been published in the nineteenth century. It's organized by name, location, and subject. It is available on CD-ROM by purchase from Ancestry.com or the library's Web site, <www.acpl.lib.in.us>.

STEPS FOR SOLVING GENEALOGICAL PROBLEMS

STEP ONE: Present a clear and reasoned account of the problem under study. The kinds of problems in genealogy that require a systematic approach to research include:

- Beginning research on a family line not previously investigated. This includes researching a family that has not had anything published on it, a family for which there are published genealogies but they have poor documentation, or a family for which no current material exists.
- Correcting a tradition, belief, or material published in a pedigree or family sketch. Many genealogical errors have been in print for years, and it often takes new research and a creative approach to find the correct answers.
- Solving a specific identity problem for which a previous search or research has proved unsuccessful. One of the most important jobs of scholarly genealogical publications is to publish new solutions to old problems. As an example, one of the most exciting finds in recent years has been the heretofore unknown maiden name of *Mayflower* passenger Richard Warren.

Figure 1-1
Circle graph illustrating the steps in implementing a research strategy.

When defining the problem, determine what you already know. This means a careful analysis of every known and documented fact about the individual or family. This does not mean that you know only when they were born, who and when they married, and when they died. It means you pinpoint exactly where they lived, when they moved there, how they earned a living, what they believed in, and what was happening around them. Was there a war, an economic depression, a land speculation boom, major migrations in or out of the area? Who were their friends and family? Who was their minister? Where were they buried? The more you know about the people you have definitely identified as your ancestors, the easier the rest of your task will become.

This is the time to assemble and record information you have gathered. Write a biographical sketch of the individual or family you have researched, placing the events of their lives in chronological order, including specific documented events. Countless genealogists who have gone through the process of writing down what they know about the subject of their genealogical problem and checking the documentation often find that the clue to solving the problem has been in their own papers all along. This is also the time to note what you don't know. This is a great help in directing further research, but it is remarkable how often this step is not included among researchers' notes. I usually have a separate page headed "Things I don't know, but would like to."

STEP TWO: Learn what others already know, or think they know.

This is the "search" step. If you are a careful and systematic researcher you will confirm what you have been told by others, whether in an informal family group sheet or a published work. If your experience is like mine, you will find that many times people cannot tell you how they know what they think they know. This, of course, makes your task harder—you must verify the information to make sure it's not just a family legend. It's amazing how many people are not the slightest bit interested in documentation until they need it from someone else.

Naturally you don't want to repeat work that someone else has done, especially if it was done well. The best finds are good, well-documented genealogies and family articles published in scholarly journals. They may not be easy to locate for a particular family, but they are worth the effort if you find that a good scholar has worked on your family. "Examples of 'Search,' " below, gives you examples of where to look for this material, but always keep in mind that this is a search, not research.

EXAMPLES OF "SEARCH"

A genealogical search of existing dates and literature might consist of:

- Placing queries online or in genealogical magazines.
- Corresponding and communicating with other genealogists.
- Searching online databases such as the Family History Ancestral File, the International Genealogical Index, Ancestry's World Family Tree, the online Genealogical Forum, and other online family Web sites and family name databases.
- Searching census indexes, published on CD-ROM or online.
- Reading published genealogies and family articles.
- Examining the Periodical Source Index (known as PERSI) and then ordering pertinent articles to read.
- Using various other "arm-chair" searches in published literature for the region of your interest.

Some genealogists never move beyond this step—they are always looking for someone else who can provide the answers they seek. When they hit a brick wall, they just continue to look for someone who knows the answer rather than digging into the records themselves. They never become true researchers—they just search forever.

SEARCH AND RESEARCH

Search: "Seek data on James Caffey Jr. and his wife, Susannah. They resided in Morgan County, Missouri, in the 1840s. Where did they come from and where did they go?" I placed this query in *The Genealogical Helper*, November/December 1994. I received several answers, but none referred to the correct family.

Research: The Morgan County, Missouri, Deed Book 5:367 revealed that James Caffey and wife, Susan, of Camden County, Missouri, sold their right, title, and interest to land that had belonged to Nicholas Coffman, deceased, late of Morgan County. Nicholas Coffman was enumerated in Jefferson County, Tennessee, on the 1830 census, p. 282, as age fifty to sixty years. His household consisted of two females twenty to thirty and thus of marriageable age. James "Coffee" married 21 December 1832, Jefferson County, Tennessee, Susanna Coffman. No Caffey family was found in Jefferson County, but there were several in adjoining Grainger County. I was convinced I had found the geographic origin of James Caffey of the burned county of Camden, Missouri.

The research required a step-by-step process and called for moving beyond the primary records of the county of residence (burned Camden) to Morgan County, where the grantee lived. I then had to read Morgan County's deeds carefully and understand what terms such as "all right, title and interest" meant. From there it was a simple, logical procedure backwards.

STEP THREE: Decide what records to use.

Some records are likely to provide more information about the problem than others, so it's wise to evaluate them before delving into your research. You will have to decide priority, availability, and ease of use based on your access to the records you need and how well they have been preserved. We all hope that our problem can be solved by the primary records that genealogists most commonly use. These include census records, family Bible records, vital records, wills, obituaries, probate files, pension applications, and other original or microfilmed records likely to provide genealogical information. We check the more recent census records for places of birth and relationships. We comb attics and basements, and then contact cousins, hoping for family Bible records. We order birth and death certificates if the family of interest was living in the twentieth century. We hope for detailed obituaries. As our expertise increases, we learn to check wills, probate administration applications, and the pension files of former soldiers—all of which can reveal interesting family details. When we gain more expertise, we learn to look for the division of land among heirs, often called land partitions.

Many people, unfortunately, quit when the easily accessible records do not yield results. Sometimes they don't know where else to search or how to better use the data they have already found. **Many records containing valuable information are harder to find—they aren't indexed and are more likely to yield indirect evidence.** These records include diaries, circuit court records, county order books, tax records, federal land records, newspaper accounts, county court records (sometimes called quarterly sessions records), and deeds that appear to be only simple land transfers but have deeper implications if analyzed more carefully.

Reminder

Gathering enough data to point to a possible conclusion may be a relatively short undertaking or it can take years. Often it can be frustrating and time-consuming, depending on the individual and family involved, their propensity for creating records, the time period in which you are working, and the locale. Some geographic areas have preserved many old records; others are literally a wasteland.

STEP FOUR: Analysis is the most crucial step in the research process.
The data and records you have gathered need to be analyzed both separately and as a group. Often when the records gathered over a long period of time are analyzed carefully, new answers, perspectives, and clues emerge.

As you gather records for the specific family or individual you are researching, ask the following questions:

a. What does the record add to what I already know? Does it support or contradict information I have already found?

b. Other than my ancestor, who else was involved in creating or witnessing the record? Who was mentioned in it? Are they likely to be "official" participants or associates of my ancestor? Have these individuals appeared in any other records my ancestor created?

c. Would other records have been created either before or after this one to complete its purpose? Often we find a record that generated other documents, but we fail to follow the trail the record reveals. For instance, a quitclaim deed may record an individual or couple who are selling their right, claim, and interest in a parcel of land. The quitclaim may not tell how the interest in the land was acquired. Was it an inheritance or a part of an inheritance? What part of the total share of the inheritance did the individual possess? Other deeds made to complete the process of clearing the title may answer those exact questions.

For instance, if you were researching the Zumwalt family in Franklin County, Missouri, checking deeds would be very helpful. You would discover that on 1 January 1833, John Zumwalt and his wife, Mary, sold to William Coshow their right, interest, and claim to land they had inherited from John's father, George Zumwalt.[1] That might be all you would look for if you descended from John, but what if you want to learn about other descendants of George and no other Zumwalts are mentioned? You might check the index for the other name in the deed: William Coshow. This investigation would lead you to a deed made in 1841 in which William Coshow and wife, Elizabeth, sold to George C. Zumwalt their "right, title and interest, it being a one undivided seventh part which descended to John Zumwalt as an heir and was then sold to William Coshow."[2] This leads to another suggestion when using deeds. Many deeds are recorded at the same time by the grantors, and it is wise to look for several pages on either side of the deed of interest. In this case, you would find two more pertinent documents on the page preceding and the one immediately after: David Crow and his wife, Elizabeth, sold to George C. Zumwalt their one-seventh part of the estate of George Zumwalt Sr., deceased, that descended to Elizabeth as one of the heirs; and John Keller and his wife, Nancy, sold to George C. Zumwalt all right, title, and interest which descended to Nancy as one of the heirs of George Zumwalt, deceased.[3] You now know of at least three heirs: John Zumwalt, Elizabeth Crow, and Nancy Keller—and probably a fourth, George C. Zumwalt. At this point, I would try to locate additional deeds by checking the grantee index for the person who is purchasing the property rights of the individual (or individuals), in this case George C. or George Zumwalt. Incidentally, neither the Keller nor Crow marriages were recorded in Franklin County, where the deeds were made. One was not recorded at all. The only record for the Keller marriage was the above deed.

d. Are there clues recorded here that are not directly related to this record but could lead to additional records or other people to be studied?

Let's look at two case studies that were solved using the steps above and asking the questions I have outlined.

THE SEARCH FOR LEMUEL BLANTON

When I started looking for the origins of Lemuel Blanton, the prospects for finding him looked dim because I knew only two things about him.

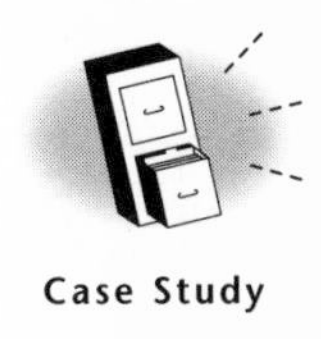

Case Study

1. Lemuel Blanton purchased forty acres in NE1/4 of NE1/4 section 18 township 32 range 23 west of the 5th Principal Meridian.[4] This area became Polk County, Missouri, in 1835.
2. Lemuel Blanton married Mary Ann Rogers 8 November 1831 in Crawford County, Missouri. They were married by John P. Campbell of Campbell township.[5] This area became Greene County in 1833 and Lemuel Blanton was on the first tax list taken that year.[6] No one named Rogers was listed.

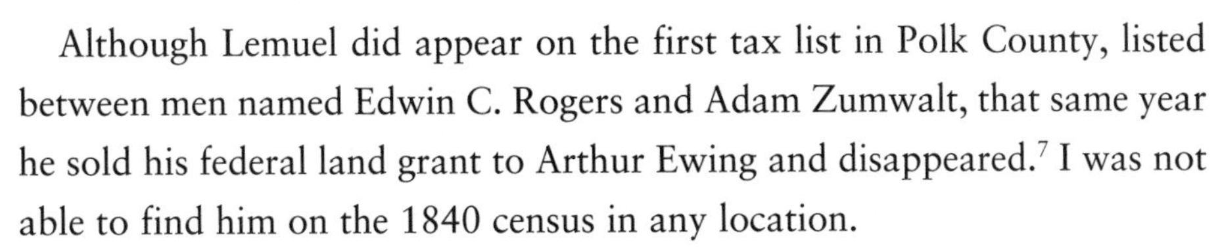

Although Lemuel did appear on the first tax list in Polk County, listed between men named Edwin C. Rogers and Adam Zumwalt, that same year he sold his federal land grant to Arthur Ewing and disappeared.[7] I was not able to find him on the 1840 census in any location.

I did find a man named Ledwell D. Blanton listed as head of household on the 1830 census in Crawford County, Missouri.[8] There were several males twenty to thirty years old in this household, and I wondered if one might have been Lemuel. I spent a good deal of time tracking this Ledwell back to his origins and marriage to Nancy Davis in Hopkins County, Kentucky.[9] There was nary a sign of Lemuel anywhere along the path.

Next I decided to investigate the man to whom Lemuel sold his land, Arthur Ewing, and also searched for the name Rogers, the maiden name of Lemuel's wife. To determine Lemuel's neighbors in what became Polk County, I had to look at a township-range map. The most helpful township-range maps use a form that not only shows adjoining sections, but the sections adjoining in other townships and ranges as well (see Figure 1-2 on page 12).

Lemuel's land was in the northeast corner of 18, so I examined neighbors in sections 7 and 8 as well as those in section 17. Just one mile west is section 13 township 32 and a new range—24 instead of 23. By looking at other federal land entries, this investigation led to fifteen immediate neighbors. This is the list in alphabetical order:

Figure 1-2
Township-range map.

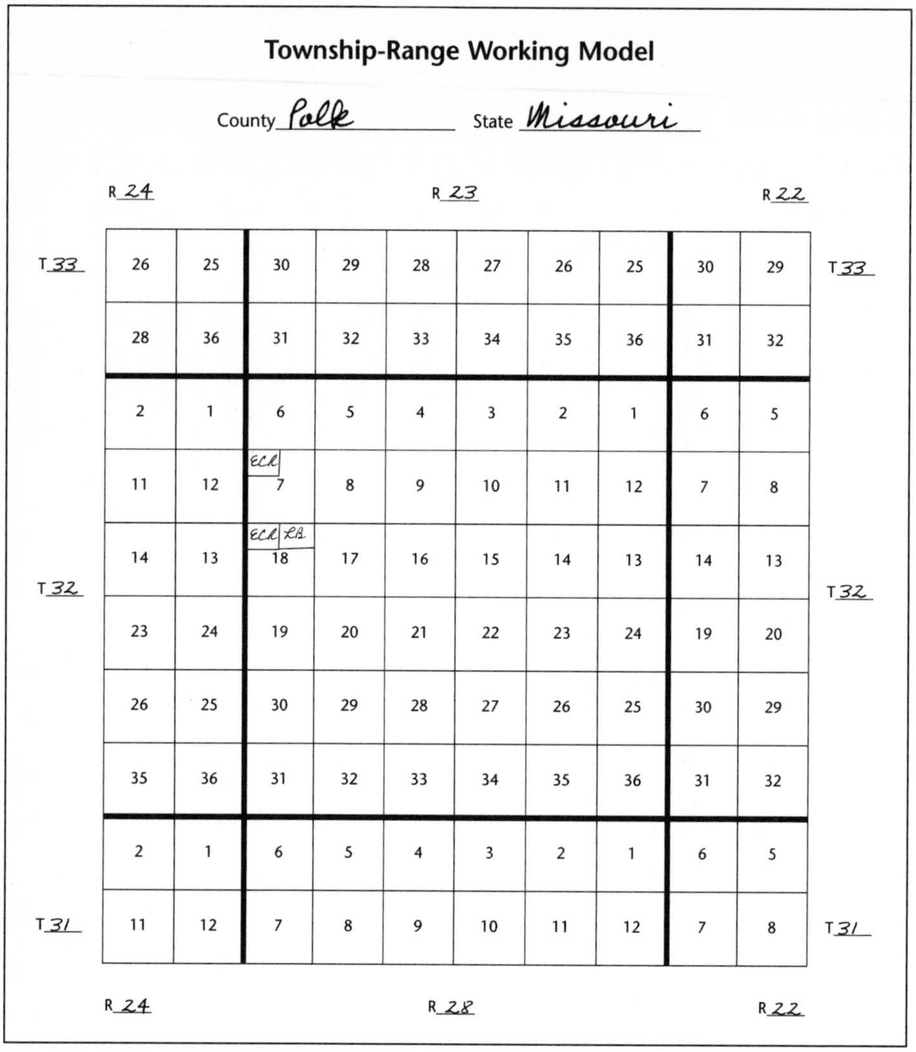

Township-Range Working Model

County *Polk* State *Missouri*

R *24* R *23* R *22*

Township										
T *33*	26	25	30	29	28	27	26	25	30	29
	28	36	31	32	33	34	35	36	31	32
	2	1	6	5	4	3	2	1	6	5
	11	12	ECR 7	8	9	10	11	12	7	8
	14	13	ECR LB 18	17	16	15	14	13	14	13
T *32*	23	24	19	20	21	22	23	24	19	20
	26	25	30	29	28	27	26	25	30	29
	35	36	31	32	33	34	35	36	31	32
	2	1	6	5	4	3	2	1	6	5
T *31*	11	12	7	8	9	10	11	12	7	8

R *24* R *28* R *22*

James Boone	James Mitchell	Henry A.H. Russell
Samuel H. Bunch	Morris Mitchell	Jesse Scroggins
Michael N. Crow	Morris Mitchell Jr.	William Stevens
Abraham Foley	Morris R. Mitchell	William Thompson
Reuben M. Hill	Edwin C. Rogers	Samuel Tindell

I started with the obvious man—Edwin C. Rogers. He bought a parcel that adjoined Lemuel's and also sold it to Arthur Ewing. The last record Rogers produced in Polk County was in May 1838, when he filed a claim against the estate of Henry A.H. Russell, another neighbor of Blanton and Rogers.[10] I traced Russell, and although I found his origins, no one named Rogers or Blanton appeared in his earlier records.

I checked the 1850 census indexes for several states that were likely outward migration points for Missouri residents. Edwin C. Rogers and Lemuel

Blanton surfaced again as neighbors in Fannin County, Texas (see Figure 1-3 below). Lemuel's land entry there stated that he had arrived there in December 1837 as a married man with a family. Edwin C. Rogers affirmed that he had arrived at the same time, as a single man. A man named Joseph D. Rogers also arrived at that time and purchased land next to the other two.[11]

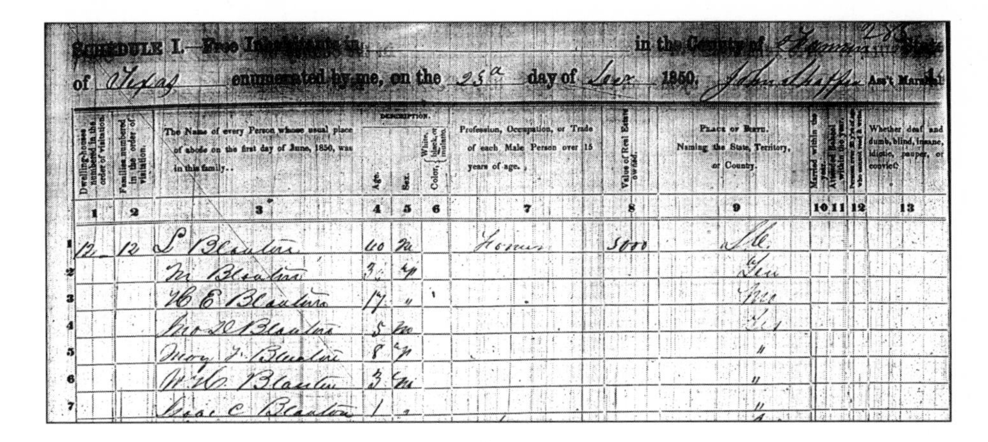
SCHEDULE I.—Free Inhabitants in [illegible] in the County of Fannin State of Texas enumerated by me, on the 25th day of Sept 1850. [illegible] Ass't Marshal.

Dwelling	Family	Name	Age	Sex	Color	Profession	Value of Real Estate	Place of Birth
12	12	L Blanton	40	M		Farmer	500	N.C.
		M Blanton	3[illegible]	F				Ten
		H E Blanton	17	"				Mo
		Jno W Blanton	5	M				Tex
		Mary J Blanton	8	F				"
		W H Blanton	3	M				"
		[illegible] C Blanton	1	"				"

Figure 1-3
1850 census, Fannin County, Texas.

The 1860 census (see Figure 1-4 below) gave more information but confused the situation. Lemuel's wife was now Martha instead of Mary Ann. In addition, the only Blanton tombstone inscription I could find in Fannin County was for Martha Blanton, born 18 January 1816 (death date gone from the stone). This matched the census ages for the woman in both 1850 and 1860. No marriage records for Lemuel Blanton surfaced in Fannin County.

I decided to check for probate records. Joseph D. Rogers left a will in

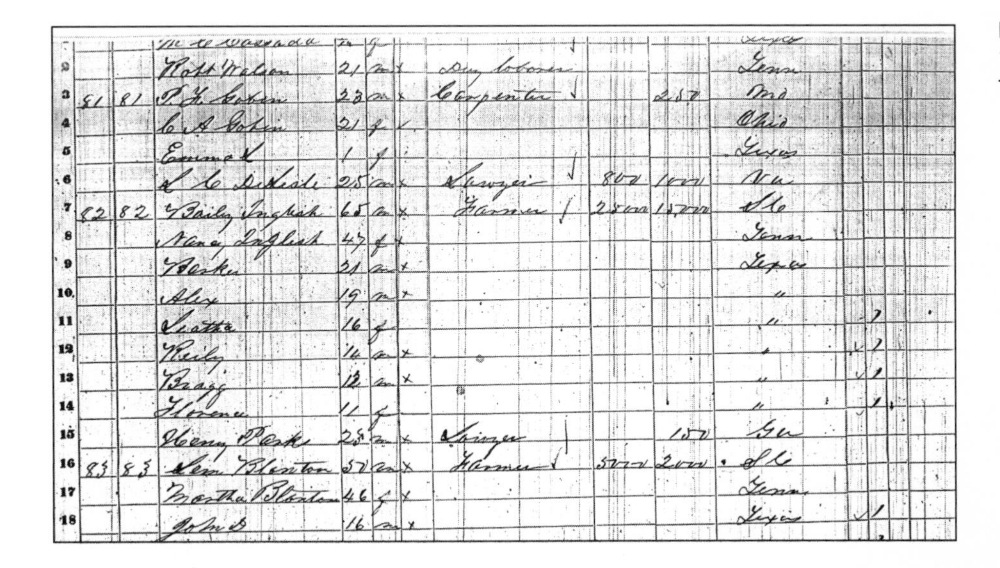

Line	Dwelling	Family	Name	Age	Sex	Occupation	Real Estate	Personal Estate	Birthplace
2			Robt Wilson	21	m	[illegible]			Tenn
3	81	81	P. F. Cohen	23	m	Carpenter		250	Md
4			C A Cohen	21	f				Ohio
5			Emma L	1	f				Texas
6			L C DeLisle	25	m	Lawyer	800	1000	Va
7	82	82	Bailey English	65	m	Farmer	2500	1500	N.C.
8			Nancy English	47	f				Tenn
9			[illegible]	21	m				Texas
10			Alex	19	m				"
11			Martha	16	f				"
12			Reily	14	m				"
13			Bragg	12	m				"
14			Florence	11	f				"
15			Henry Park	25	m	[illegible]		150	Ga
16	83	83	Lem Blanton	50	m	Farmer	5000	2000	N.C.
17			Martha Blanton	46	f				Tenn
18			John B	16	m				Texas

Figure 1-4
1860 census, Fannin County, Texas.

1842, naming sons Joseph J. Rogers and Edwin C. Rogers, but no daughter named Blanton. Lemuel Blanton, however, did serve as a witness to a codicil drawn at the same time, reconfirming some connection between the two families. I next looked for a combination of the surname Rogers and Blanton in Tennessee. Another dead end. Rogers was simply too common a surname and no one named Joseph Rogers was listed on the 1830 census index in Tennessee. Dead end.

We need to more carefully analyze what we know so far:

1. Lemuel Blanton's wife was Mary Ann Rogers in 1831 in Missouri.
2. One of the children living in the home in 1850 in Texas was born in Missouri, and she was the eldest, born about 1833, so the Texas and Missouri family was linked.
3. There is an age gap between the second and third child on the 1850 census. Perhaps there was a second marriage. Perhaps the new wife was a Britton or Stephenson, the other surnames in the 1850 household.
4. There is little doubt that the Edwin and Joseph Rogers and the Blanton families were connected, probably through Lemuel's marriage to Mary Ann Rogers, but neither were on the 1830 census in Missouri, nor could either be located before the marriage. We need to go to the next steps.

STEP FIVE: Look for a trail.

When you have analyzed each record concerning or involving the ancestor you are researching, you are likely to see a pattern of behavior, clues to other places or records to search, and a recurrence of names to be tracked. We have a trail from Missouri to Texas, and we have a number of families that are connected, both in Missouri and Texas. We have two new surnames—*Stephenson* and *Britton*—to check. I did, but nothing helpful surfaced. I studied the Rogers family. I learned a lot, including the fact that in his later years, Edwin C. Rogers became a Christian mystic. But he never passed on any revelations to me about where he came from.

I had followed the steps, looking at all the records I could find, pursuing a trail of clues and recurrences of names and associates, eliminating some people while keeping others on the back burner. Nothing. It was time to return to Step One. I had to construct a new hypothesis, and that required examining what I already knew to see if I could locate new people and new records to pursue.

Remember, Step One is to determine what you already know. This means a careful analysis of every known and documented fact about the individual or family. What had I missed the first time? I looked again. There was one association I had not followed. In 1831 Lemuel and Mary Ann were married in Campbell Township by John P. Campbell. Lemuel was on the 1833 Greene County tax list. That means Lemuel and Mary Ann were living in Greene County, while Ledwell Blanton, although in what was Crawford County, was relatively far away (see Figure 1-5 below).

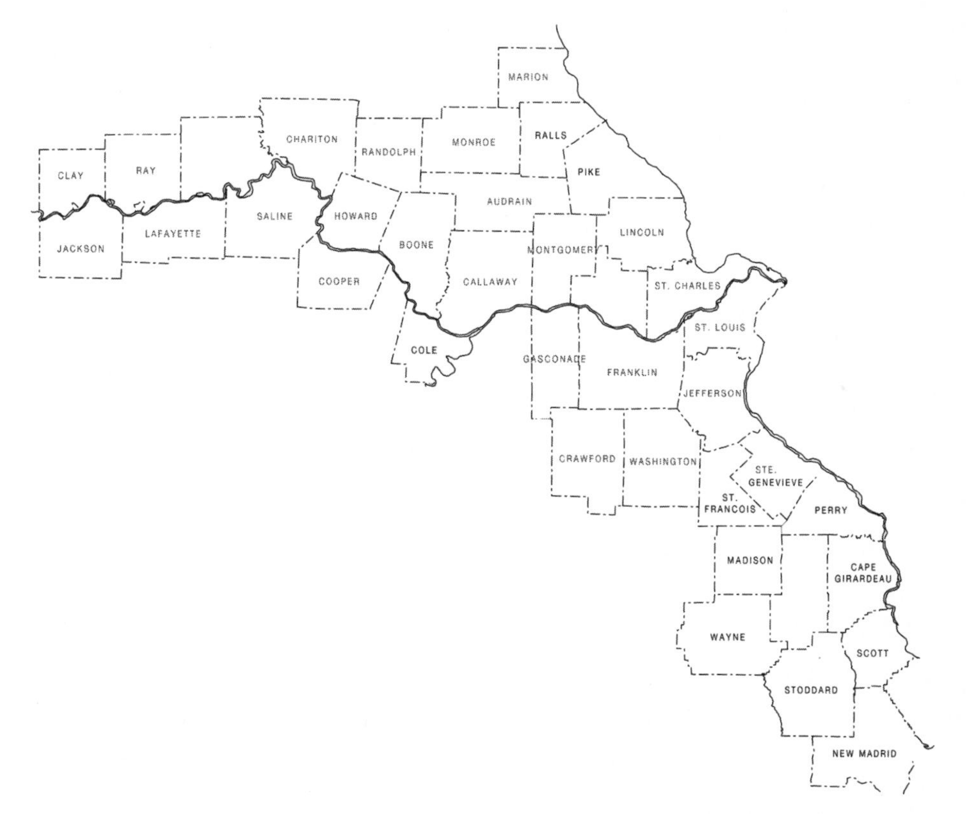

Figure 1-5
Map of southwest Missouri, 1831 county boundaries. Greene County was organized in 1833 and was about one hundred miles southwest of Crawford.

In 1831 there was only a small settlement of pioneers in the part of the state where John Polk Campbell and Lemuel Blanton were living. Most of these settlers were from Tennessee. They were ignored by the 1830 census taker and few records were available. Among the small number of families living there was a man named Joseph Rountree. Like John P. Campbell he was from Maury County, and he kept a diary about his journey from Tennessee to southwest Missouri. It was preserved in the manuscript division at the University of Missouri at Rolla. I sent for a copy.

> Entry from 15 February 1831: "It continued to snow this day and yesterday a little. This day most intolerable cold. We proceeded on traveling six or eight miles. We met Joseph H. Miller and Lemuel Blanton coming to meet us. Great joy."

Joseph Rountree knew the two men who had welcomed him. Therefore, they must have come from Maury County, Tennessee. Once I had that connection and a specific place to look, I could turn to the more traditional genealogical records for more pieces to the puzzle.

Lemuel Blanton was the son of John D. Blanton, who died in Maury County, Tennessee, leaving a number of children (note that Lemuel's eldest son was John D.). Lemuel had always retained his Tennessee ties, and after his first wife's death, he had returned to Tennessee to marry on 20 July 1839 in adjoining Williamson County, Martha Nicholson. Martha was the sister of the wife of William Blanton, Lemuel's brother. Williamson County was also the home of Lemuel's first wife's family, the Rogerses, and they were among the other families of the area that moved to southwest Missouri. Everything fell into place once the right clue surfaced. The connections were all as they should have been.

When you take the steps outlined in this problem-solving strategy, one of two circumstances arises. You either hit a dead end as I did with Lemuel in Texas, or the trail becomes wider, the clues more prevalent, the light brighter, and the direction clearer. You know you are on the right track.

If a dead end occurs, you return to step one and reexamine what you know. If no clear direction emerges, then basic knowledge and assumptions must be questioned, and perhaps a new hypothesis devised. Either the researcher must reanalyze the records already found for clues that were overlooked—as I did with the marriage location and justice of the peace—and/or obtain more pertinent information, as I was able to do with the Rountree diary.

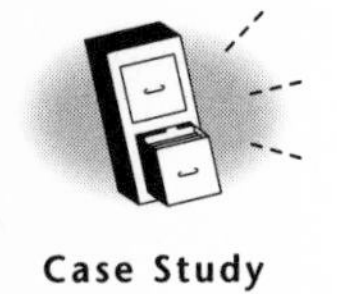

Case Study

THE PHILLIPS FAMILY OF BOONE COUNTY, MISSOURI

One more case will illustrate this strategy for solving genealogical problems before we move to specific types of problems in the later chapters. The Phillips family well illustrates a common downfall for so many genealogical researchers, even very experienced ones. Experienced genealogists research the entire family, including the collateral families they are able to identify, as well as the neighbors. They examine all the records they can find, but they still hit a dead end. Their failure results either from neglecting to investigate a faint glimmer of a light that, with just a little more energy, could have become a beacon, or from neglecting to put the records in the context of a community, rather than just in the context of a family.

Descendants of the Phillips family of Boone County, Missouri, had searched for the family's origins for many years with no success. Hiram,

John Y., and Warner Phillips were early settlers in the area of Missouri Territory that became Boone County in 1821. Using family records, land records, associations, newspaper clippings, probate files, and published nineteenth- or early twentieth-century local history books (sometimes known as "mug books"), the family had deduced that the three men were brothers and that Jane Huddleston was their sister.

The family had accumulated a great many records and I found no reason to believe that their research was faulty. From their work, the family configuration appeared as follows.

STEP ONE: What do we know?

John Y. Phillips was born about 1789, probably in Virginia, as he was apparently the eldest and both his brothers were born there; died of typhoid fever on 24 September 1847 in Boone County, Missouri; married Margaret [—?—] who preceded him in death. In his will, John Y. Phillips named three sons, John Y., Theodore, and Warner.[12] The loose papers in the probate packet named his children as Harriet, Newton, Theodore, Warner, John Y., Ann P., Ellen, and Austin Phillips.[13]

Hiram Phillips was born about 1792 in Virginia and married 1818 in Bourbon County, Kentucky, to Elizabeth Cave. He served in the War of 1812 and received a bounty land for his service.[14] He spent most of his long life farming in Boone County. His twelve children were Ellen, James, William, Augustine, Addison, Richard, Sarah, Hiram, Elizabeth, Joseph, Martha, and Isabella.[15]

Warner Phillips was born about 1794 in Virginia; died 24 March 1881 in Boone County; married Catharine Hutchings. The 1880 census gave his parents' birthplaces as Virginia. Needless to say, there were a number of families with the Phillips surname that lived in Virginia in the early 1800s. Warner and Catharine were the parents of eight children: Joseph B., four sons born between 1827 and 1844 who all died in infancy, Franklin W., Ann, and Catharine M.[16]

Jane Phillips Huddleston died in Boone County, Missouri, in 1849. She left a will appointing her brothers Hiram and Warner Phillips as her executors. Legacies went to her children John H. and Cordelia A.[17]

Onomastic Evidence?

Many genealogists know that naming patterns can be particularly important if there is an unusual name involved or a pattern of repetition in the family. This can often lead to other siblings and parents. Although the brothers used each other's names when naming their children, the only unidentified names that were repeated were Ann and Ellen. No given name was repeated that might have led to a possible father.

Other than the marriage for Hiram and Elizabeth Cave, no other recorded marriages were found for any of the family members in either Virginia, Kentucky, or Missouri. All of the children for each of these couples were born in Missouri, and the three brothers appeared as the first settlers in Columbia Township of Boone County by 1821, the year of statehood.

Other family members had found more information. The annotated cemetery inscriptions of Boone County, Missouri, reported that the "Phillips Family came to Boone County from Bourbon County, Kentucky."[18] In addition to Hiram's marriage there, his wife's father, Richard, had given permission for the marriage. Richard Cave was found in the tax and land records of Bourbon County, and followed his daughter to Missouri. Yet nothing was found in Bourbon County for either of the other Phillips brothers, their sister, or any clues to their parentage. An article in the *Missouri Historical Review* stated that, "Warren and J.B. [*sic*] Phillips came from Scott County, Kentucky."[19] "Hiram Phillips is also said to have come from Kentucky but exact county unknown." More study was done in Scott County. No results. These two "genealogical" statements stymied researchers for years.

The Phillips descendants had studied the War of 1812 bounty land application for Hiram Phillips. He served in Johnson's Regiment of Mounted Kentucky Volunteers. Later he was a sergeant in James Coleman's Regiment of Mounted Volunteers. Although the application gave his marriage date and place, there was no further information regarding his place of enlistment or origin.

I checked the probate records for each of the brothers. Everything confirmed they were related and every associate in Boone County led back to Bourbon County. And yet, the brothers were of age before they left Kentucky, and although all of their later associates appeared on the tax rolls of Bourbon County, they did not. No one named Phillips appeared on the 1810 census for Kentucky that had males in his household of the right age to be John, Hiram, and Warner.

The break in this problem came in reanalyzing records the family already had. The crucial question was one mentioned earlier: "Who else was involved in creating, or is mentioned, in the records? Are they likely to be 'official' participants or associates of the individual under study?" I had tracked the associates. What about the official—the commanding officer in Hiram's regiment? Where did he come from? I made a search—a bibliographic search.

The Report of the Adjutant General of the State of Kentucky listed all the officers that were in Hiram's regiment in the War of 1812. Perhaps I could find them on the 1810 Kentucky census. One out of the six appeared in Bourbon County; the other five were enumerated in Harrison County.

And there I found the parents, William and Ellen Phillips. Every record one could hope for was there: the father's will naming all of his children, the land distribution, the powers of attorney from Missouri—things we genealogists dream we'll find. One of the questions that had frustrated earlier researchers was why the father, William Phillips, was not on the 1810 Kentucky census. From the land records, we learn that he apparently was moving that year. The other blind spot for earlier researchers was that supposed "genealogical" records showed that the family was in Bourbon and Scott counties, when the parents actually resided nearby, and did not appear in the records the descendants searched (see Figure 1-6 below).

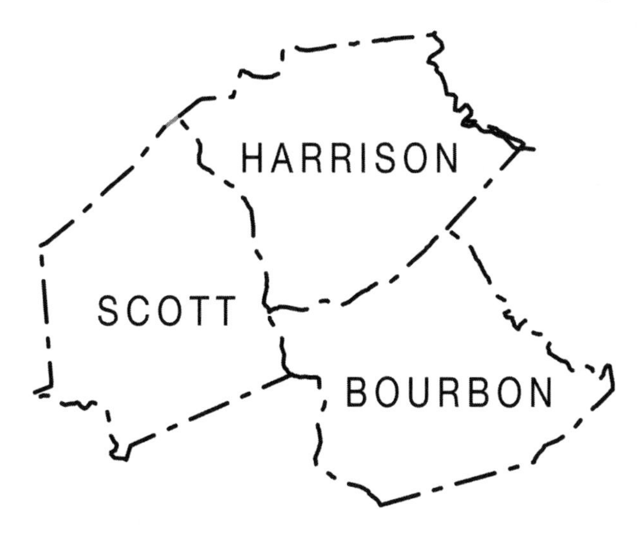

Figure 1-6
Kentucky counties, 1803.

The answer to identifying John Y., Hiram, and Warner Phillips was broadening the search to include a set of individuals not related to the family, but associated with the family and community at a crucial time. It was by following the steps and asking the questions detailed above that solutions were found to difficult problems. Now that we have a basic structure for problem-solving, let's turn to some of the specific puzzles we genealogists encounter in our research.

---

1 Franklin County, Missouri, Deed Book B:404.

2 Franklin County, Missouri, Deed Book D:448.

3 Franklin County, Missouri, Deed Book D:448, 449.

[4] United States Land Sales in Missouri, Vol. 5:372. Family History Library film 984767.

[5] Crawford County, Missouri, Marriage Book 1:30.

[6] *Greene County, Missouri, Tax Assessors' List 1833–1834–1835–1843* (Springfield, Mo.: Ozarks Genealogical Society, 1988), p.2.

[7] Maxine Dunaway, *183() Tax Assessment Book for Polk County, Missouri* (Springfield, Mo.) Maxine Dunaway, ca. 1984, p.3. Bureau of Land Management, Springfield Land Office, Tract Book 14:198.

[8] Crawford County, Missouri, 1830 census, p.180, household of Ledwell D. Blanon.

[9] Hopkins County, Kentucky, Marriage Licenses 1821–1826, unpaginated; also Marriage Books 2:10.

[10] Polk County, Missouri, Probate Book A:5.

[11] *Minutes of the Board of Land Commissioners, Fannin County, Texas*, p.50, copied at the General Land Office by Gifford White. Typescript at the Family History Library, Salt Lake City.

[12] Boone County, Missouri, Will Book B:840.

[13] Boone County, Missouri, probate file 771.

[14] Hiram Phillips, War of 1812 Bounty Land Warrant 27904-80-55. National Archives Records Administration, Washington, D.C.

[15] Virginia Easley DeMarce entry on the Ancestry World Tree Project: Boone County, Missouri.

[16] Ibid.

[17] Will of Jane Hudleston, Boone County, Missouri, Will Book B:798-9. The will was proved 9 February 1849.

[18] Floyd Strader, *Tombstone Inscription of Boone County, Missouri*, 1981.

[19] James M. Wood, "Settlement of Columbia, Mo.," *Missouri Historical Review* 3 (April 1900):187.

Finding Births, Marriages, and Deaths Before Civil Registration

The civil registration of births, deaths, and marriages did not begin on a statewide level in the United States until relatively modern times. Most began in the late nineteenth or early twentieth century. Even when they did officially begin, the laws and practices were determined at the state rather than federal level. Thus, there is tremendous variation from state-to-state when they began, the consistency with which they were kept, and the enforcement of the laws. Generally, we can't expect complete registration until the first quarter of the twentieth century.

For complete information on when states began regularly keeping birth, death, and marriage registrations, and where those records can be found, see *The Family Tree Resource Book for Genealogists* (Cincinnati: Family Tree Books, 2004). Internet users can check <www.vitalrec.com> or <www.cyndislist.com/usvital.htm> for similar information.

Vital records in most areas of this country were originally kept as part of the public health movement of the late nineteenth century, and can first be found in the mortality schedules that accompanied federal population reports. Attempts were made to gather information about types, causes, prevalence, and duration of disease.

From their inception, New England towns kept vital registration, and even though compliance was far from complete these records are immensely helpful. However, in this chapter we are speaking of the statewide civil vital registration which first began in Massachusetts in 1841, but was not instituted in many other locales until much later. Usually states began recording marriages before births and deaths. Kentucky and Ohio began recording marriages at the county level in the 1780s and early 1800s, while

Pennsylvania did not begin the statewide civil recording of marriages until 1883, and South Carolina not until 1911. So, before you begin research in a particular state, be sure to determine when civil registration began. Those records are easily attainable and an important part of your research.

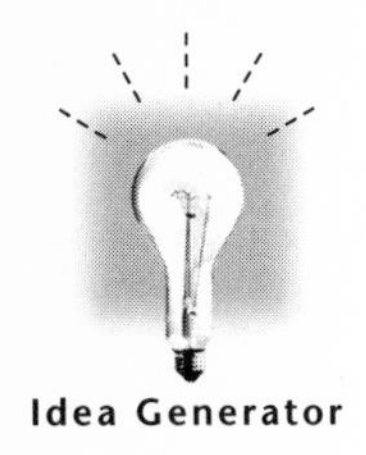

When no vital records are available, what is the genealogical researcher to do? This chapter is designed to provide you with a multitude of alternate resources that can help you discover the dates that you seek. There is no guarantee you will find the birth, marriage, and death records for your ancestor in any of these sources, but when you do, the search is very rewarding. The first half of the chapter will focus on substitutes for vital registration. The majority of these records will be found for the nineteenth century, although it is possible to locate them for earlier time periods. The distinguishing feature is that these are more or less accurate substitutes for the *dates* of birth, death, and marriage that we lack. In the second half of the chapter, I will discuss what to do when researching earlier time periods on the frontier or in other places where no exact dates can be found and the researcher must estimate the date needed. We'll focus on what to do when we don't have a date of birth, death, or marriage, and how we can document that the event actually occurred and reasonably estimate when.

When working with vital records, we must always be concerned about the accuracy of retroactively dated events, whether they be from civil registration, Bible records, tombstones, or stone tablets engraved by Aunt Tillie. Nothing is the gospel truth and these dates can't be stated with absolute certainty. They depend upon both the memory and the recording accuracy of human beings, and thus they are always susceptible to error. The dean of American genealogy, Donald Lines Jacobus, related a story of his professional work and difficulty with a client in an article that originally appeared in *The American Genealogist.*[1] A girl named Anna was born in 1764, some four months after the marriage of her parents. The birth and marriage were recorded in the town records, and the baptisms and marriage were written in the church records. All were in complete harmony.

However, Mr. Jacobus was hired to trace this ancestry by a "very pious lady" who would be disturbed to find an out-of-wedlock conception on her family tree. In the course of time, the lady noticed the discrepancy between the marriage and birth dates and wrote Jacobus, telling him that he had made an error and that her ancestress Anna was born in 1765. He replied it was not his error and cited his sources. She was not satisfied. She sent him a copy of Anna's tombstone, on which the date of death and her age in years, months, and days appeared. When figured back this agreed perfectly with the year 1765, instead of 1764. Not to be outdone, Jacobus photocopied the town records. In reply, the client sent a photocopy of a Bible record made by Anna's son in which he had entered the birth dates of both parents, and which showed Anna's birth correctly according to day and month in 1765. At this point, Jacobus gave up the struggle. He accepted that the moral of the story is that we often lack dates for birth and marriage, but that is not how genealogy is derived. We should try to be accurate, but proving the line of descent is what's important. Jacobus stated the point clearly: Does it really matter if Anna was born in 1764 or 1765, since her father acknowledged paternity by marrying her mother?

"Proving the line of descent is the essential thing. So far as dates are concerned, we should try to be accurate, but should not make a fetish of it."
—Donald Lines Jacobus

FAMILY SOURCES

Nevertheless, we all hope to find dates of birth, death, and marriage, for this is the foundation on which we build our genealogy. The first place to look for these important dates is within the family: Bibles, letters, journals, notes on the backs of photographs, obituary notices, marriage certificates, funeral cards, family histories, engraved jewelry, etc. Do not overlook the possibility that an obscure notation or reference tucked away where it doesn't belong could be the only reference to a date you need. Just use caution and be sure to carefully inspect any gem found in family sources. A postcard is the only reference my husband's family has been able to locate specifying the death date of Justus Cobb, his second great-grandfather, even though the county in which he died has been combed for additional information (see Figure 2-1 on page 24). His tombstone reads only "Father," with no dates.

Diaries and journals can reveal important information. If you can find those still within your family you are indeed fortunate, but don't neglect the diaries and journals of neighbors, local physicians, ministers, and "busybodies." New England families were particularly good at keeping those important diaries. For example, Samuel Sewall of Boston kept a diary faithfully from 1674 to 1729. Fortunately, it has been published.[2] He recorded the only death date I have been able to find for my husband's ancestor, Captain Daniel Henchman, who died in 1685.

> *Monday, Oct. 19th* About Nine aclock [*sic*] at night News comes to Town of Capt. Henchman's Death at Worcester last Thursday; buried on Friday. Very few at His Funeral, his own Servants, a white and

Figure 2-1
Postcard announcing Justus Cobb's death.

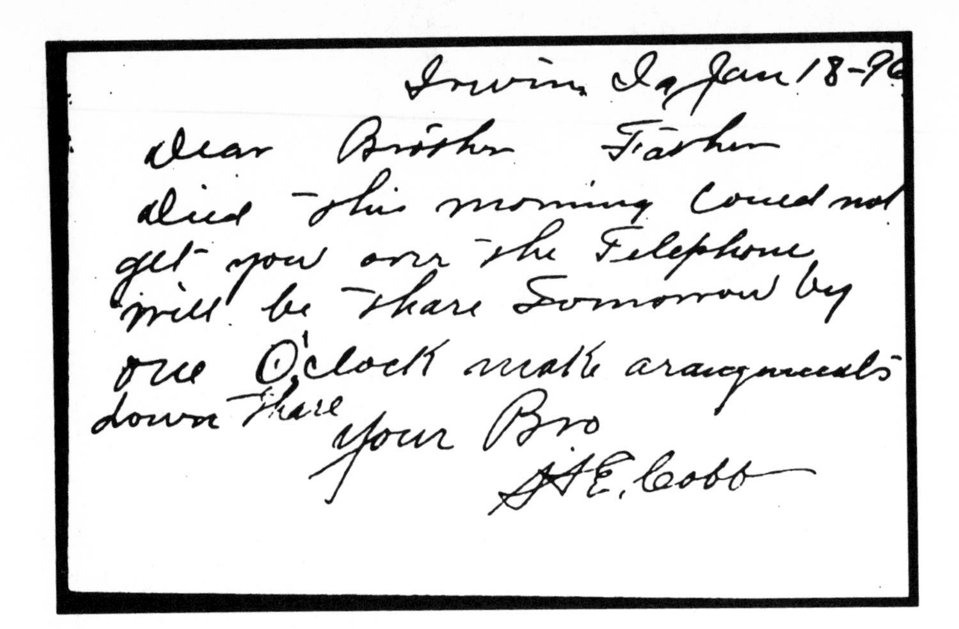

Irwin Ia Jan 18-96
Dear Brother Father
died this morning could not
get you over the telephone
will be there tomorrow by
one O'clock make arangements
down there
your Bro
H. E. Cobb

black, carried him to, and put him in his Grave. His Wife and children following and no more, but one or two more.

Although New England kept excellent vital records in the colonial period, death dates are the least likely to be complete—especially for children. In researching my Robinson family history in Massachusetts, I located this reference to the death of a cousin in 1745 that was not recorded in the Westborough vital records. It was taken from the annotated published diary of the Reverend Ebenezer Parkman.[3]

10 December 1745: At the Funeral of Mr. Seth Rice's Daughter.

Just out of interest, I compared a number of deaths at random that were recorded in Ebenezer Parkman's diary against the vital records of Westborough. I found that only 33 percent of those recorded by Parkman were also in the vital records. Thus, it behooves a researcher to learn the identity of the local minister and learn whether his diary has been preserved.

Some diaries and journals are extant from the 1630s. **Four excellent sources for locating them are:**

Arksey, Laura, Nancy Pries, and Marcia Reed. *American Diaries: An Annotated Bibliography of Published American Diaries and Journals.* 2 vols. Vol. 1: 1492–1844. Vol. 2: 1845–1980. (Gale Research, Book Tower, Detroit, Mich. 48266, no date.)

Forbes, Harriet. *New England Diaries 1602–1800.* (Topsfield, Mass.:

published by the author, no date.) Available at the Family History Library.

Matthews, William. *American Diaries: An Annotated Bibliography of American Diaries Written Prior to the Year 1861.* (Berkeley: University of California Press, 1945.) Diaries are listed alphabetically under the year the first diary entry occurs.

Matthews, William. *American Diaries in Manuscript 1580–1954.* (Athens, Ga.: University of Georgia Press, 1974.) Over 6,000 items of published and unpublished diaries from 350 libraries.

The National Union Catalog of Manuscript Collections (NUCMC) also contains many references to diaries and can be found in print at most large and university libraries. It is a gold mine of information on various unpublished works and where they are available. It is also available online through a subscription service, Archives USA, to which many libraries subscribe.

TOMBSTONES

The next most common substitute for a birth or death record is the date recorded on the tombstone. When you use such dates as corroboration, be sure you indicate that the source is the tombstone. The individual who was buried there probably did not order the tombstone, nor did he supervise the carving. There is a common sequence for purchasing a tombstone and a number of things can go wrong in the process.

- The memory of the individual ordering the stone may not be accurate.
- That individual may not transmit the information accurately.
- The individual receiving the information from the purchaser may not record it accurately.
- The individual producing the stone may not accurately carve the information transmitted to him.
- The stone may not be preserved well enough to allow an accurate reading. Watch out for this problem particularly when you are reading a transcription of the dates rather than looking at the stone itself.

A tombstone I found clearly reads, "Sarah S. dau. of W. & S.A. Fleener born Aug. 24, 1885, died Aug. 5, 1867" (see Figure 2-2 on page 26).

As it is obvious the stone is wrong, the genealogist must analyze what the dates *should* be and try to find other records that support or contradict those guesses. Perhaps the birth date is wrong and should be 1865. Perhaps

Figure 2-2
Picture of Fleener tombstone.

the death date should be 1887. Perhaps the birth and death dates were reversed, and Sarah was born in 1867 and died in 1885. What other records could help us to determine which date is correct? The census is our first stop and here, we luck out. Sarah does not appear on the 1870 census with her parents and there is a space between Lydia, age seven, and William, age two. It fits that the birth year could have been 1865 and Sarah did not live to be in the 1870 census.

CHURCH RECORDS

The records maintained in many churches are another common alternative for both birth and death records. It seems that clergymen were more prone to record baptisms than births, probably to ensure that the newborn babe would be prepared for heaven if premature death should occur. Churches that have particularly good vital registration records include Quaker, Lutheran, Dutch Reformed, Catholic, Episcopalian, and Presbyterian congregations. A tremendous array of religious denominations and sects exist in the United States and their records are usually more difficult to locate here than they may be in European countries, where only one or two denominations are common. *The Source: A Guidebook of American Genealogy* edited by Loretto Dennis Szucs and Sandra Hargreaves Luebking, rev. ed (Salt Lake City: Ancestry, Inc., 1997)

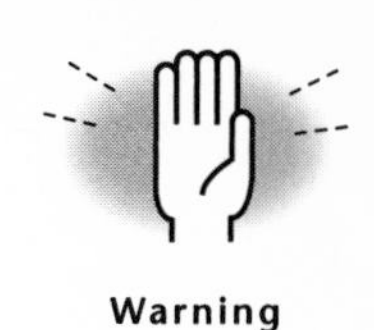

provides some suggestions on where to begin your search for the records of specific denominations. **Too often we assume these records don't exist because they have not been published or microfilmed.**

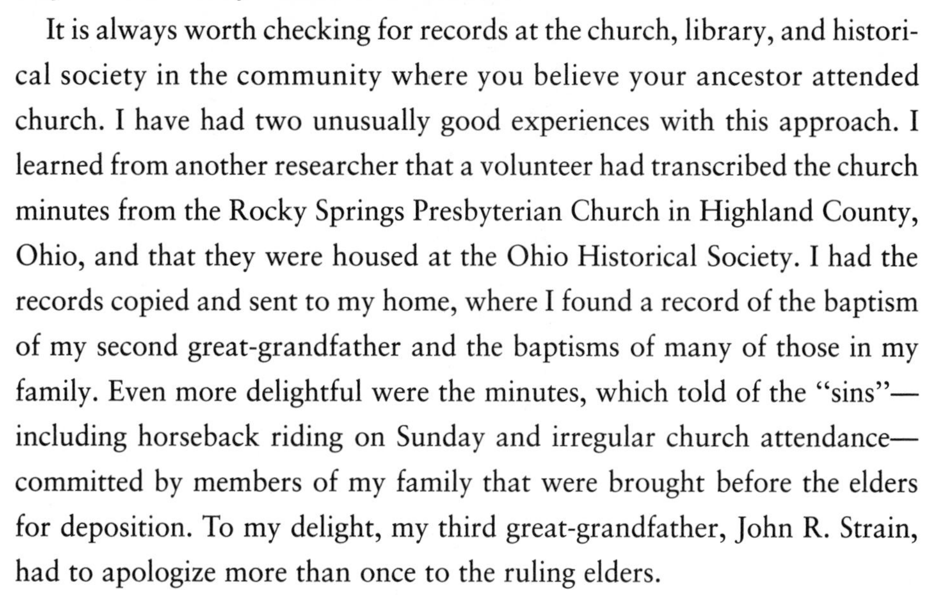

It is always worth checking for records at the church, library, and historical society in the community where you believe your ancestor attended church. I have had two unusually good experiences with this approach. I learned from another researcher that a volunteer had transcribed the church minutes from the Rocky Springs Presbyterian Church in Highland County, Ohio, and that they were housed at the Ohio Historical Society. I had the records copied and sent to my home, where I found a record of the baptism of my second great-grandfather and the baptisms of many of those in my family. Even more delightful were the minutes, which told of the "sins"—including horseback riding on Sunday and irregular church attendance—committed by members of my family that were brought before the elders for deposition. To my delight, my third great-grandfather, John R. Strain, had to apologize more than once to the ruling elders.

On the other hand, researching Butler County, Pennsylvania, from my home in Missouri brought nothing but frustration. Finally, on a trip there in the 1980s I visited the courthouse, which allowed me to sort out many of the dilemmas I had encountered. In addition to there being a plethora of people named Hoffman in the area, I found two men named Michael Hoffman born the same year and both married to women named Mary. However, I was most interested in finding the ancestral home and, as the naturalizations had not provided the location, I had just about given up hope. To my surprise, translated versions of the marriage, death, and baptismal records of St. Peter's Reformed Lutheran Church in Zelienople, Pennsylvania, were housed in the town's historical society. There, I found the following entry in the death records for my second great-grandfather:

> Casper Hoffman born in Breunings in Gausersan 21 December 1803; married in 1830 to Eva Boehm with whom he had six children; came in 1848 to America; died in Cranberry Township, Butler County 13 October 1872.

What a gift! I photocopied the translations. I also copied the originals of the records, which were kept in the kitchen cabinet of the house behind the reconstructed church. Although the translation of the records was very good, it did contain at least one omission from the originals: the birthplace of my second great-grandfather. Remember that if there is one mistake in transcribed records, it is most likely to be for the ancestor that you are seeking.

As your research moves to the frontier regions of the upper south and middle west, you will encounter the more evangelical churches, such as various sects of Methodists and Baptists. The likelihood of finding vital registration in these churches is slim. These denominations primarily kept membership rolls, and usually the most useful information you can glean from these is a death citation.

Hidden Treasures

When researchers think of church records, they usually think of the minutes or regular records of the church's proceedings and activities. **Too often, denominational newspapers are overlooked.** Some excellent obituaries were printed in the late nineteenth century, for ordinary church members as well as the more prominent ministers. One of the advantages of religious newspapers is that they cover a wider geographic area than local church registries. Thus, one can trace migration patterns as well as locate vital records in ancestral towns. I don't know how I would have ever found the origins of James Miller if it had not been for an obituary in a published abstract from a newspaper:[4]

> James Miller died April 25 1852 at his residence at Ebenezer, Greene County in his 77th year. He was born in Shenandoah Co., Virginia and migrated to Clarke County Kentucky. He was a Methodist from early life. He moved from Kentucky to Greene County, Missouri in 1836. Left children and grandchildren.

Tip

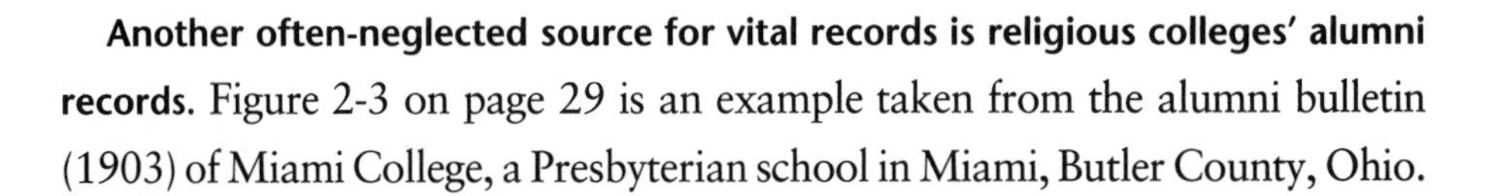

Another often-neglected source for vital records is religious colleges' alumni records. Figure 2-3 on page 29 is an example taken from the alumni bulletin (1903) of Miami College, a Presbyterian school in Miami, Butler County, Ohio.

NEWSPAPERS

Newspapers can be a wonderful substitute for vital records even though they are not always completely accurate. Although comprehensive obituaries did not become common until the late nineteenth century, short notices of deaths and marriages were usually included from the beginning of newspaper publication. Whether your ancestor or his family members appear will, of course, depend on their prominence, their proximity to the town where the newspaper was published, and the drama of their demise. In other words, a man dragged to his death by a horse team was more likely to make the paper than a woman who died in childbirth.

From the *Vermont Gazette*:

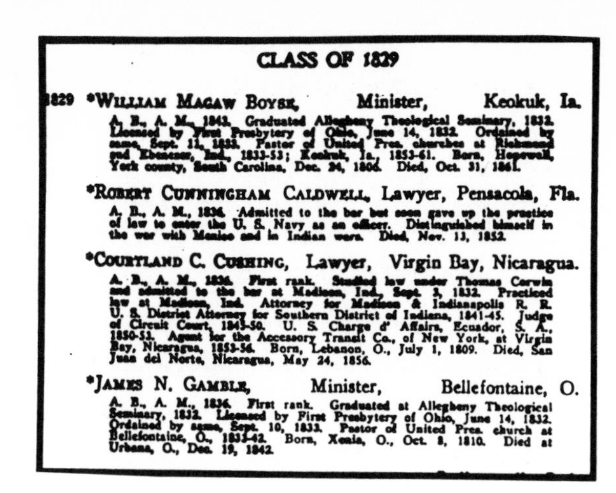

CLASS OF 1829

1829 *WILLIAM MAGAW BOYSE, Minister, Keokuk, Ia.
A. B., A. M., 1843. Graduated Allegheny Theological Seminary, 1832. Licensed by First Presbytery of Ohio, June 14, 1832. Ordained by same, Sept. 11, 1833. Pastor of United Pres. churches at Richmond and Ebenezer, Ind., 1833-53; Keokuk, Ia., 1853-61. Born, Hopewell, York county, South Carolina, Dec. 24, 1806. Died, Oct. 31, 1861.

*ROBERT CUNNINGHAM CALDWELL, Lawyer, Pensacola, Fla.
A. B., A. M., 1836. Admitted to the bar but soon gave up the practice of law to enter the U. S. Navy as an officer. Distinguished himself in the war with Mexico and in Indian wars. Died, Nov. 13, 1852.

*COURTLAND C. CUSHING, Lawyer, Virgin Bay, Nicaragua.
A. B., A. M., 1836. First rank. Studied law under Thomas Corwin and admitted to the bar at Madison, Ind., Sept. 3, 1832. Practiced law at Madison, Ind. Attorney for Madison & Indianapolis R. R. U. S. District Attorney for Southern District of Indiana, 1841-45. Judge of Circuit Court, 1845-50. U. S. Charge d' Affairs, Ecuador, S. A., 1850-53. Agent for the Accessory Transit Co., of New York, at Virgin Bay, Nicaragua, 1853-56. Born, Lebanon, O., July 1, 1809. Died, San Juan del Norte, Nicaragua, May 24, 1856.

*JAMES N. GAMBLE, Minister, Bellefontaine, O.
A. B., A. M., 1836. First rank. Graduated at Allegheny Theological Seminary, 1832. Licensed by First Presbytery of Ohio, June 14, 1832. Ordained by same, Sept. 10, 1833. Pastor of United Pres. church at Bellefontaine, O., 1833-42. Born, Xenia, O., Oct. 8, 1810. Died at Urbana, O., Dec. 19, 1842.

Figure 2-3
Miami College Bulletin, 1903.

23 September 1791: Died in Addison by act of lunacy, Mr. Simon Smith, age 50 years. He left a widow and ten children. His body was found hanging by the neck with his face within ten inches of the ground. Inquest brought verdict of insanity.

29 September 1800: We hear from Orwell that Mr. Jesse Marks, in sailing on Lake Champlain from Mount Independence to Ticonderoga, accidentally fell overboard and was taken up, almost instantly dead. He was in the 36th year of his age.

When you read newspapers, do not limit yourself to the small section reserved for birth and marriage notices or obituaries. Birth and death announcements can appear in other sections as well, especially if the event was unusual in some way—if it occurred in a peculiar place or there were multiple births.

Here are two death notices buried in news stories from *The Bolivar Weekly Courier,* Bolivar, Missouri:

10 July 1856: "Last Monday morning Milton Davidson heard a disturbance among the chickens. He was about to fire his rifle, but thinking the report would disturb his wife, he decided to step outside the door, but in doing so, he fell, the gun discharged and the ball entered his wife's head penetrating the skull just above the right eye killing her instantly."

This news story can certainly be viewed with a jaundiced eye, but it does report the death of Mrs. Davidson. The story, however, was not over. From *The Springfield Mirror,* Springfield, Missouri:

> 31 July 1858: "Milton M. Davidson of Polk County, was struck by lightning on the 20th inst. and immediately killed."

It's possible there *is* justice in the world.

Now consider this birth notice from the *Spring River Fountain* (Lawrence County, Missouri):

> Triplets in Polk County born April 24 [1869] to Mr. and Mrs. Judge James Human of Humansville, two boys and a girl, averaged 6 lbs. He is age 69 and has had 3 wives, is paternal relative of some twenty-five children.

Newspapers also contain letters from citizens who migrated and later wrote back to inform the community of deaths of former citizens.

> *The Stockton Journal*, Stockton, Missouri, 3 May 1888: William P. Conway of Independence, Oregon wrote his father, Dennis Conway, announcing the death of William Tatom, which occurred in Oregon a few days since. He emigrated from Cedar County to Oregon in 1850, accompanied by Thomas Hartley, Mr. Edwards and others. His family followed three years later.

> The *Springfield Express*, Springfield, Missouri, 6 May 1881: Died at Navarro Mills, Texas, April 25th, 1881, Richard H. Younger, formerly of this county. Deceased was brother-in-law of the late Dr. G.P. Shackelford and a nephew of Judge J.T. Morton.

Col. Blodgett, master of several wagon trains west, published a list in 1852 of over a hundred and fifty graves he found along the Oregon Trail from Devil's Gate [Wyoming] to the Missouri River. I submitted this list to the *National Genealogical Society Quarterly*, where it was published in December 1988, pages 302-04.

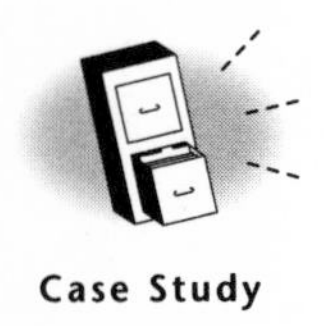
Case Study

CASE STUDY

I had terrible difficulty establishing the death date of Rebecca McConnell Strain, my second great-grandmother. She had applied for and received a military pension for her husband's service in the War of 1812. The last notice in the pension file was a complaint from her son, James Strain, that Rebecca's pension payment was supposed to have been transferred to the pension office in Topeka. In the letter, dated November 1876, he stated that his mother was 86 years old and "a great deal troubled about it." At that time,

James Strain was living in Concordia, Kansas. Searches were made of the cemetery, probate, and death records. No sign of Rebecca Strain.

I began a week-by-week search of the local newspaper, starting with the issues from when I knew she was living in Concordia—November 1876—hoping a death notice would appear. The first notice in the *Concordia Empire* was a nice surprise. On 23 February 1877, the newspaper reported that "Mrs. Rebecca Strain has just attained the age of 87 years. She was prostrated by a recent illness but is again able to sit up and handle her knitting needles." Before finding this, I had only a year for her birth. Surely I was close to finding the death notice. She couldn't have lived a lot longer and was unlikely to be traveling at that age. *Wrong!*

The following spring the newspaper reported that she had boarded a train and left Concordia: "It is with great regret that we hear of the purposed [*sic*] departure of three of our most respectable and respected people: Mrs. Rebecca Strain, mother of Jas. Strain, Esq., Mrs. Margaret Gilmer, mother of Dr. Gilmer, and Miss Franky Gilmer, sister of the Doctor." *Where did she go? And who were these people with her?*

A month later, on 15 June 1877, the newspaper reported, "Mrs. Rebecca Strain, Mrs. Margaret Gilmer and Miss Franky Gilmer, left Concordia for their future home in Illinois . . . Mrs. Strain and Mrs. Gilmer will reside in Sandoval." Although hope of finding a death notice dwindled, I kept reading. On 27 September 1878, the *Concordia Empire* notified its readers, "Died at Sandoval, Ill. Sept. 20, 1878, Mrs. Rebecca Strain, mother of James Strain, Esq. of this place, in the 89th year of her age."

Success in finding dates of birth, death, and marriage in newspapers does not require any particular skill. It does, however, require patience and tenacity—two critical traits for a successful genealogist. Searching newspapers also requires innate curiosity and the ability to distill important items from a nongenealogical context. Mrs. Gilmer was not just a traveling companion for Mrs. Strain. She was a previously unidentified daughter.

Reminder

COURT RECORDS

Coroner's reports are issued when an inquest is held to investigate unusual or unknown circumstances surrounding a death. When the inquest is complete, the report includes the causes of death and other valuable information (see Figure 2-4 on page 32). These records are public, and although difficult to locate, they may be kept in the coroner's office of any court of record, whether city, county, or state.

Figure 2-4
Coroner's report on Daniel W. Foster.

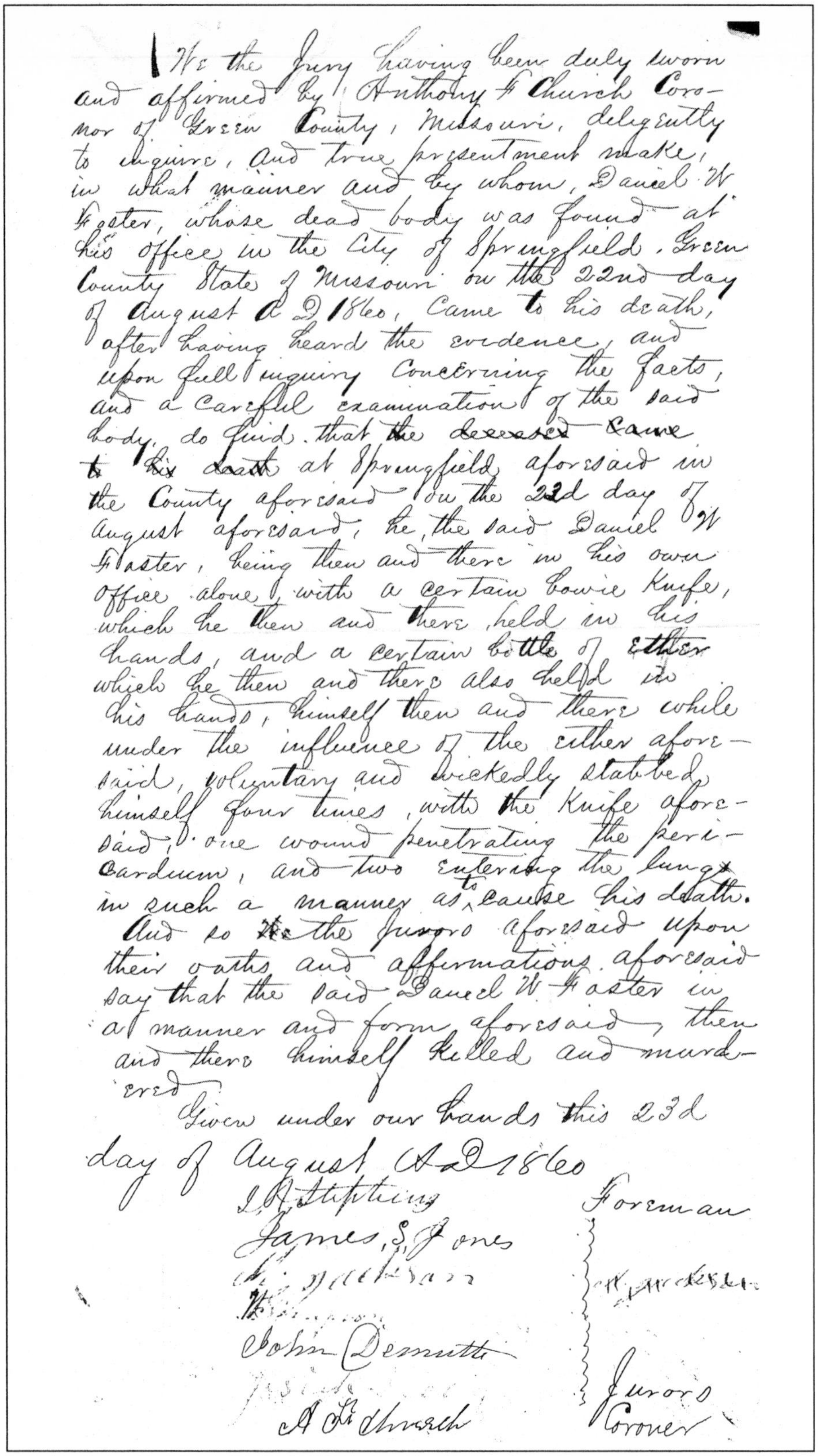

We the Jury having been duly sworn and affirmed by Anthony F Church Coroner of Green County, Missouri, deligently to inquire, and true presentment make, in what manner and by whom, Daniel W Foster, whose dead body was found at his office in the City of Springfield, Green County State of Missouri on the 22nd day of August A D 1860, Came to his death, after having heard the evidence, and upon full inquiry Concerning the facts, and a Careful examination of the said body, do find that the deceased Came to his death at Springfield aforesaid in the County aforesaid on the 22d day of August aforesaid, he, the said Daniel W Foster, being then and there in his own office alone, with a certain bowie knife, which he then and there held in his hands, and a certain bottle of ether which he then and there also held in his hands, himself then and there while under the influence of the ether aforesaid, voluntary and wickedly stabbed himself four times, with the knife aforesaid, one wound penetrating the pericardium, and two entering the lungs in such a manner as to cause his death.
And so the Jurors aforesaid upon their oaths and affirmations aforesaid say that the said Daniel W Foster in a manner and form aforesaid then and there himself killed and murdered

Given under our hands this 23d day of August A D 1860

J. R. Stephens [illegible] Foreman
James S Jones
[illegible]
[illegible]
John Dennith
[illegible] Jurors
A F Church Coroner

Elizabeth Barnes was buried in an unmarked grave in Greene County, Missouri. The newspaper states only that she "died within the past weeks." The application for letters of administration listed her exact death date and her heirs (see Figure 2-5 below).

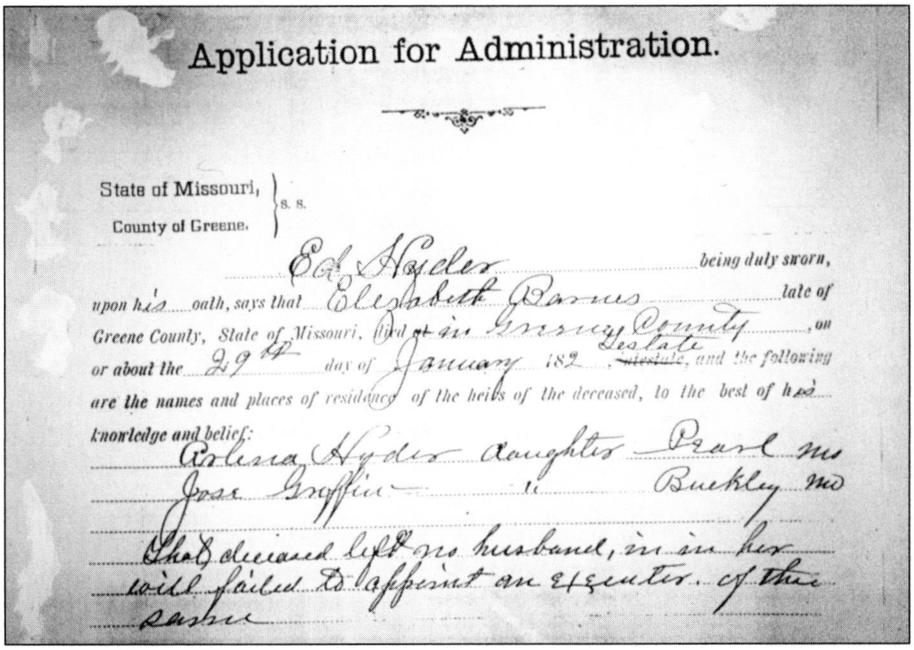

Application for Administration.

State of Missouri, } S. S.
County of Greene.

Ed Hyder being duly sworn, upon his oath, says that Elizabeth Barnes late of Greene County, State of Missouri, died in Greene County, on or about the 29th day of January 182 testate, and the following are the names and places of residence of the heirs of the deceased, to the best of his knowledge and belief:

Arlena Hyder daughter Pearl mo
Jose Griffin " Buckley mo
That deceased left no husband, in in her will failed to appoint an executor of the same

Figure 2-5
Application for administration concerning Elizabeth Barnes estate.

If the death date cannot be found in the probate record, or if the probate record is missing, other court records may be helpful. In the case of James H. McBride (see Figure 2-6 below), the circuit court minutes of June 1873 gave his date of death as 1863—ten years previous. In November 1873, the court minutes state that both the widow and a daughter of James McBride had also died (see Figure 2-7 on page 34). Interestingly, James H. McBride did not die in the county where this record was created. He died a hundred miles to the east, but had left property in Greene County that needed disbursement.

Although birth dates in court records are relatively rare, I have found a few

GREENE COUNTY, MISSOURI
CIRCUIT COURT MINUTES
BOOK M PAGE 285

June 7, 1873

The court further finds that afterwards, to wit, on the first day of November 1863, the said James H. McBride departed this life intestate.

Figure 2-6
Circuit court minutes providing the death date of James H. McBride.

in apprentice or guardianship records. Following is an example of the latter, when in January 1807 the names and dates of birth for Joseph Gash Sr.'s children were recorded: "John Gash will be 21 years April 19 1816, Rachel Gash will be 18 years February 19 1815, William Gash will be 21 years old March 11 1820 and Joseph Gash will be 21 years April 14 1822."[5]

Figure 2-7
Circuit court minutes proving the death of James McBride's two wives.

GREENE COUNTY, MISSOURI
CIRCUIT COURT MINUTES
BOOK M PAGE 476-477

November 20 1873

And, the court finds that Mildred A. McBride, the tenant in dower, as well as Allison McBride have both departed this life ... leaving the other plaintiffs ... entitled to one-sixth.

In this case, the family's births were registered in the Record of Negroes and Mulattoes, Randolph County, Illinois, Family History Library film 975014:

> The following list contains the names and ages of the family of Mumford Jones, a colored person, residing near Edin in the County of Randolph and State of Illinois.
>
> Mumford Jones born 21st March 1792
> Elizabeth Jones born 20th December 1810
> Wm. Riley Jones born 27th January 1831
> Thomas Warren Jones b. 9th June 1833
> Delia Matilda Jones born 12 August 1835
> Jasper Newton Jones born 31 August 1837
> Marion Houston Jones born 25th December 1840
> George Washington Jones born 9th January 1842
> Columbus Lafayette Jones born 2nd September 1844
> Martha Ann Jones born 1st January 1847

Depositions in court cases for civil or criminal actions will often begin with the individual identifying himself and giving his age.

PENSION FILES

In order to qualify for various veteran benefits and pensions, the applicant often gave his own birth date, the date of his marriage, and, for Civil War pensions, a list of births and deaths for each of his children. **The later the time period of the benefit, the more vital information you are likely to find.** If an individual or his widow was receiving a pension there should be a date for when that person was dropped from the rolls, and often the exact date of death appears (see Figure 2-8 below).

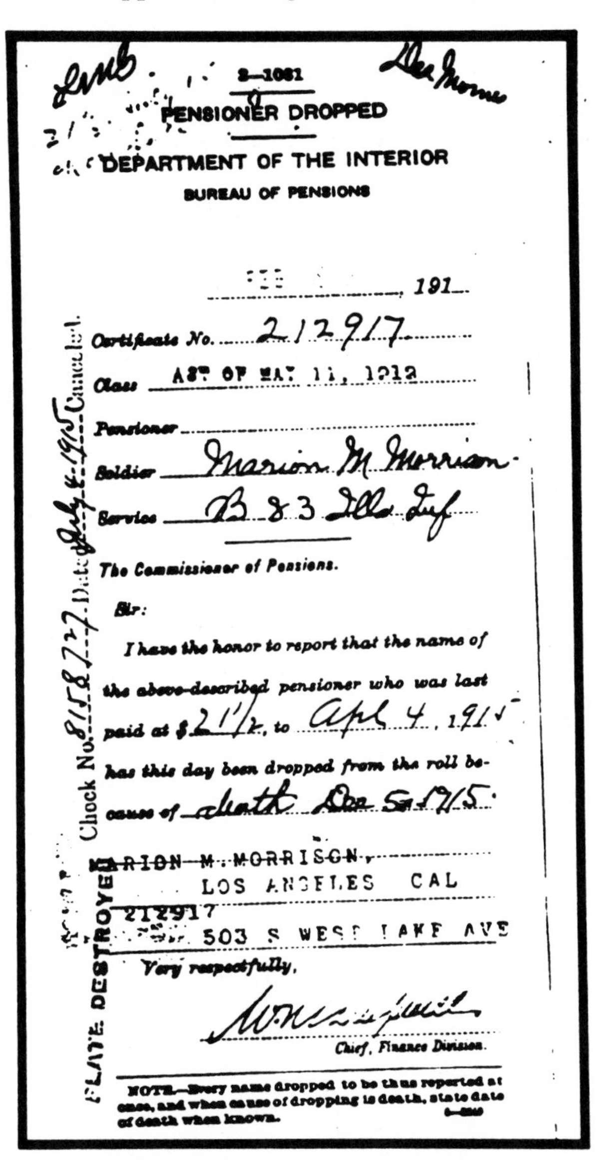

3—1061

PENSIONER DROPPED

DEPARTMENT OF THE INTERIOR

BUREAU OF PENSIONS

191

Certificate No. 212917

Class ACT OF MAY 11, 1912

Pensioner

Soldier Marion M Morrison

Service B 83 Ill. Inf

The Commissioner of Pensions.

Sir:

I have the honor to report that the name of the above-described pensioner who was last paid at $21 1/2, to Apl 4, 1915 has this day been dropped from the roll because of death Dec 5 1915

MARION M. MORRISON,
LOS ANGELES CAL
212917
503 S WEST LAKE AVE

Very respectfully,

Chief, Finance Division.

NOTE.—Every name dropped to be thus reported at once, and when cause of dropping is death, state date of death when known.

Check No. 8158727 Date July 4 1915 Cancelled

PLATE DESTROYED

Figure 2-8
Department of the Interior record of Marion Morrison's Civil War pension being dropped due to her death.

If the benefit application doesn't supply the date you need, another source you can check is the Final Payment files, a chronological list of payments made by the government. A card index is available. The microfilm is NARA's T7-18 (23 rolls), entitled "Ledgers of Payments 1818–1871 to U.S. Pensioners Under Acts of 1818 through 1858, From Records of the Office of the Third Auditor of the Treasury." At the Family History Library, these records are available on rolls 1319381 and 1319403.

MORTALITY SCHEDULES AND CENSUSES

Don't forget to check the mortality schedules for the years preceding the censuses of 1850, 1860, 1870, and 1880. The census takers were told to report the deaths that occurred in the community within the previous twelve months. Although these lists are not complete, they provide valuable information if your ancestor is named. The mortality schedule was the only record we could find for the death of my husband's aged third great-grandfather (see Figure 2-9 below).

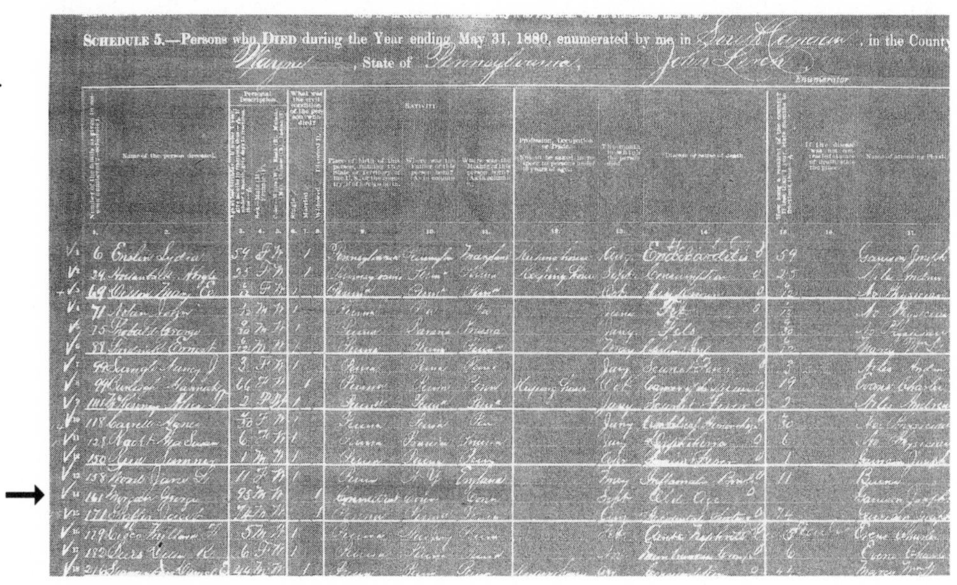

SCHEDULE 5.—Persons who DIED during the Year ending May 31, 1880, enumerated by me in , in the County , State of

Figure 2-9
Mortality schedule proving the death of George Morgan.

A few states were encouraged to conduct a special state census in 1885 with the promise of partial reimbursement from the federal government. The states that conducted this census were:

- Arizona
- Colorado
- Florida
- Nebraska
- New Mexico
- North Dakota
- South Dakota

Schedule 5 of this series was a mortality schedule and included name, age, sex, color, place of birth, parents' place of birth, occupation, and cause of death for every person who died within the year ending 31 May 1885.

You must know the state and community of your ancestor to determine whether special censuses were conducted there, and if so, what items were listed. For instance, New York did not begin to keep statewide marriage registration until 1880, but the 1865 and 1875 state censuses contain the names and dates of marriages recorded in the previous year. In Kentucky, school censuses were taken in 1888. Not all have survived, but those that did contain birth dates for the children attending the school. Local variations like this do occur and it is important to watch for them.

DIVORCE RECORDS

The exact date of marriage can often be found within the divorce record. Obviously, that there was a divorce is direct evidence that a marriage occurred. Divorce records can be located in county court minutes or in private legislative acts. Table 3-1 of *The Source* (first edition), pages 86-88, gives the divorce courts for each state and suggestions for locating the records. Divorces, of course, were also reported in newspapers—especially if the spouse had absconded to places unknown, which was typical. The *Vermont Gazette* (Bennington, Vermont) reported the exact date of marriage in this divorce announcement:

> December 21, 1800, Samuel Crafts of Pittsford, Rutland Co., Vermont, petitioned for divorce. He stated that he married Phebe Hill of Pittsford on 8 November 1796 and executed his duties as husband until January 1799, when Phebe was said to be guilty of the crime of adultery and lived in "lewd connections with another person."

ESTIMATES FOR BIRTH, DEATH, AND MARRIAGE DATES

Prior to the mid-nineteenth century, and before that period outside of New England, few exact references to births, deaths, and marriages exist. Instead, the researcher must use inferences, approximations, a process of elimination, and a thorough knowledge of human behavior—as well as an understanding of the legal and social customs of the time period—to arrive at a reasonable estimation of the needed date.

Records To Help Estimate the Time of Birth

Idea Generator

1. Count backward from the time of the first marriage or the birth of the first child to get an approximate age for both parents. A good rule of thumb is eighteen to twenty-three years for a female's first marriage and twenty-three to twenty-eight years for a male's first marriage—allowing a few years for a margin of error. Rural residents and those of lower socioeconomic class tended to marry and begin their families earlier than townsmen and those of higher economic class. Enthusiasm and inadequate birth control almost always produced the first child within two to three years. One must remember that the first child may not survive, and that there is always the possibility of the lusty eight-and-a-half-pound "premature" baby who

arrives only four months *after* the marriage. Wise researchers always keep in mind that they are working with human beings, who had the same interests, faults, proclivities, and needs as human beings do today.

2. The age at which a woman stops having children may also be a clue to when she was born. It is extremely unusual for a woman to have children after the age of forty-five. When a woman has a number of children and then stops for a period, then suddenly another child appears, at least three possibilities must be considered.

a. She is taking care of a grandchild (possibly one of those lusty premature babies mentioned earlier) or a relative's child that she and her husband may have adopted.

b. She has had a menopausal baby. If so, keep alert to see if that child is "void of intelligence," "defective," or "dependent." There is a much higher likelihood of a child being born with Down's syndrome or other birth defects if the mother is over the age of forty. Also, the likelihood of twins increases if the mother is over forty—particularly if there is not a history of twins in the family. If you find one of these situations to be the case, the child is probably biologically hers rather than a relative's.

c. She is a second wife with the same given name as the first wife, and is thus much younger than you think. You may encounter this situation more frequently before 1850, when women are often difficult to locate in the records. A good clue is a significant passage of time in which her name does not appear in the records. Or the opposite may occur. If you are "leapfrogging" across decades and primarily using the census to document your family, ten years is more than enough time for a woman to die in childbirth and a man to remarry and produce additional children. I have speculated that men marry wives of the same name to avoid embarrassing mistakes during moments of intimacy. James M. Beall of Russellville, Logan County, Kentucky, was more cautious than most. He erected a gravestone there in memory of his three wives, all named Sarah.

3. The legal age of consent is important when estimating a date of birth. It is important to know the laws of the community for the period. When could one buy and sell land? Usually individuals couldn't sell land until age twenty-one, although they could acquire it at an earlier age. When did the law allow the witnessing of deeds, the signing of bonds, the witnessing of wills, the choosing of a guardian? In colonial times in Massachusetts, someone as young as

fourteen could witness a deed and choose a guardian. In many states and colonies, if a guardian was chosen *for* the children, they were under fourteen. If the children came into court and chose their own guardian, they were fourteen or over. Sometimes the court minutes reflect a child's dissatisfaction with the manner in which the estate was handled, or he may have wished to exercise the authority of maturing years, so he would ask for a change of guardian as soon as he reached the age of fourteen. If the court minutes are complete, we can also find when the children reached maturity (usually eighteen for girls and twenty-one for boys), as they usually dismissed their guardian and signed a receipt for whatever was left of the estate. A desire to reach maturity and control the money prompted many a dependent child to release and relinquish his guardian very soon after reaching the age of consent.

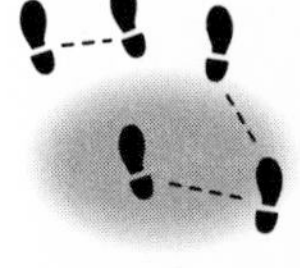

Step By Step

Following is an example of how estimations can be made for birth years. In this case, I had birth dates for only two of the seven children known to have inherited from their father, Moses Foren. The others were estimated from changes of guardianship and marriage dates and all fit well within the known three marriage dates of Moses Foren.

Moses Foren married (1) Morgan Co., Alabama, 1821, Lucretia Rice.

Moses Foren married (2) Hardeman Co., Tennessee, 27 April 1824, Ceely Ragan.

Moses Foren married (3) Greene County, Missouri, 3 February 1835, Mahala Farmer.

There were seven parts of the estate to be divided among the children. Here I have estimated the birth years for these seven children:

i. Lucretia born 1822/1823, as she was married by 1839, to Theophilus Cobb.

ii. Mary Ann born 1825, as she had reached age fourteen by May 1839, when she chose her guardian.

iii. Martha Jane born 1826, as she had reached age fourteen by November 1840, when she chose her guardian.

iv. Elizabeth born 1828/1829, as she had married in 1846, James Wood.

v. William C. born 20 February 1831 in Hardeman County, Tennessee (from his death record); he had reached age fourteen by September 1845.

vi. Celia born late in 1832, as she had reached age fourteen by January 1847.

vii. Filey Ann born 12 December 1835, as she died 15 March 1857, age twenty-one years, two months, three days.

Beginning with just the ages of the fifth and seventh children and the marriages for two, I could reconstruct the rest of the family from the guardianship papers.

4. When do taxes begin? When do taxes end? Many of the colonies and states required taxation of white males at age eighteen, others at twenty-one. You simply have to know the law of the particular area in which you are working. You can find these laws in the legislative chapters on "Revenue." For instance, I am currently working in early Missouri. The first revenue act of 18 December 1822 taxed all free white males above age twenty-one. The next, passed in 1825, exempted men over sixty-five, one in 1833 exempted men fifty years and over, and in 1835, the legislature settled on a law that taxed all free white males over twenty-one and under fifty-five years of age. The variations can keep you on your toes, but it can also help make your estimations more accurate—who would pay taxes when they no longer have to?

5. Time and type of migration can be an excellent clue to age. Age is a crucial variable in the analysis of migration trends. *When* people move, *where* they move, and *how often* they move all are influenced by age. A young, single man is the most likely to initiate the exploration of new country, to strike off on adventures, and—since he is also the most likely type to get in trouble with the law—the most likely to find it necessary to become scarce for a while. The established, mature man with a family of half-grown children is more likely to migrate with extended family, or to a location where family members and people from his previous community have already settled. The older person (widowed or with grown children) is likely to move only to where close family members have already established homes.

PROBATE RECORDS

Probate records can help you estimate the year of birth for an ancestor in several ways. If the testator's (one who leaves a will) brother or brother-in-law is appointed executor of the estate, the testator's children are probably minors. Usually an older testator will name an adult child or his wife as his executor. A middle-aged woman, often with the help of someone close to her, will retain the responsibility of handling the estate. However, if the wife is very young she may relinquish her right. Whomever she chooses to replace her as executor is probably a relative of hers, and this can give good suggestions regarding her family. If she is quite old, she will probably relinquish her responsibility to administer or execute in favor of a child.

Often, you will find this relinquishment in the loose probate papers.

The contents of the will itself can give you clues to the ages of the individuals involved. How is the wife provided for? Will she live with a son, or have access to a corner of the house and a portion of the garden? The testator may not expect her to remarry because of her age. Or is the testator careful to provide for her *only* until the time of her remarriage? If he expects her to remarry, he probably wants to make sure her second husband does not have access to his children's money. Does the testator name grandchildren, and do his granddaughters have married names? Doing some arithmetic will help you estimate the age of this testator.

\di'fin\ *vb*

Definitions

Loose probate papers are the files kept in probate packages that consist of original accounts, receipts, distributions, and other papers not recorded in the probate books.

LAND RECORDS

Important

Deed books may be the most versatile of all the records we use. You never know what will be recorded in a deed book. Although it is rare to find birth dates within deeds, they can give you a clue to the age and physical health of the grantor. In order to avoid probate court, fathers may begin to sell or give land to their children as they reach maturity and/or marry. An aged man or woman may also sell property to a son or son-in-law in exchange for care during the remainder of his and his wife's lives.

> Franklin County, Missouri, Deed Book B:269 6 December 1833, Mary Pepper of Franklin County, for $1 paid by William Pepper of Jefferson County, Missouri, who had obligated himself to maintain Mary during her natural life with good and decent boarding and lodging, and in return she granted 40 acres of land in Franklin County. She further granted him all of her household and kitchen furniture and livestock.

The following unusual deed even provided a specific date of birth, as well as clues to family connections.

> Cole County, Missouri, Deed Book B:197: 17 February 1835, John Walker of City of Jefferson certified that James C. Wills, a negro who was 21 years of age on the 12 November 1833, was born in my house while his mother, a freed woman named Nancy, belonged to me. Nancy was set free by the will of Courtney Walker, recorded in Jessamine County, Kentucky. Nancy lived with Walker until she was 25 years of age, at which time she was entitled to her freedom as well as her offspring. James has lived with me from the day of his birth until he came of age and is to be considered a free man since 12 November 1833.

Records to Aid in Estimating the Time of Death

1. Probate. A common method for estimating death is to assume that a death occurred between the time an individual made his will and the time it was proved in court. If he died intestate (without a will), the *first* letters of administration will be issued by the court within two to three weeks of his death; creditors do not want to wait long after an individual has died to be paid what is owed them, and that process can't begin until the bond has been filed and the letters of administration issued. There are times when the letters of administration may be delayed, perhaps due to the death or relocation of an administrator, or an extension of settlement due to disputes, so you must be alert to those circumstances. A new administrator may have been appointed if complaints were made about the original one by those standing to inherit or by creditors who are not being paid promptly.

Receipts in the probate packet may indirectly give you the date of death. First, find the last date the deceased rendered some type of business.

From Figure 2-10 below, we know John Griffis was alive 5 January 1842. Next, try to locate the receipt for the date the coffin was built (see Figure 2-11 on page 43) or the shroud was purchased (see Figure 2-12 on page 43).

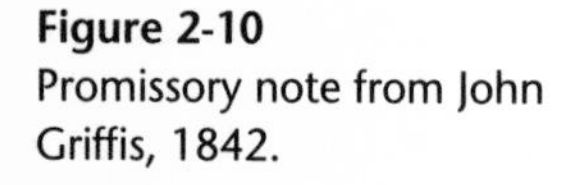

Figure 2-10
Promissory note from John Griffis, 1842.

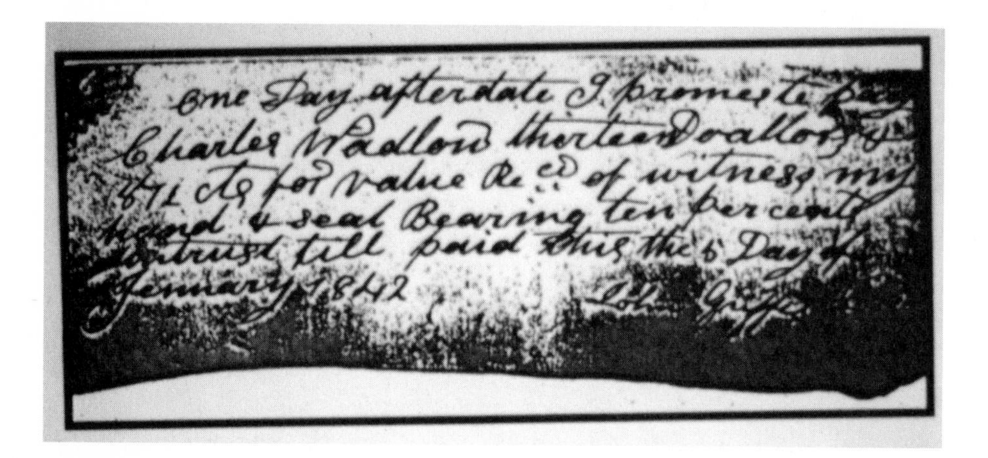

One Day after date I promise to pay
Charles Wadlow thirteen dollars &
71 cts for value Rec'd of witness my
hand & seal Bearing ten per cent
intrust till paid this the 5 Day of
January 1842 John Griffis

The last doctor's visit can give an excellent idea of when death occurred. In this instance, Dr. Terrell last visited on May 31, the coffin was built in June, and the widow relinquished her right to administer the estate on June 6. When did John Griffis die?

Research Tip

If a probate case remains open for some time but there is no indication of dispute or legal entanglements, the closing of that estate may indicate that the widow has now died. Charles Wildish died in 1898 in Waukeshau, Wisconsin. His estate was settled in 1916. Why? Because his widow died that year.

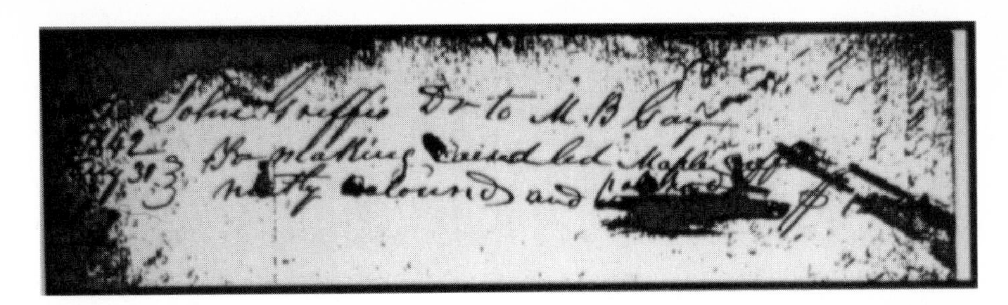

John Griffis Dr to M B Gray

Figure 2-11
Record of John Griffis' estate.

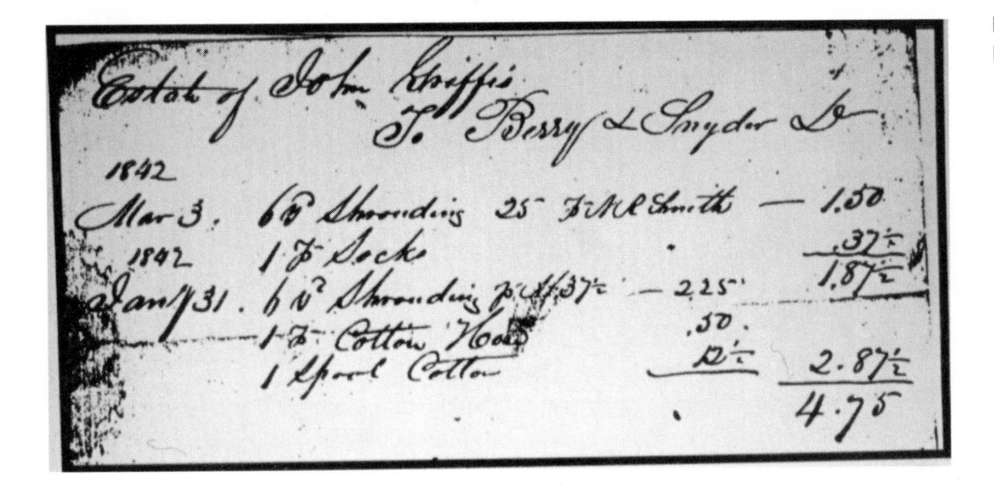

Estate of John Griffis
To Berry & Snyder Dr

1842
Mar 3. 6 yd Shrouding 25 — 1.50
1842 1 pr Socks .37½
1.87½
Jany 31. 6 yd Shrouding — 2.25
1 pr Cotton Hose .50
1 Spool Cotton .12½ 2.87½
4.75

Figure 2-12
Record of John Griffis' estate.

Cornelia Southern of Greene County, Missouri, died in 1898. Her land was not sold until 1909. Why not? Her husband had just died.

2. Large gaps in the ages of children recorded in census records may indicate the death of a child or child-bearing wife. This clue can help you determine possible remarriages.

3. Circuit court minutes can be an overlooked source for estimating a death date. Figure 2-13 on page 44 is an example of Greene County, Missouri, circuit court minutes reporting a death in a case that had nothing to do with probate proceedings.

4. Tax lists are one of the better ways of tracking individuals over discrete time periods. If you are able to follow an individual for several consecutive years and then he suddenly drops off the tax roll, three possibilities arise: he moved away, he reached the age of exemption, or he died. Clues to a death written on the tax rolls are notations such as "Henry Musselman's widow," "Peter Brubaker's Ex" (meaning executor), or "Christian Hershey's estate," as were found in Lancaster County, Pennsylvania, records. Kentucky has an excellent set of early nineteenth-century tax lists; the widow may be listed for one or two years after her husband's death, but then she will drop off even though she is still alive.

Figure 2-13
Circuit court minutes proving the death of Druery Merritt.

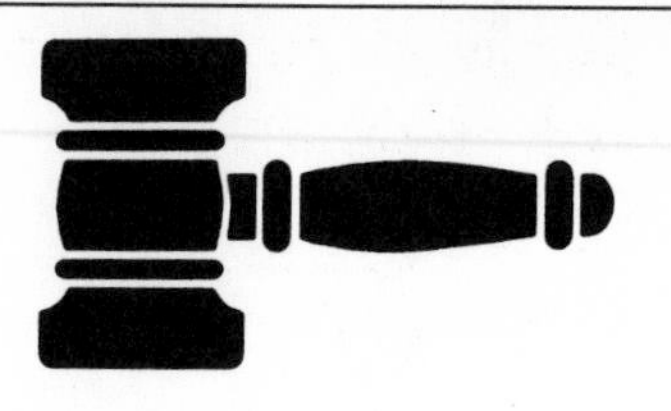

Greene County [MO] Circuit Court Minutes

April Term 1839

DRUERY MERRITT vs. BENJAMIN KIMBERLING

Now at this day appearing to the satisfaction of the Court that the said Druery Merritt is deceased and it is considered by the Court that said suit be dismissed.

Following is an example of finding a death date using tax records. It also shows the importance of distinguishing individuals of the same name.

The death date of Joshua Cornell of Greenwich, Connecticut, born ca. 1667, was unknown to researchers. He left no probate records, no deeds, no tombstone, and there was no mention of his death in the Quaker records—but I know that he died in 1743. I found the date using tax records. Both Joshua Cornell Sr. and Joshua Cornell Jr. were taxed a number of years in a row, including

1742:	Amount as given
Joshua Cornell Sr.	53-8
Joshua Cornell Jr.	124-00

The following year only Joshua Cornell was listed, with nothing indicating that there was more than one man of that name in the neighborhood who paid taxes.

1743	
Joshua Cornell	174-17-6

Notice that he is no longer using a junior or senior designation, and look at the amount—it is almost the combination of the earlier year's taxes for both men. Doubters may suggest that the younger man died, not the elder.

Examining a few more documents in the area such as deeds, church records, or court minutes conclusively proves that the younger man was the one later creating or named in records.

5. Migration can occur in the elder years. If you are having difficulty establishing the death date of an older person who lived in one community for several years and then disappeared, most likely he or she migrated and then died in the home of a child—usually a daughter.

6. A change of name may indicate a death. If "Peggy," who was named after her grandmother, suddenly becomes known as "Margaret," this may indicate the death of the older woman for whom the child was named. "Polly" may become Mary, "Betty" may become Elizabeth, and so on. Watch for the changing of a title from junior to senior. As you may know, before the twentieth century, *junior* did not necessarily indicate that a man was the son of the man with the same name who used senior. It demonstrated only that there was an older man of the same name living in the community. See chapter eight, "Sorting Individuals of the Same Name," for a more extensive discussion.

7. Watch for legal transactions of the offspring. The division of lands previously held is an indication of death, and if the lands are sold and the heirs leave the community, both parents are likely to be deceased. Land sold "in the interest of Samuel Connelly, a minor" may be a clue to the death of a parent. Note the absence of one-third of the land of the deceased; it may be held for the widow during her lifetime, and then dispersed at her death. When the land is divided into parts and all the children are accounted for, the wife of the deceased man has predeceased him.

Clues to the Occurrence of a Marriage

1. Probate records should be checked carefully. Note wills in which the husband (or anyone with his surname) is named as a "legatee," and look for probate in the county of the husband's or wife's residence at the approximate time of marriage.

It was common during the eighteenth century for the witnesses of a will to be one person from the wife's side of the family and one from the husband's. This is not a hard and fast rule, but one certainly worth investigating. Often guardians appointed for the children will be a member of her family as well as one of his. **Guardians are almost always family members.** If you had dependent children, wouldn't you most likely choose a family member to look after any estate your children might inherit? The only exception I have

Important

noticed to this rule also gives a clue to marriage: the widow's new husband, the children's stepfather, becomes the guardian.

2. Look for deeds in which the husband was the grantee of a land parcel of unknown origin. Perhaps his wife brought the land to the marriage. Before you jump to this conclusion, however, be sure to check the many ways people may acquire land other than in fee simple. Check delinquent tax sales, civil suits, entitlement (such as military bounty land), federal land sales, and other nontraditional methods for acquiring land that have nothing to do with inheritance. Look for situations in which the husband was a co-owner with others who were not his brothers and sisters or their spouses. This may indicate lands held in common with his wife's siblings.

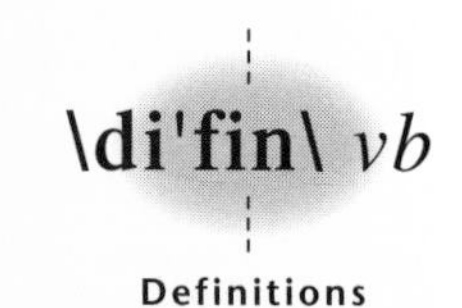

Definitions

Fee simple is property granted without limitation or condition—sold or given to a man or woman and his or her heirs absolutely, without any end or limit.

3. Quitclaims executed by a husband who may be acting in his wife's place.

> Franklin County, Missouri, Deed Book D:334: On May 4, 1841, Andrew Caldwell and wife, Nancy, sold and quitclaimed to William Bell, all right, title and interest in their undivided share of the estate of Leonard Fairer, deceased.

4. Watch for the sudden prosperity of a male ancestor that you can't account for. This may indicate inheritance from the bride's side of the family.

5. Any deeds involving a woman are worth investigating. She may be selling property she inherited from her father or husband; quitclaiming for the same reason; selling land with a son or brother; or selling lands to a child.

6. Unusual names that may be surnames can often be clues worth searching. Pressly Glenn, Holloway Cobb, Avery Morgan, and Bailey Bond were all named for the mother's side of the family.

7. Marriage contracts, often found in deed books, trust deeds, intestate land divisions, deeds of gift, equity and probate court records, quitclaims, and property settlements in divorce cases are all possible sources for marriage records and identification of a spouse. The following deed of gift does not name the husband, although most gifts to married women do. This one is especially nice, as it also names three grandchildren. As the deed was recorded in Missouri, we can assume the daughter was living there.

> Boone County, Missouri, Deed book A:67: 26 November 1821, Benjamin Lawless of Kentucky, for the natural love and affection he had for

grandchildren Minerva Riggins, William Riggins and Thomas Riggins, the children of daughter Bargellia Riggins, he gave negro girl, Nelly, age 14 years.

The following trust deed provides the residence of the father and the Tennessee residence of his daughter, her husband, and her later residence in Missouri. It can be assumed that Isaac Fulkerson was then in Virginia with his probable grandfather, Reuben Bradley, but that he either lived in Missouri or was planning to move there. Reuben's daughter, Sarah Fulkerson, and her husband Frederick were planning to move to Missouri, probably to join their son and perhaps other relatives.

Lafayette County, Missouri, Deed Book C:341: 23 July 1829, Reuben Bradley of Washington County, Virginia, sold to Isaac Fulkerson, James Sharp and Jacob Sharp of Lafayette County, Missouri, and Nathaniel Dryden of Washington County, Virginia, who is about to remove to the state of Missouri; that whereas Sarah, the daughter of Reuben, married Frederick Fulkerson several years ago and now resides in Rhea County, Tennessee and contemplates moving to Missouri in September next, and said Bradley being advanced in life and desirous to make some suitable provision for his married daughters and out of control of their husbands, with love and affection for daughter Sarah and children born to her or hereafter, conveyed to Isaac Fulkerson and Jas. Sharp in trust two negro slaves: a man about twenty-five purchased by Bradley, and a negro girl aged about nine years named Jane which Bradley intends to send to his daughter by her son for the purposes mentioned herein. Sarah may use the slave for her own use during her natural life, but without any power to sell or dispose of slaves and at her death go to her children. Filed for record in Lafayette County, Missouri 31 July 1832.

8. Cemeteries can provide inferences of marriage from inscriptions, family groupings, and even types of tombstones. A young woman (age twenty-two to twenty-eight) in a family burial plot who has a different surname from the others buried there was probably a daughter who married, died young (perhaps in childbirth), and whose husband then remarried. Look for adjoining stones with different names, but of the same shape, type of stone, and style of carving (see Figure 2-14 below).

These tombstones were probably purchased, carved, and set at the same

Figure 2-14
William F. son of G.W. & Virginia Huffman b. Dec. 25 1887 d. Mar. 17 1888. Lonnie son of H.S. & Virginia Miller b. Jan. 25 1897 d. Feb. 6 1897.

time, most likely when Lonnie died. We can assume that Virginia was first married to William F. Huffman, but by 1897 she was married to H.S. Miller.

A "stranger" in the family plot may actually be a relative who can provide clues to a woman's maiden name. Two children lie in the Strain family plot in a Monmouth, Warren County, Illinois, cemetery. Nathan Brown, a man of eighty years, was also buried in that plot. He died over twenty years after the Strain family had left Warren County. I had assumed James Strain had sold part of the plot to a stranger who needed a burial place. *Wrong!* Nathan Brown was Nancy Strain's younger brother.

Sometimes no stones exist, but there may be a record of purchases of plots. Knowing that an ancestor purchased a plot where someone whose name you do not recognize is buried may indicate the burial of an in-law or other relative. I found the unmarked graves of my great-grandparents in Prosser, Washington, because their infant grandson, who would have been my great-uncle, was in the same plot. His gravestone led me to the records that indicated who had purchased the cemetery plots.

Clues to the *date of a marriage* are:

a. the birth of the first child.
b. the sale of a parcel of land from a father to his son or son-in-law, especially if the sale was for a small amount of money, such as $50 (know the going rate for land in the area at the time to verify this).
c. the acquisition of a small parcel of land by a young man—he has either just married or is likely to be intending to.
d. movement on the Pennsylvania tax list from freeman (or inmate) to regular poll tax for a white male.

9. Correlating two dates, one in which the woman was single and one closely following in which she was married. As an example, I learned from a deed dated 14 November 1700 that Hannah, the wife of William Sumner of Middletown, Connecticut, was the daughter of Daniel Henchman of Boston. But by 1700, Hannah had been married a long time—her first child was born 22 November 1679. Could I come closer to estimating the time of marriage? Deeds again provided the answer. On 15 August 1678, along with her brother Hezekiah Henchman, Hannah witnessed a deed as Hannah Henchman, and on 4 April 1679, she was a witness to her grandmother Elizabeth Clement's deed of gift as Hannah Sumner. So Hannah Henchman was married to William Sumner between August 1678 and April 1679. In fact, unless Hannah and William jumped the gun by necessity, they were married between August 1678 and February 1679, as her first son was born in November.

Locating births, deaths, and marriages when no vital records are available requires studying a multitude of records. It demands the correlation of data rather than finding that one record of absolute proof. It means the researcher makes a logical and chronological study of the records to bring together the myriad events that re-create an individual's life—one begun by birth, connected by marriage, and ended by death.

---

[1] Donald Lines Jacobus, "Retroactive Dates and Places," *The American Genealogist* 34 (January 1967):31-35.

[2] M. Halsey Thomas, ed., *The Diary of Samuel Sewall 1674–1729* 2 vols., (New York: Farrar, Straus and Giroux, 1973), I:80.

[3] Francis G. Walett, *The Diary of Ebenezer Parkman 1703–1782* (Worcester: American Antiquarian Society, 1974), 128.

[4] "Some Obituaries and Death Notices," abstracted from the *St. Louis Christian Advocate* of the Methodist Episcopal Church, South, various volumes of *Missouri Pioneers* compiled and published by Nadine Hodges and Mrs. Howard W. Woodruff.

[5] "Buncombe County, North Carolina, Special Court Proceedings, 1798–1812," 326. FHL film 410980.

Why Does the Census Taker Always Miss *My* Ancestor?

Ancestors sometimes do not appear where we expect them to in the federal census. Too often a genealogist assumes that the enumerator "missed" the individual or family sought and abandons the search. Let's explore some of the common reasons you may not be able to find your ancestors in census reports, and I'll suggest methods to overcome this difficulty.

The federal census is a resource genealogists depend upon. It is easily accessible through microfilm, interlibrary loan, and online through such Web sites as HeritageQuest and Ancestry.com. Because it is theoretically a count of all the people then living in the United States, we deservedly have high expectations of finding the person we seek. We also know that the census contains information valuable to the genealogist. It is more than just a list of names; it contains data needed for establishing relationships, and clues to further research.

In fact, when one genealogist asks another for help, the first question the helper usually asks is "Did you find those people in the census?" A census, especially those from 1850 on, puts a person in time and space, gives him an approximate age, places him inside a residence (usually with other people who are significant to him), notes his place of birth, and offers other valuable information used by astute researchers. But what happens when the individual is *not* found in the expected census? The most common step that genealogists take is to move back another decade and try to place the person ten years earlier. Often this fails. Why can't the individual be located in the census where he *should* be? The easiest answer is that the census taker missed him. That reply—made all too often—is frequently false. Too seldom does the genealogist ask *how else* the individual might have been listed, *where else* he might have been listed, or—if he was indeed missed by the census taker—*why* he was missed, and who else might have been missed as well.

Before I develop some of these issues and list some of the reasons that individuals do not appear in an expected place in a census, first **let's transform ourselves from the person searching into the person sought.** Think about where you probably appeared on the censuses taken during your lifetime. This may give you some insight into why your ancestor is difficult to locate. Track your own life and reflect where you were or *should have* been during each decade the census was taken. Do you remember you or your parents filling out the census form? Would you be easy or difficult for a future researcher to find? Why?

Idea Generator

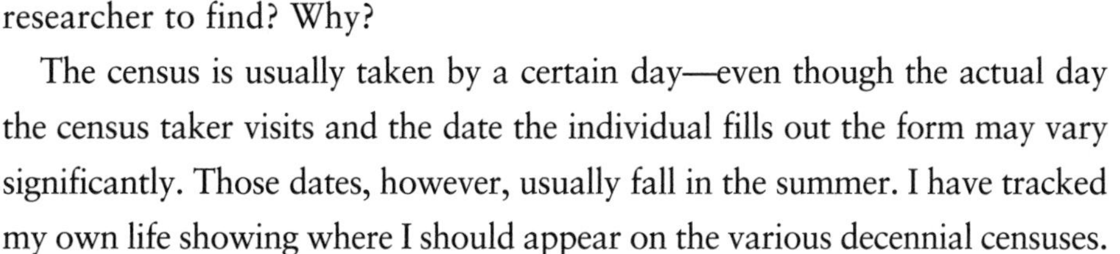

The census is usually taken by a certain day—even though the actual day the census taker visits and the date the individual fills out the form may vary significantly. Those dates, however, usually fall in the summer. I have tracked my own life showing where I should appear on the various decennial censuses.

1950	Clay County, Missouri [with parents]
1960	Clay County, Missouri or Polk County, Florida (with parents; moved in June 1960; may have been missed or may have been enumerated in both places!)
1970	Dade County, Florida (I remember filling out the form in the *fall* of 1970. In June 1970, I would have been in Clay County, Missouri.)
1980	Greene County, Missouri
1990	Greene County, Missouri
2000	Greene County, Missouri

Two significant items emerge from the above for the purposes of our discussion. First, individuals tend to be the most mobile between the ages of eighteen and forty. Of course, the childhood years are when the genealogist is hoping to find and connect a person with his or her parents. For two of the above censuses I should have been counted with my parents, but for the 1960 census, we were in transit. After finishing my education, beginning my career, and marrying, my life became more stable—as it does for many people—so I remained in one location for over thirty years.

Often genealogists begin to reconstruct a person's life from the information we find on the census. Nevertheless, the census provides just a skeleton of a family. The census is only one step in the research process. Often you find the information you seek only after have you have used the information on the census to lead you to other records about the family.

Individuals are particularly hard to find before 1850, when the census listed only the heads of households. Using information I gained from a study of 1,000 early Southwest Missouri pioneers, I believe I have found 141 of those pioneers who were not heads of households in 1830, but were listed in another household as just a slash mark in the appropriate age category. I've determined that 108 were living with their fathers, 22 with their widowed mothers, 5 with their brothers, 2 with their fathers-in-law, 3 with their stepfathers, and 1 with his guardian. It was extremely difficult for me to locate those 141 people, so I am not surprised that there are still 271 individuals out of the 1,000 whom I can't find listed in 1830. This does *not* mean that these people were not included in the census. They may be in similar situations to the ones I will describe in the next pages.

In addition to the problem presented when an ancestor is not the head of household in an expected area, an ancestor's mobility may be another major issue for those searching censuses before 1850. We think of our society as a mobile one, but many of our ancestors, particularly those living in the nineteenth century, were just as prone to move as we are. After the War of 1812, the largest migration in the history of America began—just at the time when the census provides only limited information, making it very hard to locate a pioneering ancestor. Of the 1,000 individuals who purchased land in Southwest Missouri between 1835 and 1839, only about 91 percent can be found on the next available census: the 1840. By 1850, more have disappeared from the rolls. Of those who purchased land in Southwest Missouri before 1839, 125 cannot be found anywhere on the 1850 census.

Considering the handicaps of terrain, the lack of decent roads, poor transportation, the isolation of the people, and the rigors of the job, it is amazing that the census enumerators did as well as they did. Today we often hear about undercounting in the census, and no doubt omissions occurred in the nineteenth and early twentieth centuries as well. However, it is important to remember that census takers were paid by the number of people they recorded in a county. For instance, in 1810 the pay for federal census takers was two and one-half cents per person listed. Thus, those taking the census were financially motivated to locate as many people as possible. Too often the genealogist is quick to blame the enumerator.

Warning

In fact, **there are three presumptions we frequently make when we cannot find the individual or family we seek.**

i. **Presumption of Error:** We presume the census taker was at fault. You will often hear, "A lazy census taker evaluated the neighborhood," or "The census taker only enumerated some families in the area and ignored mine," or "That census enumerator was careless and sloppy."

ii **Presumption of Blame:** We presume the ancestor was at fault. "Our family never wanted anything to do with government people," or "Hiram Hideaway must have been avoiding the census taker," or "I bet old Hiram told a wild tale to that census taker and didn't answer the questions properly. He didn't think his name or his family was any business of the government." That may have been true, but old Hiram was taking a risk. It was illegal to knowingly give false information to a census taker.

iii. **Presumption of Loss:** We presume that no important information can be gleaned from that census if the ancestor we seek is not listed.

If the researcher presumes any, or all, of the above incorrect suppositions, the result is a missed opportunity.

Discussed below are fourteen types of problems that researchers sometimes encounter when using a census. People may appear to be missing because the researcher is using finding aids rather than the census itself, or because they may be "hidden" in an unexpected section. Some people may actually be missing because they were not counted. Examples of these problems and ideas for solving them follow.

FINDING AIDS

1. What do you do when the ancestor you're researching is not found in a published computerized census index, on a CD-ROM, or with an Internet search? Far too many genealogists presume that when their ancestor is not in the census index, he was *not* in the census. The census index is a *finding aid*—that is all. *Aid* means *help* or *assistance*, not *replacement*.

Some problems are inherent when using a computerized index. See Richard Saldana's *A Practical Guide to the "Misteaks" Made in Census Indexes* (Salt Lake City: R.H. Saldana & Company, 1987) for suggestions as to how to work with these difficulties. Problems include spelling variations, complete omissions, typographical errors, and reversed first and last names.

Examples:

Roger D. Joslyn, CG, FASG, who works extensively in New York, found the following variations in the 1850 New York City census index for the common name Smith. Following the name is the Soundex code, showing that a reversal of letters leads to unexpected changes in the code.

SMITH	S-324
MSITH	M-256
SIMTH	S-322
SMTIH	S-330
SMIHT	S-324

If you are working in a small or rural county, it may be easier to just check the census itself than to figure out the index. John Biggs and William Montgomery were absent from the census index, but easily located on the census in the county expected. Caleb Headlee was indexed as "Hadley"; Jane Cawlfield as "Coffield." When the actual census was checked and the names placed in the context of the neighborhood, they were located without difficulty. The spellings differed enough to place them in unexpected areas of a large census index, but not so different that they were not immediately recognized when the names appeared in the census itself.

What *do* you expect to gain when you pick up a census index? Do you expect to find your ancestor? Narrow those expectations. Use the index to help find a *page*, not a *person*. If you find the person and page you need, fine. If you do not locate that individual, you still have no idea whether she was on the census itself. Almost everyone who has been in this field long enough can give an example of finding an individual on the census who did not appear in the index—or at least not where he was expected.

2. New problems arise with using CD-ROMs and Internet databases to search census indexes. When reading text in a census index, *Sameul* and *Goerge* are easily recognized as typographical errors. When you search a computer for a name, however, the computer will not "hit" on a misspelled name if the researcher has typed in the correct spelling. Most census indexes on CD or the Internet do not permit "wild-card" searches, making it easier to miss the individual for whom you are searching.

Example:

In just one county, Franklin County, Tennessee, I found *Smauel Baker*, *Uraih Deckard*, and *Michael Dckard* on the CD-ROM index. When I checked the actual census, all were spelled correctly. Isaac Hodges of Franklin County was indexed as Isaac "Odges." The given name William was misspelled as Will*aim* *forty-five times* on the CD-ROM of

Robertson County, Tennessee, alone! Some CD-ROM census indexes are even worse than the printed ones.

3. Some compiled census materials are done very well; others are incredibly sloppy. If you are using a published census odds are that, even if you find the individual you are seeking, not all the information included in the census will be included in the publication. Again, if you don't find the individual you are trying to find in the publication, this doesn't mean he wasn't in the county. If the compiler is not familiar with the handwriting of the period, the enumerator's style, or the families in the community, the name may be garbled. Some names and letters are easily misread.

Examples:
Elias Powell was transcribed as "Lewis" Powell, Benjamin Snyder as Benjamin "Sngou," Hanny Denny as Hannah "Deury," Lewis Oldfield as Lewis "Aufield," John Toler as John "Soler"—and I could provide dozens more examples. When the actual census was examined by a researcher who knew the families, these individuals were easily found.

4. You may think that unusual names would be easy to trace—but not in the census! While common names often can be deciphered even when poorly written, unusual ones can't. Many of these names could be determined by a knowledgeable researcher who is familiar with the family and the community, but they are not likely to be found simply with a computerized search.

Examples:
Demarcus Hopper transcribed as "Demasters" Hopper, Sampson Cordel as Samuel "Carde," Thomas Journigan as Thomas "Jonekin," and Reanos Thompson as "Remus" Thompson.

Some initials and letters are harder to distinguish than others. The names *Daniel* and *David* may be difficult to differentiate; the letters *M*, *H*, *N*, and *W* may also be difficult to discern from one another.

Examples:
John S. Wills was transcribed as John S. "Mills," John C. Henson as John C. "Oten," Jesse Hiller as Jesse "Miller," and James Wilson as James "Nelson."

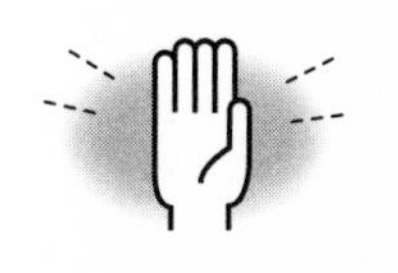
Warning

The researcher must also watch for double names or prefixes that are read and indexed incorrectly.

Examples:

Amos Hill Briant should have been Amos *Hillbrant*, John D. Rosset should have been John *Derosset*, John P. Pool should have been John *Pettipool*, and Mathew M. Peak should have been Mathew *McPeak*.

5. Another problem with compiled censuses is the ditto mark (") that census enumerators often used to designate repeats. One who compiles the census may attempt to be helpful by translating those ditto marks into surnames, but this may mislead the researcher. For example, in the 1850 printed census of Greene County, Missouri, the publisher substituted a surname for the ditto marks; thus households #1619, #1620, and #1621 all appeared to be named Johnson.

#1618 Thomas Simmons, age 63, born North Carolina
#1619 Bethena Johnson, age 28, born Tennessee
#1620 Michael Johnson, age 26, born Missouri
#1621 Amos Johnson, age 24, born Tennessee

The microfilmed copy of the census shows that the elder man was named *Simmons*, members of household #1619 were named *Johnson*, and households #1620 and #1621 were dittos—presumably of *Johnson*. However, because at least two of the younger persons listed, Bethena and Amos, are known to be Thomas Simmons's children, the census taker must have meant the dittos to indicate copies of *Simmons* rather than of *Johnson*. Bethena Johnson had been born a Simmons but was widowed; Amos was her brother. When the census taker used the ditto marks, he made a mistake; the publication compounded his error.

Greene County, Missouri, Cass Township (heads only)
#1618 Thomas Simmons, age 63, born North Carolina
#1619 Bethena Johnson, age 28, born Tennessee
#1620 Michael " , age 26, born Missouri
#1621 Amos " , age 24, born Tennessee

6. An index may omit part of or even an entire county.

Examples:

The 1870 Collin County, Texas, census is covered on two microfilm reels, but the second roll was omitted from the index. The 1830 Marion County, Tennessee, census was omitted by the indexers; the 1870 Putnam County, Missouri, census also was overlooked. Only 128 families are indexed on Automated Archives CD-ROM 1830 index for Hamilton County, Tennessee, but 354 heads of household were listed on the actual census. Researchers are probably aware of dozens more examples.

COUNTED, BUT "HIDDEN"

These examples refer to situations where the individuals and families being sought actually appear in the census, but not as the researcher might expect. This may be because members of the family were given the wrong name, or because of the way the census itself was recorded or copied.

1. One of the reasons that people may be hidden in a census is that all household members were once assigned the surname of the head of household. This problem often occurred in households that sociologists now call a "blended family," that include members of the extended family. Perhaps not only the nuclear husband, wife, and children resided there, but also widowed daughters and their children, stepchildren, mothers- or fathers-in-law, or other more distant relatives. In many cases, all these were listed under the surname of the head of the household.

Examples:
Four children of Absalom Looney were listed under the surname *Asher* while living with their stepfather in 1850. In another case, Elizabeth Moore and her son, J.H. Moore, were given the surname *Redman* when enumerated with Elizabeth's father, Joel Redman, in 1850. Elizabeth Folks was living with her son-in-law, Vincent Thompson, in Smith County, Tennessee, in 1850, and was listed under the name of *Thompson.*

Too often, beginning genealogists assume that all children living in a household with a married couple are the couple's biological children. Carefully study the members of the household, and do not assign children to parents simply because they live together. This common mistake can lead to many false conclusions about parentage.

Eli and Susannah Cheek were listed in 1850 in Dallas County, Missouri, in dwelling #384. She was fifty-three years old and Eli was fifty-five. Also living in the household were James Cheek, age seventeen, born in Tennessee; James Patterson, age ten, and Mildred Patterson, age eight, both born in Missouri. A submitter to the LDS Ancestral File™ assigned the latter two children the middle name *Patterson* and the surname *Cheek*, making it appear as though they were children of Eli and Susanna Cheek. A more careful genealogist would have noticed the large gap between James Cheek and the Patterson children, and realized that it was unlikely for two living brothers only seven years apart in age both to be named James. Moreover, Susannah Cheek would have been forty-five years old when Mildred was born; and although it is not impossible for a woman to give birth at that age, it is unlikely. Instead, Mildred and James Patterson were probably Susannah's grandchildren by daughter Mary Cheek Patterson—who was not even mentioned in the Ancestral File as a daughter of Eli and Susannah. Apparently, James and Mildred Patterson were raised by their grandparents. Mary is not listed in the county under the surname Cheek or Patterson in 1850, although she had returned by 1860.

2. Before 1850, only the heads of households were listed on the census; everyone else in the residence was recorded with nothing more than a slash mark. These slashes, of course, represent more "hidden" individuals—particularly women who often went from their father's home to their husband's without ever becoming a head of household. Although we can never be absolutely certain that the individuals who are counted by slash marks are the people we suspect them to be, we should not ignore the possibility. If we proceed with our research as if these people did not exist because they are not specifically named in a census, we lose valuable clues to information found in other records. If those sources indicate that an individual was living in the community when the census was taken, trying to find the household in which the individual was living can lead to establishing relationships, sometimes even parentage.

Example:
In 1830, Elijah Dyer was undoubtedly the forty-to-fifty-year-old male living in Pittsylvania County, Virginia, with his eighty-to-ninety-year-old father, Haman Dyer, who remained the head of household. Elijah Dyer of Miller County, Missouri, would have fit into that category at that time; his father is believed to be Haman Dyer, and tax records indicate Elijah was living in the county, although he was not listed as a head of household.

Example:
In 1840, Sarah McNew was not a head of household in Rives County, Missouri. However, she sold land there in December 1840 and paid taxes in 1845. She is surely the fifty-to-sixty-year-old woman listed as living with her son, Frederick McNew, in the 1840 census.

3. Young people new to a community and living with unidentified relatives may easily become hidden in a census. However, you can't simply assume that they were missed by the census taker, even though positive identification may be difficult because of the limited information that is available on them. For instance, a man may be listed on the tax lists so you know he is living in the community, but not listed as a head of household. The obvious place to look is a male of the right age listed with his paternal family. The next place is a male of the right age listed with his maternal family. The next place to consider is with in-laws, if he was newly married. Knowing the collateral family may help you determine which slash mark could be the man you seek. You may never find a "hidden" individual on the census, but supplementary records can reveal he was living in the community.

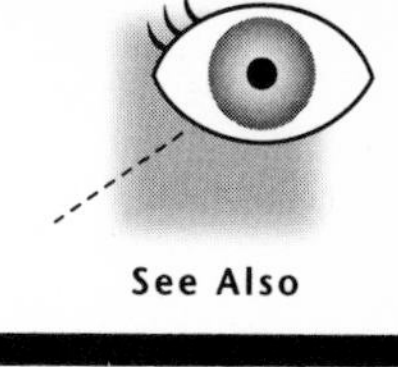

See Also

See chapter four, pages 83-86, for the case of Isaac J. Murry and the importance of locating him on the 1840 census, when he was not a head of household.

Example:
Silas Baker was an unmarried schoolteacher in Greene County, Missouri, in the 1840s. Customarily, teachers lived with various families during the school year. From other records Silas is known to have been in the county in 1840, but the household in which he was living cannot be identified. He died before the next census, so his age can only be estimated from his activities without the aid of the census.

4. Census enumerators sometimes mangled and scrambled names so badly that a mother would not be able to recognize a listing for her own child. Using phonetic spelling can help you find a hidden ancestor. How does the name *sound* when pronounced? Another method for locating a lost ancestor is to scout out the entire township where you think he should be, as well as the surrounding communities. Scroll through each page carefully to see if he might be listed under a garbled name.

Example:
A county history said that in 1835, Jonas Brown and his son-in-law, Williamson Foster, moved from Kentucky to Prairie Hollow, Missouri. I thought this would be easy to verify; I simply had to find a county on the census index in Kentucky where a Brown and a Foster were listed together. That didn't work. No Jonas Brown, no Williamson Foster listed in the state. I did find a "Jones Brown," but there were no Foster families in that county on the census. More research produced the county where Jonas's daughter was said to have married. I

found the marriage record for Nancy Brown and Williamson Foster in Clark County, Kentucky. I then returned to the census for that county. I found "Jones Brown" and next to him "Williamson Austin." The census taker didn't miss them; he just misunderstood the names. Williamson Foster was hidden under the name Austin.

Use phonetic (or creative) spelling when entering search queries into CD-ROMs or Internet databases, particularly for those individuals with unusual first names.

5. In most cases, the federal census records you will examine are government copies of documents written in the field. As Kathleen W. Hinckley notes in her book, *Your Guide to the Federal Census* (Cincinnati: Betterway Books, 2002), "The original manuscript is the one the census marshal carried when he questioned local residents. Depending on the law at the time, handwritten copies of these manuscripts were made prior to their distribution to government officials. Unfortunately, it is nearly impossible to know whether records we examine today are the originals or copies." When handwritten copies were made it would have been easy for errors to occur, such as skipping family members, moving slashes into the wrong rows, or placing individuals within the wrong family. Human error can lead to a number of problems with the census, so the researcher needs to remain alert.

6. Crucial parts of the name or enumeration might be missing or obliterated. Abbreviations may be used for the first names, or a last name may be missing entirely. The letters may be smudged or parts of the household overlooked or combined with a household to whom they do not belong. The family may give middle names or nicknames that you do not recognize. Be sure you know the nicknames common to the era and to the ethnic groups with which you are working: Nancy/Agnes, Martha/Patsy, Mary/Polly, Biddy/Obedience, Bridget/Delia, Milly/Emeline/Melissa, Gus/Augustine, Abe/Abraham, Bony/Bonaparte, Kit/Christopher, Iggy/Ignatius, or Ed, Ted, or Ned for Edmund, Edward, or Edwin. It is not unusual for the census taker simply to have copied the names incorrectly.

For More Info

See Ruth Land Hatten, CGRS, "Finding 'Missing Men' on Early Census Records: The Example of Thomas Russell," *National Genealogical Society Quarterly* 81 (March 1993) 46-50.

Example:

Jason Ashworth was listed in 1860 in Polk County, Missouri, as "James" Ashworth. The lack of any other records from that vicinity for a man named James Ashworth prove that the census taker or copier simply must have made a mistake and that "James" was actually Jason.

Example:
Greenberry was often shortened to "Green" or "G.B.," Ebenezer to "Eb," which could easily be misread as "Eli," and Constantine to "Tine."

7. You may be looking for the right man in the wrong place. **Before 1850, geographical boundaries were unclear, jurisdictions could overlap, and county and state lines often changed from decade to decade.**

Warning

Example:
Isaac Rogers lived in St. Clair County, Missouri, in 1840, which was then called Rives. He was buried in Hickory County, but he was enumerated on the 1840 census in Polk County.

Example:
James Harrison was one of the first settlers at the mouth of the Little Piney River in Missouri, arriving about 1817. While James did not move from the location where he first settled, the counties in that area were dividing rapidly. He was taxed first in Franklin County in 1819. When Gasconade County was formed in 1821, he became justice of the peace for Boone Township. Crawford County was formed in 1829, and James became clerk of the probate; his home became a pioneer courthouse. James was listed in Crawford County in 1830, the first surviving census for Missouri. By 1840 his place of residence was in Pulaski County, and he was head of household there. James left a will dated 28 August 1836, in which he called himself "of Crawford County." The will was proved in 1842 in Pulaski County. In 1857, the area where the Harrisons had settled in 1817 became Phelps County and remains so, the same house having been in five different county jurisdictions.

MISSED—BUT WHY?

Although many "missing persons" may be found by using the methods described in this chapter, there undoubtedly are cases in which the census taker clearly did not enumerate the family you seek. Following are some of the reasons for such failures that I have encountered in my own experience. It is important to see whether any of these situations apply before you abandon your search.

1. Jurisdictional or boundary confusion in a part of the state left a "hole" in the census enumeration.

Example:
In Missouri in 1840, the borders between Douglas and Christian counties and between Benton, Camden, and Hickory counties were unclear, and thus no census takers covered some areas, all assuming that some districts were someone else's responsibility. Anywhere from fifty to a hundred families were thus not counted.

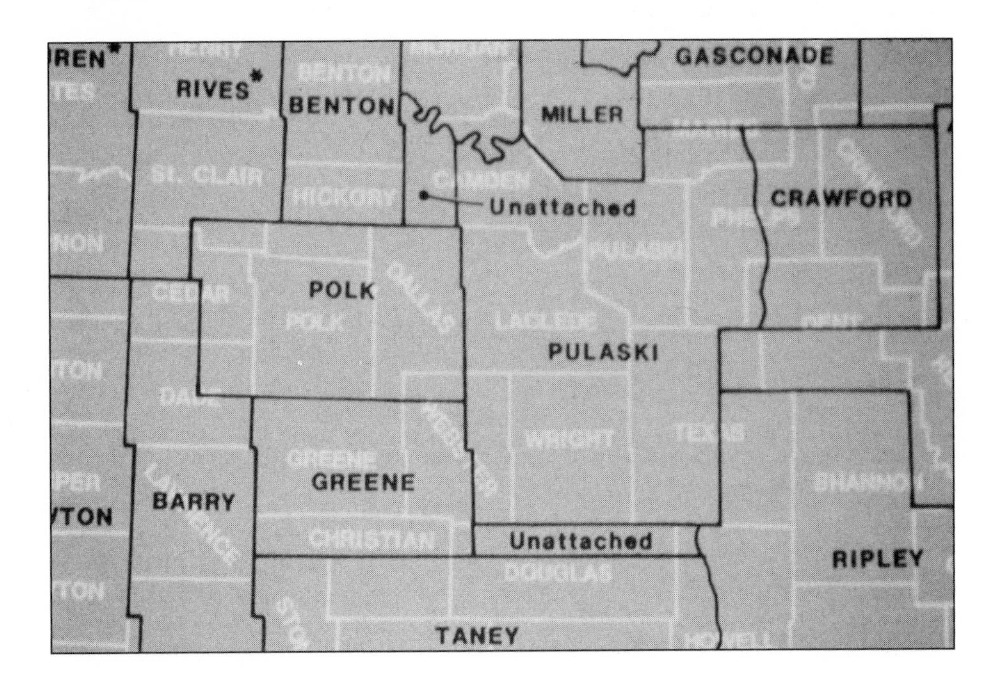

Figure 3-1
Map of the Douglas-Christian, Benton-Camden-Hickory county boundaries, Missouri.

Example:
Marcus Williams could not be found in the 1850 California census. The answer was simple. He was living in San Jose County—a county whose 1850 census is simply lost.

2. Geographic isolation of the family may result in omission from the census. Learn the trail of the census taker by matching contemporary roads and neighbors. Once you determine his route, you will know if he omitted one family, several families, or an entire area.

Example:
Greene County, Missouri, was founded in 1833. That part of Missouri was under the administrative jurisdiction of Crawford County, but census maps indicate that the individuals who were living in that area should have been listed under Wayne County. They were not listed in

either county; so although we know from other records that these people existed, they don't appear in the census because they simply were not counted.

3. Life events such as births, funerals, marriages, unexpected trips, and summer vacations may have taken families away from their usual place of residence at the time the census taker was in the area.

Example:
Frances B. Whitney was not found in the 1860 census. She married in October of that year. She was a schoolteacher and may have been living with a family who probably didn't think of her as a family member, or who perhaps forgot that she had been with them in June by the time their neighborhood was canvassed in October. Perhaps the family with whom she was living in August knew she wasn't with them in June, so they didn't list her. (See Connie Lenzen, CGRS, "Proving a Maternal Line: The Case of Frances B. Whitney," *National Genealogical Society Quarterly* 82 [March 1994]: 17-31.)

Example:
James Strain died in Cloud County, Kansas, on 25 January 1880. As he was the probate judge at the time, his death received front-page coverage in the local newspaper. He did not appear on the mortality schedule, however, nor was his family listed on the 1880 census. The family appeared to be there during the month of June, as "Johnny Strain" was credited by the local newspaper with saving the life of another child on June 24. Why was the family missed? An extended trip during the summer months seems the only explanation, but this has not been established.

4. The family may have been migrating during the census year and thus may have been in an unexpected place, or they may have been so new to a location that the enumerator simply didn't know they were there. Although the winter months were the preferred times for travel because roads were frozen and passable, if the family was moving livestock, they may have waited until grass was available in the spring or summer. Some may have told a census taker they were "just passing through" when he asked about their residence and thus were not counted; others may have been unknown to members of the community because they had not yet settled.

Consult other documents to determine how long the family remained in the old location and by what date they must have left. Check additional records to establish at what point they had definitely arrived in the new community. If you cannot produce such evidence, you may still be able to locate the family later in an unexpected place. Unless a family was making the big jump to California or Oregon, many migrants seemed to go back and forth between their old homes and their new ones. Often they would clear the land and begin establishing a homestead, then return for other family members—or to settle old business, such as a parent's estate. They might be out of the neighborhood temporarily just at the time the census taker was passing through. They *should* have been listed, but weren't.

Perhaps the family moved into a *new* territory. The area may not yet have been surveyed, or officially organized or attached. Perhaps it was too distant from the seat of government for newcomers to be noticed. In essence, anyone living in unorganized territory was squatting, and the census taker may not have been aware of them. The territory may not have been organized well enough to conduct a careful and comprehensive census. Oregon and California, for example, experienced such floods of new settlers in the mid-nineteenth century that census takers simply could not keep up with the constant flux. We know there are huge gaps in the censuses of both these areas.

Example:
Jacob Alderman appeared in probate court in May 1850 in Polk County, Missouri, asking for guardians to be appointed for John J. and Lucinda Alderman, but did not request that he become one. He cannot be found on that county's census, nor in any neighboring counties or states. He was not on the local 1851 tax list. The conclusion is that he moved that summer from Missouri to an unknown location.

Example:
Walter Anderson and family migrated to California in 1847, and contemporary documents record his presence there soon after his arrival. Before 1850 the family moved to what became Mendocino County; they were among the first Anglo settlers in that area. Although they are listed in the 1852 California state census, they do not appear in the one for 1850.

5. The family was new to the area, so the enumerator was unaware of them even though the community was organized and functional. **Newcomers**

were more likely to be among the missing in a census, because neither the census taker nor the neighbors may have become acquainted with them. This would be true especially if the terrain were mountainous or hilly and the family had settled in a remote "holler."

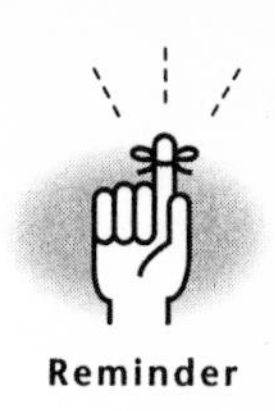

6. The family was enumerated, but not in the expected place. Perhaps they moved for a short time to a location unknown to you. As new territories opened, people often moved into them for short periods of time to determine whether the area was suitable for permanent settlement. Sometimes they stayed; sometimes they became "go-backers" who returned to prior residences. If such moves occurred during the year the census was taken, you may think that the family was missed, when actually they are listed in a different location.

Example:
An extensive genealogy of the Dooley family produced a detailed biographical sketch of a man I was researching. Yet, the compiler did not know that for about four years, between 1836 and 1840, John Dooley had lived in Southwest Missouri. He does not appear in the 1840 census there, nor in the area where he lived in 1850. Where was he in 1840? Apparently, he was missed because he was between a residence in Southwest Missouri and one in the northwest part of the state.

7. Sometimes a family moved but did not follow normal migration patterns, or did not move with the expected neighbors and friends.

Example:
Some Kentucky migrants can be found listed in the northwestern third of Illinois in the 1830s. This is not where one would expect southerners to migrate because the area has an entirely different climate. However, that area was the site of early 1812 bounty land warrants. Most of these migrants did not remain long and moved within a few years to areas that were more familiar, or to which extended family members had already moved.

8. Death and the remarriage of the spouse may obscure the individual for whom you are searching. Of the 1,000 pioneers of Southwest Missouri that I have been studying, 180 had died before the 1850 census. I wonder how many of the 95 I have not been able to locate had also died by this time, but have been "lost" because their spouses had either died or remarried. When a frontier woman was widowed, the likelihood that she would remarry within ten years was very high. Yet, unless marriage records for the time were complete, the

woman you are looking for may be listed under a name she no longer carried. Her first husband is absent from the census because he was no longer alive, while she is hidden within it because she had changed her name.

The importance of studying communities is emphasized over and over in methodology and problem-solving lectures. Knowledge of your ancestor's neighborhood as well as the collateral family can often prove valuable when looking for a "missing" name on the census. As a final lesson on the importance of community when working with the census, let's examine the case of William R. Devin. In a local Missouri history, he was said to be from Lincoln County, Tennessee. However, he is not listed in the printed 1830 Lincoln County census, which was compiled by a reputable publisher. When I checked deeds in Lincoln County, I learned that he purchased land there in 1829 and 1832. Family records stated that his son was born there in 1830—but I still couldn't find him in the census. I studied records of his land purchases and sales, and because they were surveyed on the metes and bounds system, I learned the names of his neighbors. I then located those neighbors on the printed census and found William's brother Clayton listed under the surname "Divins." I then went to the microfilm copy and started two pages ahead of where Clayton and the neighbors were listed and examined each name. In the process, I learned how that census taker fashioned his *D*s. Once I detected that pattern, I was able to locate William—whose name appeared as "Owen" rather than as Devin. Unfortunately, the name *Owen* is a common one that appears at least once in nearly every county. It was by knowing both William's relative and his neighborhood that I could be sure that this census listing was the correct one for William Devin.

Important

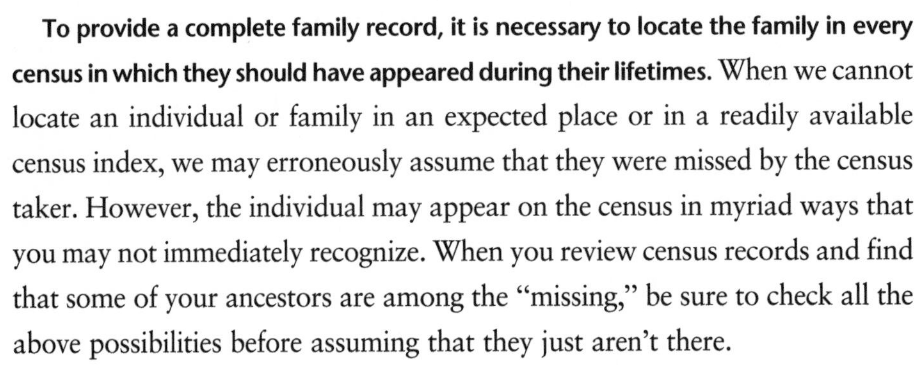
To provide a complete family record, it is necessary to locate the family in every census in which they should have appeared during their lifetimes. When we cannot locate an individual or family in an expected place or in a readily available census index, we may erroneously assume that they were missed by the census taker. However, the individual may appear on the census in myriad ways that you may not immediately recognize. When you review census records and find that some of your ancestors are among the "missing," be sure to check all the above possibilities before assuming that they just aren't there.

Consider the Collateral Kin: Genealogical Research in the Full Family Context

Perhaps the one thing that would improve the quality of research being done, more than any other single factor, would be a concern for complete families rather than just direct lines.

—VAL GREENWOOD, *THE RESEARCHER'S GUIDE TO AMERICAN GENEALOGY*

This chapter will explain and discuss *cluster genealogy*, and I must warn you, it sounds easier than it is. Cluster genealogy requires learning how to create people from just names, getting to know the people within families both as individuals and as part of the human community, and considering both predictable and unpredictable behavior from your ancestors and their friends and neighbors. It requires working with a large number of records, being able to recognize almost by instinct what is important in the record, and what can be noted or even forgotten. Cluster genealogy is not required in solving all genealogical problems—only the most difficult.

This concept was first introduced into genealogical education by Elizabeth Shown Mills in the Advanced Methodology class at the Institute for Genealogical Historical Research at Samford University in Birmingham, Alabama. She advised her students to get to know the neighbors of the ancestors they were researching. By the 1990s, the idea had started to acquire names: "cluster genealogy," "associate analysis," "the neighborhood concept," and most likely other terms as well. **Cluster genealogy requires looking at a particular family from a broader view than as a single family whose pedigree moves back in a straight line to one progenitor.** Studying ancestors in the full family context has evolved from looking not only for the brothers and sisters

Important

of an ancestor, but for other important companions in your ancestor's life as well. Not only are in-laws, collateral family, and associates identified, but these people are then anchored within their own cultural, geographic, and sociological elements. Placing your ancestor and his associates in their historical context not only fleshes them out as individuals, but restores life to their community from the dry pages of unread history books. Undoubtedly, broad family and community research is essential when it becomes necessary to solve the most difficult genealogical problems.

Studying a family within its context probably goes against what may be our very first instinct, and perhaps even the first lesson in genealogy: looking for the family surname. Surely you have encountered people at the library, conferences, or workshops who report, "I have ten thousand names in my computer database" and then ask, "What surnames are you searching?" The more advanced researchers, who have moved beyond the searching of surnames, are always stumped by this question. We are more likely to ask, "What areas are you working in?" or "For what time period?" Narrowing research to a specific locality, to established migration routes, or within a defined time bracket is more likely to aid in finding people with whom to share information.

When we begin genealogical research outside the family's own sources, we usually start with the federal census. Our first job is to find the family household on the most recent census available. Perhaps whoever helped you initially—a teacher, friend, or maybe a librarian—told you, "Don't just look for the ancestral family, but write down every person of that surname living in the county." Those of us searching families named Johnson, Davis, or Miller, as well as the ubiquitous Smith and Jones, probably groaned audibly. When I began searching my maiden name, Hoffman, in western Pennsylvania, I found myself writing down the names of several dozen Hoffman families—many of whom turned out to be not even slightly related. This is usually the first lesson in searching surnames.

You will also find that printed genealogies devoted to families of one surname are sometimes comprehensive, but more often they follow one line for several generations before beginning to cover sisters, brothers, aunts, uncles, and cousins in the late nineteenth or early twentieth century. Indeed, it was common in the late nineteenth century to believe that most people of a certain surname descended from one individual, such as in the case of James Rising of Suffield, Connecticut, or the proverbial "three brothers who came over together." In-depth research has found that rarely to be true. An even less likely scenario is that of a family who came to America together and then separated, with one brother who went south, one brother who went west, and one brother who stayed put. The *one* thing a new immigrant didn't want to happen in his new world was to lose contact with the few people he might know from the old country.

As we learn more about genealogy, we also find that family organizations, newsletters, and reunions usually are devoted to people searching a particular surname or descending from an individual, usually an early colonist. My mother's family always held the Molzen family reunion on May 2. None shared my amusement when I learned that May 2 commemorated the birthday of my great-grandmother—a woman who had been born a Jensen, not a Molzen.

Most genealogists, when they begin their search, are interested primarily in the direct line. On the other hand, there are those who begin by compiling a family history for their grandchildren and include the spouses, in-laws, and female lines (sometimes referred to as "indirect lines"), and they are far ahead of those of us who start by trying to see how far back we can go. The goal of tracing one line backward as far as possible narrows your research to gathering data on certain surnames. Before long, you will find yourself with drawers and filing cabinets full of information on families that are not even slightly related to you. Often, tracing just a surname will lead you on a wild goose chase, or to claim ancestors that later prove to be unrelated to you. Then we have to admit we've been chasing what the well-known genealogist Milton Rubincam called "former ancestors." And then there are those dead ends. Every genealogist encounters dead ends: ancestral lines that stymied people who had been searching for years before we were ever born, and that now stymie us.

More and more of those genealogical puzzles have been unraveled and solved in the last twenty years. Almost every time you pick up a good genealogical journal, you will find an article about a newly discovered relationship, ancestral line, or place of origin. What has changed in our research to make these discoveries possible? New sources show up, of course. Computerized indexes and documents on the Internet have made some material easier to search, and no doubt more people are searching. But research methods have changed as well. **More genealogists are researching families as people connected through relationships, not just through a common name.** We investigate our ancestral families as people who have emotional bonds as well as blood ties, people who have a common history, common traditions, and a commitment to one another. These bonds, relationships, and commitments—and the records that document them—are the factors that can lead to a genealogical

Important

breakthrough. Relationships—be they among neighbors, collateral kin, friends, or significant others—are critical to producing the records that make the connections we seek.

FAMILY NETWORKS

To illustrate, let's look at a theoretical example that shows the complexity of names within an extended family. The local newspaper, *The Possum-Trot Postings*, reported a birthday party given for a seventy-year-old resident, Mrs. Jacob Mitchell. Among the children and relatives who attended were Susan Ackason, Lydia Masters, Allen Boyer, Alice Goodman, James Marquis, Fred Short, Hattie McCormick, James McFarland, and Mary Jane Powell. It is difficult not to notice that all these individuals have a different surname. Yet the newspaper said they were all related. Could all of them have been born to Mrs. Mitchell? If so, under what name were they born? What surname is the one of interest? How could you possibly tell from just the information given?

Extensive research could show that Mrs. Sarah Mitchell, whose maiden name was Boyer, married Jacob Mitchell as her third husband. Her first husband was Peter Marquis, so James is her child by her first marriage. So is Hattie, who married: (1) Edward Short (thus Fred is her son and Mrs. Mitchell's grandson), and then (2) Alfred McCormick. Mrs. Mitchell's second husband was Martin Powell, and children by him include Susan, who then married an Ackason; Lydia, who married Charles Masters; Alice, who married Thomas Goodman; and Mary Jane, who has remained single. James McFarland is Mrs. Mitchell's son-in-law by her deceased daughter, Barbara. Although James McFarland is not Mrs. Mitchell's descendant, his children would be. Allen Boyer is Mrs. Mitchell's brother. Thus, it's not at all farfetched to have ten surnames within a single nuclear family.

It is fascinating to see how this network of family relationships can develop when studying real people. To illustrate this situation, I examined the relationships of ten people who purchased land from the federal land office in Springfield, Missouri:

Daniel Berry	Joseph H. Miller
Lemuel Blanton	William Polk
Ezekiel Madison Campbell	Lucius Rountree
Matilda Jenkins	John D. Shannon
Daniel Bird Miller	John R. Sturtivant

At first this appears to be a list of unrelated surnames, yet Figure 4-1 below shows that each one was connected to another on the list. In this case, the names with stars next to them are the people who actually purchased land. The circles denote brothers and sisters, the solid lines show parents and children, and the infinity symbol (∞) indicates a marriage. Ten different surnames, and yet all are connected by a family relationship. The myriad documents these people generated in their lifetimes show these surnames appearing over and over. A study of any whole community will reveal the same pattern.

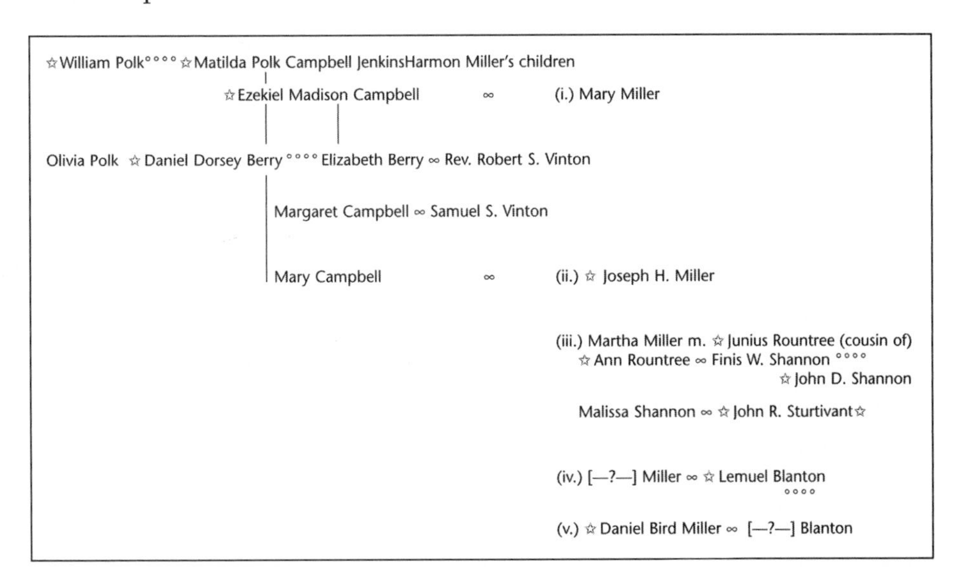

Figure 4-1
Collateral relative chart of William Polk.

Before recent times, relationships through marriage were not distinguished greatly from relations by blood. A woman may think of herself as belonging to the family of her birth name (usually called a maiden name), but that is not necessarily the name by which others recognize her or the one by which she is identified in records. It is, however, the people who bear or once bore this name with whom this woman shares a commitment and an emotional relationship. Therefore, it is those people—not those of her husband's surname—with whom she is most likely to have personal or business dealings that will reveal genealogical connections, especially when she is young. Considering one surname will reveal only a small portion of the people in the family you are researching.

REASONS TO STUDY COLLATERAL LINES

Studying the collateral family will bring many benefits to your genealogical research. First, the more people under investigation, the more records you are likely to find that have been created and survived. Rarely does just one

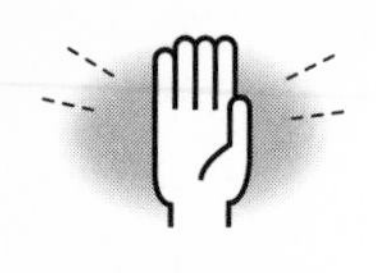

Warning

Too often the genealogist focuses research on those individuals bearing the surname and often only in the direct lineage. For this reason, records which may clarify relationships, "prove" ancestral connections, or add evidence to support a hypothesis can be overlooked. The researcher needs to view genealogical research as discovering intricacies of a family network rather than finding links in a chain.

record provide us with a solid genealogical connection. In most cases, it is many records woven together like strands in a web that weave a solid conclusion. More people simply produce more records for you to study.

Second, studying the entire family helps us to learn about migration patterns, places of origin, and destinations. The same pattern of names will emerge both in the community the group came from and in the community where they later settle. For example, from a well-documented published genealogy, I knew that Matthew Boswell married Edith Rogers and moved to St. Clair County, Missouri, from Henderson County, Tennessee. Rogers is a common surname. How might I find Edith's parents? I could begin searching for families named Rogers in Henderson County, Tennessee. However, I decided to follow a better clue gleaned from the published genealogy: Edith and Matthew Boswell were buried in the Robinson Cemetery in Hickory County, Missouri.

Whenever possible, try to visit cemeteries to see how the graves lie, as this can give marvelous clues to family relationships. The Robinson Cemetery did not disappoint me.

At the bottom of Figure 4-2 below are the gravestones for Matthew Boswell and his wife, Edith. Now look at the people buried in that same row:

Matthew Boswell d. 1852, age 60
Edith Boswell, wife of Matthew d. 1854, age 45
Lydia Rogers, wife of D.R., 1770–1859

Figure 4-2
Robinson Cemetery, Hickory County, Missouri.

Daniel Rogers 1760–1838
John P. Rogers 1812–1876
Isaac Rogers b. 1814–1883
Zilpha Rogers 1810–1832

After getting a specific name to search for in Tennessee from the gravesite—Daniel Rogers—I found that he was listed as head of household in the 1830 Henderson County, Tennessee, census. The households next to him were those of Mary Boswell and Edward Boswell. Matthew was also head of household in Henderson County, but listed twenty-three pages away on the census. I might have searched dozens of families named Rogers if I had started in Henderson County rather than looking for Edith's own family in Missouri.

Third, study collateral relatives to find ancestry. Second and third cousins with many different surnames share a common ancestor. Those cousins may have records that your direct ancestors didn't create. Or you may discover your ancestry by the back door. You may not be able to prove that your ancestor is the son of a certain man. However, if you can prove that an individual is your ancestor's brother or sister, and you can prove the parentage of the sibling, you automatically find the parents of your ancestor.

In 1850 a woman named Sarah Cassett appeared on the census with the individual I was studying, John E. Spangler. There were many families named Spangler living in Adams County, Pennsylvania, at that time. After finding far too many named John, Jacob, and Abraham, I decided to investigate the less common name of Cassett. David Cassett married 10 April 1834 in the Lutheran Church at Gettysburg, Pennsylvania, Sarah Spangler. Was it the same woman with John Spangler in 1850? No one named David Cassett appeared in the 1850 census. No one named David Cassett left a probate record, but

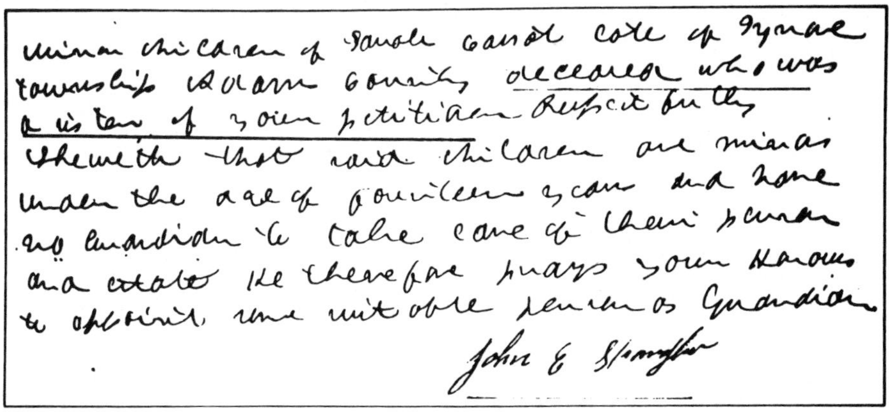

minor children of Sarah Cassett late of Tyrone
township Adams County deceased who was
a sister of your petitioner Respectfully
sheweth that said children are minors
under the age of fourteen years and have
no guardian to take care of their person
and estate He therefore prays your Honours
to appoint some suitable person as Guardian
John E Spangler

Figure 4-3
Petition of John Spangler to become the guardians of Sarah Cassett's minor children.

surprisingly, Sarah E. Cassett did. She died intestate, leaving minor children. John E. Spangler applied for guardianship and the record gave his relationship to the deceased: "she was a sister of the petitioner." (See Figure 4-3 on page 73.)

He then identified her father, and therefore his own, as William Spangler. (See Figure 4-4 below.)

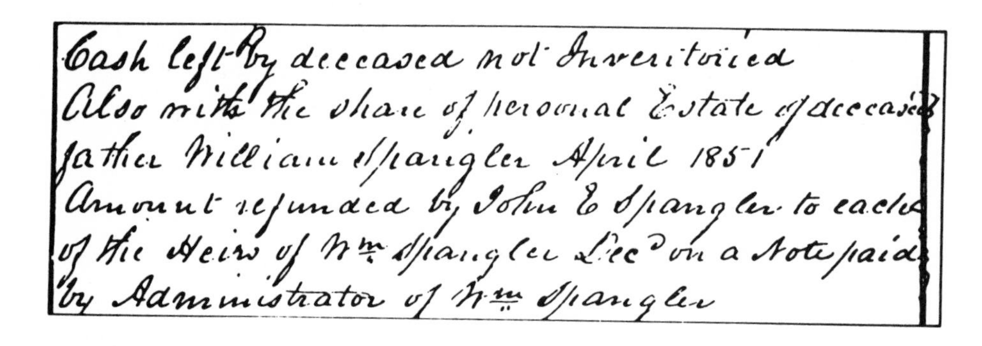
Cash left by deceased not Inventoried
Also with the share of personal Estate of deceased
father William Spangler April 1851
Amount refunded by John E Spangler to each
of the Heirs of Wm Spangler Dec'd on a Note paid
by Administrator of Wm Spangler

Figure 4-4
Identification of John Spangler and Sarah Cassett's father as William Spangler.

Guardianship records are invaluable to genealogists, because the people appointed guardians of minor children are almost always family members. They may be from the wife's side or the husband's, but the vast majority of the time they are relatives. If something tragic happened to young parents, wouldn't you expect family members to assume the care of the small children?

The fourth reason to study collateral relatives is to find the ones who died single or without children. It is common for people with no children to have more money than those who do. In order to find the many brothers, sisters, and perhaps cousins of your solitary ancestors, the best method is to locate the probate or will of those siblings who did not marry or who died without children. Often their wills named nephews and nieces, brothers and sisters, and sometimes even parents. Intestate proceedings may be even more important than wills, because the court would have insisted that all property owned by the deceased must be distributed to all the heirs according to the probate laws in effect at the time.

The following deed abstract, which names thirty-three heirs, is just one of many such examples:

> St. Francois County, Missouri, Deed Book C:364 The November 1842 term of the circuit court divided land among the heirs of James Caldwell late of St. Francois County, deceased. They jointly claimed a parcel of land being part of 640 acres granted by the U.S. Government and containing 257 acres. The deceased died leaving no children, but left a widow

Mrs. Meeke Caldwell, now residing in county and numerous family of brothers, sisters, half brothers and sisters, and their descendants many of who are unknown and who reside, if they are living, in parts unknown. Petitioner Edwin C. Sebastian (according to James Caldwell's will, Edwin was his adopted son) gained, through purchase, the rights of the widow. At his death, deceased left known heirs and legal representatives, to wit; Samuel Kinkead of St. Francois County, Walter C. Kinkead, James Kinkead, John Hampstead, the father and guardian of heirs of Meeke Hampstead, deceased, Thomas Sappington and wife, Mary Ann, and several heirs of Andrew Kinkead, deceased, are heirs of Mary Kinkead, deceased, who was an "own sister" of James Caldwell, deceased, and entitled one full share of his estate John Conway, Samuel Conway, Joseph Conway, James Conway, James Pollock and Ann his wife and Fountain Conway, several of whom live in St. Louis County, John Hampstead and wife, Lucinda, these last named are heirs and descendants of Elizabeth Conway, deceased, and a half sister of James Caldwell and entitled to ½ share; also Ephraim Caldwell, Joseph Caldwell, several heirs of John Caldwell, deceased, and two sisters whose names are unknown, all heirs and descendants of William Caldwell who was a full brother of James, deceased and entitled to one full share; also Caldwell Byrnside and Samuel Moore and wife, Ann, and divers others whose names are unknown, all heirs of Ann Byrnside, deceased, who was a half sister of the said James Caldwell and entitled to ½ share; also several heirs of Kinkead Caldwell whose names and residence are unknown, said Kinkead being half brother and entitled to ½ share; also heirs and descendants of Samuel Caldwell, deceased, all of whom are unknown to petitioner, but are said to reside in the state of Kentucky, the said Samuel being a half brother to deceased and entitled to ½ share; also John Caldwell, Mathew Caldwell, Sally King, George King and wife, Anness, and also Walter Caldwell, all of whom are half brothers and sisters to said James, deceased, and each entitled to ½ share. Distribution was as follows: Mary Kinkead heirs were to have one whole share, Elizabeth Conway's heirs were to have one-half share; William Caldwell heirs one whole share; Ann Byrnside's heirs one-half share, Kinkead Caldwell heirs one-half share, Samuel Caldwell's heirs one-half share, Mathew Caldwell one-half share, John Caldwell one-half share, Walter Caldwell one-half share, Sallie King one-half share, George and Anness King one-half share.

Putting the family together from this deed and one other that was recorded a few pages away—naming those called "unknown heirs" in the deed above—carried the line for the common surname *Caldwell* back to Kentucky and then to Virginia, three generations previous to the man who died without children.

The fifth reason to study collateral relatives is that they probably generated documents that can be used to circumvent holes created by missing or destroyed records. For example, if our ancestors settled in a county whose records later burned, we may find surviving records for collateral relatives to reconstruct information that was lost.

The sixth reason is to establish genetic links. More and more, genealogy is seen as an important tool for tracing patterns of inherited traits and illnesses. More than three thousand out of ten thousand known diseases and medical conditions have a strong hereditary component, and new ones are found every day. People who are aware of their predisposition to certain diseases can do much to help themselves, either by changing their diet or behavior, or by early detection of a potential problem. Genealogists can make people aware of their genetic family history. Moreover, studying the genes of cousins may also help prove or disprove ancestral lines. It is vital to remember that biology has no relation whatsoever to surnames—genes strictly follow bloodline descents.

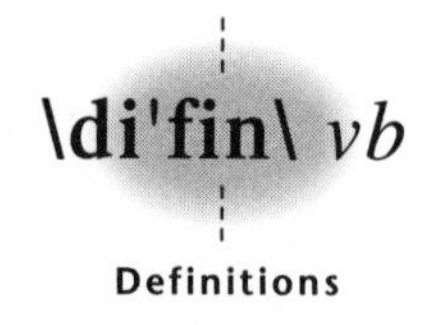

And finally, studying collateral kin may reveal naming patterns, identifying unusual given and middle names used by a family. **Called *onomastics*, the study of names can aid in finding those missing links and branches.** If you are researching a common surname, given names of several family members can make it easier to distinguish your Brown or Jones from the others.

FINDING THE COLLATERAL FAMILY

The first step in creating the web of a collateral family is becoming familiar with the kinship terms used during the time period you are researching. You must remove cultural and time blinders that may lead you to assume that terms used a century or two ago have the same meaning today.

M. Halsey Thomas, who edited *The Diary of Samuel Sewall 1674–1708*, attempted to identify in his annotations all the people to whom Sewall referred. He commented, "Sewall uses the word *cousin* as we would kinsman. His parents, uncles and aunts, siblings and children were called by our terms, but all other relatives near and remote, connected by blood or marriage, were cousins. Our footnotes show how remote some of these relationships were." Unfortunately, Thomas was not always able to discern the relationship, but surely Samuel Sewall knew exactly how those people were related to him. Thus, it is worth investigating what, exactly, the relationship was when a colonial diary or account book refers to a "cousin."

Kinship terms can become very important in analyzing the records that use them. Following are some of the terms used in American society to identify collateral relatives. In the colonial era, terms such as *cousin* and *nephew* had different meanings than in modern times. An "in-law" was usually a stepparent, a "cousin" could be a nephew, and a "nephew" could be a grandchild.

KINSHIP TERMS

Affinity: A relationship that exists because of marital ties. The contemporary term for these relations is "in-laws."

Augmented family: An extension of the nuclear family that includes people bound together by law and marriage, rather than by blood. Examples include half-siblings, adopted children, stepchildren, stepparents, and stepsiblings.

Aunt: In American society, can refer to a woman in four different relative positions: father's sister, mother's sister, father's brother's wife, mother's brother's wife.

Brother: In addition to the obvious meaning, can include the husband of one's sister, the brother of one's wife, the husband of one's sister-in-law, a half-brother, or a stepbrother. Genealogists must also be aware that "brother" may refer to a member of one's church.

Collateral family: Refers to relatives who are "off to one side" (i.e. not in the lineal ancestry) but who share a common ancestor. In western society, these people are called aunts, uncles, cousins, etc.

Consanguinity: Refers to persons who share common descent or biological heritage.

Cousin: A very general term in American society referring to someone with whom you share a common ancestor. It can refer to a relative occupying a position on either the mother's or father's side, and may also refer to someone related only by affinity. If this person is in a different generation, the term *removed* is used to designate the number of generations separating individuals: i.e., if you are two generations apart from a cousin, that person would be your *first cousin, twice removed.*

Extended family: A term used to describe families of more than two generations within a household or relationship.

Full sibling: One who has the same biological mother and father (thus the same ancestry) as another individual. A ***half-sibling*** has one of the same parents (and therefore shares only one side of the lineage) as the other.

In-Law: In contemporary society, a term used to designate someone to whom you are related by your own marriage or that of a sibling. In colonial society, this term also referred to relationships created by the marriage of a parent, currently called step relationships. Thus a "mother-in-law" in the seventeenth century may have been a father's second wife.

Natural child: Can be a confusing term. Sometimes researchers find this term and conclude that it denotes an illegitimate relationship. Rather, it is meant to indicate a relationship by blood rather than one by marriage or adoption. An illegitimate child may be called "my base son" or "my bastard son," or even "my alleged son."

Nephew/Niece: The child of a sibling (or a half-sibling, or a stepsibling, or a spouse's sibling, or your sibling's *spouse's* sibling). Because the term derives from the Latin term *nepos*, meaning *grandson*, it is possible that an early colonial reference may have this meaning.

Now wife: Can fool a researcher into assuming that the testator of a will using this term had a former wife. While this may be true, it is more likely the testator is indicating that the bequest is intended only for his present wife and not necessarily for any subsequent wife he may have. Donald Lines Jacobus wrote, ". . . it is to be doubted whether any other legal phrase has fooled so many of our most experienced genealogists."

Nuclear family: A family group consisting of mother, father, and dependent children.

Stepsibling: Is one related by virtue of a parent's marriage to an individual with children by a former marriage or relationship. While there is no relation by blood, there can be strong ties of emotion and tradition between stepsiblings.

Uncle: In American society may refer to a man in four different relative positions: father's brother, mother's brother, father's sister's husband, or mother's sister's husband.

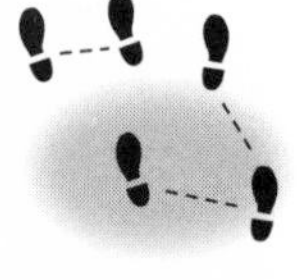
Step By Step

RESEARCH STEPS IN COLLATERAL FAMILY STUDY

Let's outline the research steps that can help you identify collateral relatives and use the records they produced or are mentioned in to analyze relationships.

The easiest ways to identify relatives are through vital records, recorded marriages, bequests in wills, estate divisions, and land partitions. But because collateral family members may be more difficult to identify, we must look at the family's recorded associates, including witnesses at weddings, witnesses of wills, executors of estates, guardians, grantees and grantors of land, sponsors at baptisms, and of course, unidentified individuals appearing in their households in the census. Investigate those who joined the church at the same time as your family, who filed for land at the same time, and who supported their pension applications. If an individual applied for federal land by preemption (land granted by reason of residence and improvements for a specified time, depending on the congressional act), he would have needed individuals to support his statements regarding when he settled, whether he was married, and whether he had a family. The individuals supporting his claims often were family members. You can find these affidavits in the federal land case files, filed by the case number and land office to which the individual applied (see Figure 4-5 below).

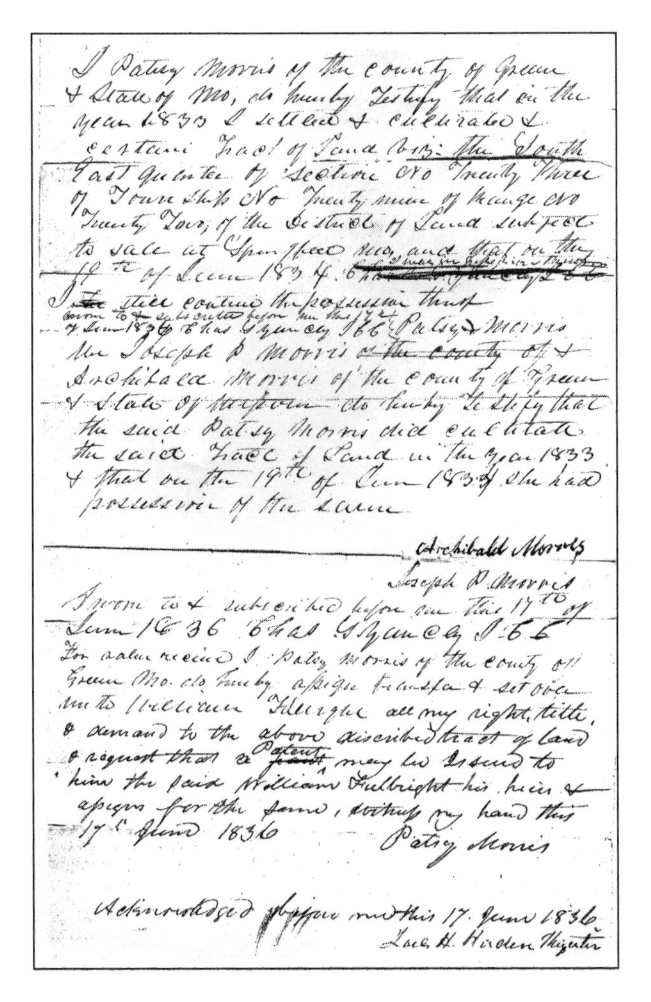
I Patsy Morris of the county of Green & State of Mo, do hereby Testify that in the year 1833 I settled & cultivated a certain Tract of Land viz: the South East Quarter of Section No Twenty Three of Town Ship No Twenty nine of Range No Twenty Two; of the District of Land subject to sale at Springfield Mo, and that on the 19th of June 1834 [illegible]
I still continue the possession thereof
Sworn to & subscribed before me this 17th of June 1836 Chas S. Yancey J.C.C. Patsy Morris
We Joseph P. Morris ~~of the county of~~ & Archibald Morris of the county of Green & State of Missouri do hereby testify that the said Patsy Morris did cultivate the said Tract of Land in the year 1833 & that on the 19th of June 1834 she had possession of the same

Archibald Morris
Joseph P. Morris
Sworn to & subscribed before me this 17th of June 1836 Chas S. Yancey J.C.C.
For value received I Patsy Morris of the county of Green Mo. do hereby assign transfer & set over unto William Fulbright all my right, title, & demand to the above described tract of land & request that a Patent may be issued to him the said William Fulbright his heirs & assigns for the same, witness my hand this 17th June 1836
Patsy Morris

Acknowledged before me this 17. June 1836.
[illegible] H. Harden [illegible]

Figure 4-5
Affidavit of Patsy Morris, Bureau of Land Management, Springfield, Missouri, land office, case file #233.

You can also identify collateral family by looking for unusual given names, names uncommon to the time period, names that could easily be surnames, or names that appear repeatedly in the records.

When researching the Nathan Brown family in Preble County, Ohio, I found that a man named Nathan B. Caldwell was mentioned in the records of my family. It would have been negligent not to check into the family of this Mr. Caldwell. Further research showed that he was the son of Mary Brown, daughter of the immigrant Nathan Brown, and wife of William Caldwell, which obviously couldn't be right. It alerted me to look for other people with the name "Nathan B," and I found that Nathan B. McDill, Nathan B. Magaw, and Nathan B. Wilson were also related to each other.

Your research with names, however, must take into account popular naming patterns outside the family. Naming children after such patriotic figures as George Washington and Thomas Jefferson was common, and military notables such as Francis Marion, Wade Hampton, Sterling Price, and Nathanael Greene were also popular namesakes. A child could also be named for a renowned minister, such as James Guillian, Cyrus Byington, John Knox, or Lorenzo Dow, or a political figure such as Albert Gallatin, James Knox Polk, Martin Van Buren, or even for the doctor who delivered the baby. When studying naming patterns, know your history and chronology. A child born in 1800 may have been named for the heroic "Swamp Fox" of the Revolutionary War, Francis Marion, but the Francis who was born in 1870 was more likely named after someone in the family who had been named for the "Swamp Fox."

Evaluating naming patterns can be a helpful tool in research, but it can also take you far astray. We may never know what motivated our ancestors to choose some of the names they did. Perhaps they respected a particular member of the community, or read an interesting book and named their child for one of the characters, or were intrigued by a charismatic minister who had passed through the neighborhood the night before the child was born. Do examine naming patterns, but be ready to discard a theory if no data from other sources can be found to support it. Onomastics offers wonderful clues, but creating a relationship based only on naming patterns is fraught with danger.

Warning

Don't just look at your ancestor's records in order to identify relatives. Study everything he did as well. For whose child was he guardian? Whose will did he execute or administer? To whom was he indebted? Family members are often more willing to loan money.

William Cawlfield of early Greene County, Missouri, left a detailed probate record, but I couldn't connect any of the individuals mentioned in it to him, nor could I use it to identify his wife, who he apparently married after he moved to Missouri. The probate records gave me no clues as to his previous location. Because some of his associates had come from Tennessee, I checked the 1830 Tennessee census index, but found no one named Cawlfield.

William Cawlfield served as administrator for a man named John Fitch while Thomas Cawlfield served as bondsman. I then searched that probate record. I learned that James and William Cawlfield had served as guardians for two of John Fitch's children. Owen Cawlfield owed John Fitch money and Jane Cawlfield attended the estate sale. That many associations between the Cawlfields and the Fitches were too many to ignore. I looked for a John Fitch in the 1830 Tennessee census index and found him in Bedford County, Tennessee. On the same page was "Owen Coffield," with one male twenty to thirty years old living in his household. The household also included Jane Coffield, a fifty-to-sixty-year-old woman who had several children living with her, including one male age fifteen to twenty and two males ages twenty to thirty, who were later identified as Thomas and William Cawlfield of Missouri. John Fitch had married Margaret Cawlfield.

But how to find William Cawlfield's wife? William Cawlfield had died as a relatively young man. Who was involved in his estate? He left minors, so I investigated the guardians of his children. In this case, they were Benjamin Boone and Alfred Horsman. How do they fit? If they weren't from his side of the family, perhaps they were from his wife's. Onomastics was helpful in this situation, as were the surviving county marriage records. Two of William Cawlfield's children were named Daniel Boone Cawlfield and Rebecca Bryan Cawlfield. Alfred Horsman married Mary Boone 23 April 1841, Greene County, Missouri. Levica Cawlfield was too young to be a daughter of Daniel Boone, but finding the probate of Nathan Boone, Daniel's youngest son, who died in Greene County, wasn't difficult. There was the proof of Levica's marriage to William Cawlfield. Benjamin Boone was her brother, Alfred Horsman her brother-in-law.

After identifying the collateral relatives or those you believe may be related, record the data for those families. Always list your sources. Avoid grouping the individuals into family units until you find supporting data. Hasty assumptions and conclusions can quickly take you far afield. You will still gather data on families who are not related to you just as you did when you gathered only surnames, but because these families lived in the same community and were affiliated with your ancestors, your search is much more likely to be productive.

Search the records produced by any families you feel may be connected. It's easy to protest that following every collateral family will produce too many surnames to keep track of. True, you can't possibly remember all those names, but a computer will help—it's amazing what that little search tool can turn up in your files. But you can also benefit from using slightly different methodology and tactics than you used while searching for surnames only.

First, geographically bracket the community in which the family lived. Notice I do not say *county*—usually a community is smaller than a county, and may overlap county and even state boundaries. It becomes a community because the people who live there share common backgrounds, beliefs, traditions, and values. For instance, I soon learned that what became known as the "Coon Creek" settlement in St. Clair County, Missouri, consisted primarily of individuals related to one another; the same was true of those who settled on "Twelve Mile Prairie" in Dallas County, Missouri. You identify those communities from the local histories, including county and church histories. Often a community organized around the church of a particular denomination. Knowing who founded that church and its early members often leads to information about family relationships.

Notes

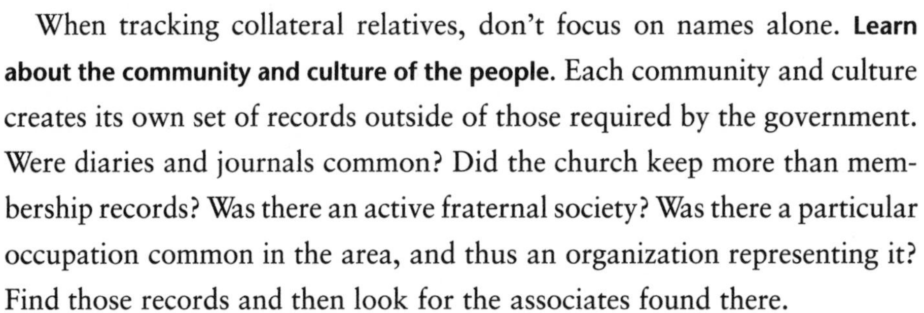

When tracking collateral relatives, don't focus on names alone. **Learn about the community and culture of the people.** Each community and culture creates its own set of records outside of those required by the government. Were diaries and journals common? Did the church keep more than membership records? Was there an active fraternal society? Was there a particular occupation common in the area, and thus an organization representing it? Find those records and then look for the associates found there.

I try to make the people I am studying real people. I want to make them live again. Surely you know the personality and idiosyncrasies of your living relatives and friends. Try to learn the personality and idiosyncrasies of your ancestors and their associates as well. I attempt to find something unique about each person I study so that I can remember them. For instance, Alexander Appleby was the man who spent his wife's entire inheritance in less than ten years. James Thompson was a judge, so I call him that. Dr. Gilmer was arrested in Concordia, Kansas, for selling liquor to a patient when Kansas was a dry state. The Reverend Marion Morrison was a great-uncle to actor John Wayne. Professor John Valentine (who knows where he got that name?) Brown died in St. Louis the night before he was to make a speech. Anna Wherry Strain was one of the first women mayors in Kansas—elected before women could vote. Allie Glenn was orphaned when she was four, and her brother Harvey died in a Civil War hospital in Vicksburg, Mississippi. I can remember individuals better when I think of them as real people rather than just names.

SUMMARY

When studying collateral family lines you must first identify the individuals, then record the data they created, noting the names of those who show up repeatedly in your family's records. At some point, you will know instinctively that some relationship stronger than a casual business or community connection must exist. Perhaps the record that proves a connection will never appear, but with enough evidence, the conclusion will still be a firm one. New evidence may emerge that proves your hypothesis incorrect, but you are much less likely to be wrong when you can demonstrate that strong associations, connections, interactions, and mutual records exist among individuals than if you try linking them purely on the basis of "the name is the same."

RESEARCH STEPS

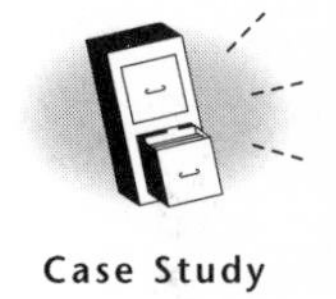

Case Study

The following case study illustrates the steps outlined in this chapter. The objective was to find the family and origin for Isaac J. Murry. The only thing I knew when I began was that he entered forty acres of land at the Springfield, Missouri, federal land office in 1838. He was not head of household in 1840, but was on the 1850 census.

1850 Boone Township, Greene County, Missouri
Isaac J. Murry, age 35, farmer, real estate value $700, born Tennessee
Nancy H., age 28, born Tennessee
Leonidas, age 6, born Missouri
Cirelda, age 4, born Missouri
Viola M., age 2, born Missouri
William Davis, age 17, born Missouri

When you encounter a genealogical problem with a man in his thirties, try to find a family for him. The odds that he came alone as a farmer from Tennessee to Missouri are not good. He most likely had family in the immediate vicinity. There were many families named Murry and Murray in

Greene County—too many in fact. The problem was that none of the males were the right age to be Isaac's father. Now what?

My first step was to identify known neighbors from the census, as these are always potential relatives. The listing showed: Stephen Dorrell, Elizabeth Glass, William Graves, Nicholas Walker, Andrew Carter, then Isaac J. Murry; and on the other side: James H. Ragsdale, Wm. C. Woodwin, Thomas Alexander, Guien Leeper, Casander Robinson, and Alexander Davis.

The second step was to look for unusual names. Did any of the immediate neighbors, or anyone in the township, have any of the unusual names Isaac had given his children? No, none of these families had a child named Isaac, Leonidas, Cirela, or Viola.

The third step was to check marriages: Did he marry in Greene County? Yes. On 24 July 1842, Isaac J. Murry married Nancy H. White. But there were no families named White in the neighborhood.

The fourth step was to look at another individual living in the household: William Davis. My immediate reaction was disappointment that his surname wasn't *Latulipe*, or something just as unusual, rather than the common one of *Davis*. I generally assume that people living in the household are related, and that helps guide my search for records.

Because I knew that Nancy's surname was White when she married at age twenty, William Davis probably was not her brother. Perhaps he was a laborer.

Any Davis families in our small neighborhood search?

1850 Boone Township, Greene County, Missouri
Alexander Davis, age 30, farmer, $350, born Tennessee
Lavina J., age 28, b. Virginia
James H., age 10, b. Tennessee
Sophronia A., age 7, b. Tennessee
Julia A.E., age 6, born Tennessee
Mary E.J., age 6, b. Tennessee
Alletha C., age 3, born Missouri
Guien A., age 1, born Missouri

The unusual name *Guien* appeared in the Davis family, and a Guien Leeper was head of household in this small neighborhood. Did Guien Leeper marry someone named Davis? No, Guien Leeper married 28 April 1839, Greene County, Missouri, Malinda Murry. Aha! Even better. Now we have a new family to study. Isaac is no longer alone, he has a probable sister.

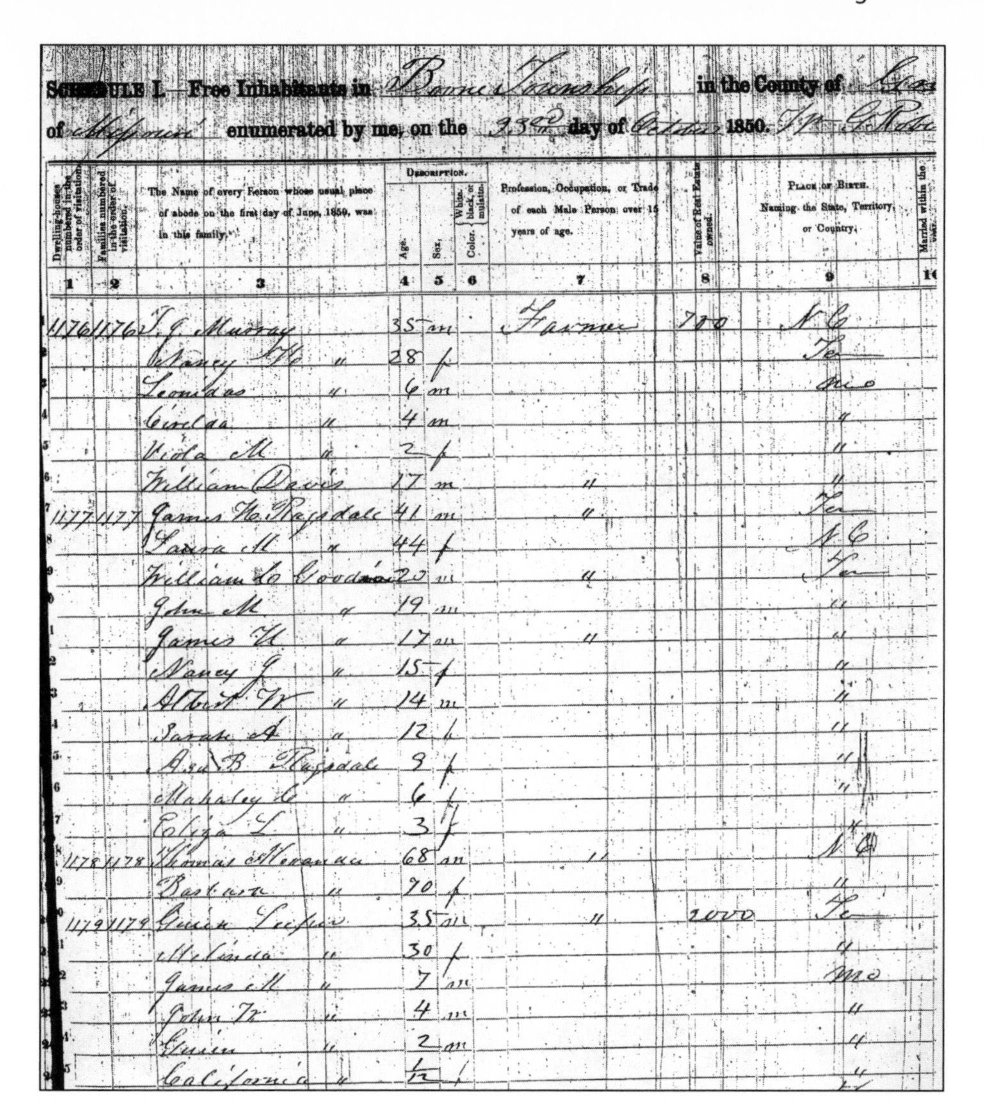

SCHEDULE I.—Free Inhabitants in Boone Township in the County of Greene of Missouri enumerated by me, on the 23rd day of October 1850.

Dwelling-houses numbered in the order of visitation.	Families numbered in the order of visitation.	The Name of every Person whose usual place of abode on the first day of June, 1850, was in this family.	Description: Age.	Sex.	Color. White, black, or mulatto.	Profession, Occupation, or Trade of each Male Person over 15 years of age.	Value of Real Estate owned.	Place of Birth. Naming the State, Territory, or Country.	Married within the year.
1	2	3	4	5	6	7	8	9	10
1176	1176	T. G. Murray	35	m		Farmer	700	N C	
		Nancy H "	28	f				Tn	
		Leonidas "	6	m				Mo	
		Cirelda "	4	m				"	
		Vida M "	2	f				"	
		William Davis	17	m		"		"	
1177	1177	James H. Ragsdale	41	m		"		Tn	
		Laura M "	44	f				N C	
		William L. Goodin	23	m		"		Tn	
		John M "	19	m				"	
		James W "	17	m		"		"	
		Nancy J "	15	f				"	
		Albert W "	14	m				"	
		Sarah A "	12	f				"	
		Asa B. Ragsdale	9	f				"	
		Mahaley E "	6	f				"	
		Eliza L "	3	f				"	
1178	1178	Thomas Morrow	68	m		"		N C	
		Barbara "	70	f				"	
1179	1179	Guien Leeper	35	m		"	2000	Tn	
		Melinda "	30	f				"	
		James M "	7	m				Mo	
		John W "	4	m				"	
		Guien "	2	m				"	
		California "	1/12	f				"	

Figure 4-6
Guien Leeper household, 1850 Greene County, Missouri, census.

1850 Boone Township, Greene County, Missouri
Guien Leeper, age 35, born Tennessee
Malinda, age 30, born Tennessee
James M., age 7, born Missouri
John W., age 4, born Missouri
Guien, age 2, born Missouri
California, age 1 month, born Missouri

What can we learn from a brief review of this household? Let's look at the names. One child was obviously named for his father, but as we know that Malinda's maiden name was Murry, could the full name of the child "James M." be James Murry Leeper, named for Malinda's father? From the census records, I also guessed that in 1850, Malinda's husband was suffering from a bad case of "gold fever."

Malinda Murry Davis was even younger than Isaac J. She was just nineteen when she married in 1839, and in that year Isaac would have been twenty-four. Two young people on the frontier. Were they likely to have gone west alone? Who do young people live with before they start their own families? Typically they would live with their own parents, but we can't find a man with the correct name who would be the right age. However, they must have come to Missouri with someone with whom they had a relationship whose name we don't know.

As I mentioned earlier, Isaac Murry purchased his land in 1838, but he was not head of household in 1840. Who was he living with in 1840? He was not with Malinda and her new husband Guien Leeper, nor any other family named Murry in Greene County. In other words, no one named Murry had an extra male in the household between the ages of twenty and thirty.

Let's go back to the neighborhood as it appeared in 1840. Who from the community of 1840 was living in the area where Isaac purchased his land? I looked for a household with an older head (male or female) and a male age twenty to thirty. I looked at thirty families. Only four fit the criteria: the families of William Folden, Thomas Alexander, Isabell Lay, and Thomas Simmons. My search had narrowed considerably.

Returning to Isaac's neighborhood in the 1850 census, only Thomas and Barbara Alexander remain in the immediate area. I checked their neighbors in 1840 and was pleased to find families headed by Samuel Davis, John Murry, and James Murry. Surely we have identified the cluster where Isaac fit. We now have an older family and several associates for whom to search.

Further investigation reveals that Barbara Alexander was a sister to Isaac Julian, another early settler of Greene County, Missouri. She had married a man named [—?—] Murry who died before 1830. Isaac Julian—an uncommon name—was a head of household in Monroe County, Tennessee, as was Barbara Murry. Her household contained slashes in the age categories that fit both Isaac J. Murry (undoubtedly named for Barbara's brother) and Malinda. About 1837, Barbara Murry married a widower, Thomas Alexander, and they came to Missouri with her five children, three of whom were grown and already married. They were John Murry, James Murry, and Elizabeth, wife of Samuel Davis. Soon after arrival her youngest children, Isaac Julian Murry and Malinda Murry, both married. And here is where the families of Murry, Julian, Alexander, and Davis settled. (See map on page 87.)

There is no doubt that a study of collateral family lines will solve many

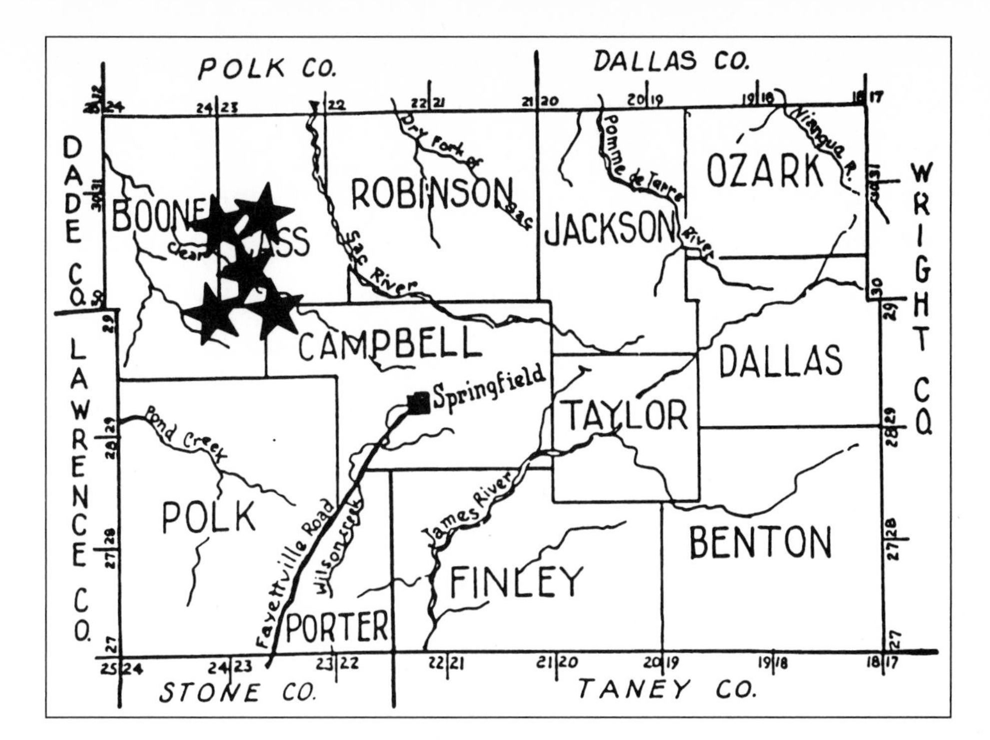

Figure 4-7
Map of Greene County, Missouri. Note the northwest corner.

genealogical dilemmas. **Remember that the key is relationships and people, not just names.**

HELPFUL PRINCIPLES WHEN RESEARCHING COLLATERAL FAMILY LINES

A family is made up of relationships; not just names.
Implications for genealogical research: Name changes are frustrating for a researcher, but a relationship remains no matter how many times the individual's name changes.

Sociologists have found that the strongest kin ties appear between women. The strongest and most enduring bond occurs between mothers and their grown daughters.
Implications for genealogical research: The best family sources for genealogical data are probably held by people with a different surname than the one you are tracing.

Studies suggest that, in Western society, ties to the wife's kin are stronger than those to the husband's—unless the male ties are crucial to the husband's occupation.
Implications for genealogical research: The researcher needs to know the occupational and economic relationships of the family as well as the blood ties.

Social relationships among kin are not broken by geographic mobility.

Implications for genealogical research: This is particularly important when one is dealing with records lost through fire, flood, or neglect. Records detailing family relationships may have been maintained by someone geographically removed from the destruction.

Legal records left by family members who did not leave descendants often can be more helpful than the records left by those who did.

Implications for genealogical research: Never forget to obtain all the data possible on *each* member of a family.

Most genealogical literature and organizations are arranged around surnames.

Implications for genealogical research: Although searching surnames may seem the best way to find other interested researchers, it's probably not the most efficient or comprehensive method by which to conduct research. Too often important female lines are neglected.

Be sure you understand the meaning of kinship terms used in the period you are studying.

Implications for genealogical research: Many false assumptions may be made regarding lineage if a kinship term is misinterpreted. For example, *daughter-in-law* meant something quite different in colonial times than it does today.

People can be tied together in several ways: by blood, law, and emotions.

Implications for genealogical research: Limiting your research only to those who are tied by full blood to your ancestor may cause you to miss valuable clues and documents.

Be alert to clues in records that may indicate the existence of family relationships.

Implications for genealogical research: It is just as important—perhaps more so—to copy the names of those who witness probate records, are named as administrators, live next door, join the same church, or purchase land at the same time, as it is to copy all those with the same surname.

In a bilateral kinship system (as in American society, where ancestry is traced on both the maternal and paternal sides), cousins share both common relationships and ancestors as well as separate family relationships.

Implications for genealogical research: Americans are often imprecise in defining their kinship. This may present a complex situation to the genealogist who is attempting to learn exactly how (and if) two people who believe themselves to be related really are.

Until modern times, it was assumed that after marriage, spousal relatives became the same as your own.

Implications for genealogical research: The terms cousin, brother-in-law, uncle, sister-in-law, etc., were used much more broadly in the colonial era than in modern times. Assuming a relationship such as a marriage from the use of one of these terms alone is common, but presumptuous, in genealogy.

Your Day in Court

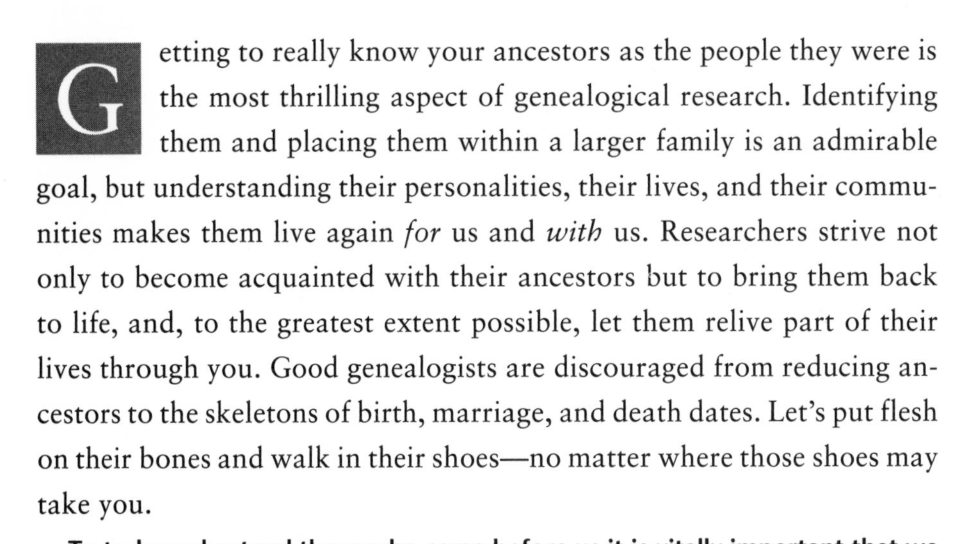

Getting to really know your ancestors as the people they were is the most thrilling aspect of genealogical research. Identifying them and placing them within a larger family is an admirable goal, but understanding their personalities, their lives, and their communities makes them live again *for* us and *with* us. Researchers strive not only to become acquainted with their ancestors but to bring them back to life, and, to the greatest extent possible, let them relive part of their lives through you. Good genealogists are discouraged from reducing ancestors to the skeletons of birth, marriage, and death dates. Let's put flesh on their bones and walk in their shoes—no matter where those shoes may take you.

Important

To truly understand those who came before us it is vitally important that we learn to live in their communities and context, not to make them live in ours. They couldn't begin to understand the world we live in, but with careful and diligent study we can understand theirs. We have records and history to study in order to better comprehend why they did the things they did, how they got along with neighbors, and how they lived in their community and time. To best perceive the people who came before us, we have to not only be familiar with the history of the times, but know what laws were in effect to govern their every-day behavior. We must know what records might have been created at the time our ancestors lived so that we have some idea of what we should be looking for. We must understand the terms that were used in those documents so that we can interpret them correctly. We can learn about our ancestors' lives by reading history books and articles describing the historical events we believe they lived through. Even more rewarding than history books are the specific documents that pertain to our own family, and court records are the key to finding them.

Within court records are a wealth of details about our ancestors. In records created for legal purposes, it is possible to find clues to family relationships, wives' identities and families, and parents' names, as well as creating a biography for an ancestor. Besides, what is more fun than finding a court case in which juicy facts are revealed about the person we are researching?

This chapter is divided into sections that describe each type of court record and how to pull the best genealogical information out of them. These records include:

- records created concerning inheritance procedures [probate].
- records created during land transactions [deeds].
- records created by officials to collect revenue for the community [taxes].
- records to settle differences between individuals, or between individuals and the State [civil or circuit, criminal].

PROBATE

Probate is the court procedure pertaining to the settlement of wills, guardianship, and the administration of estates. The probate process transfers the legal responsibility for payment of taxes, for the care and custody of dependent family members, for the liquidation of debts, and the transfer of property title to the heirs of a deceased person. This chapter assumes that you are aware of the basic definitions of a will, a codicil, a testate proceeding, an intestate administration, and a guardianship.

A variety of records can be created by a probate proceeding. *The Source*, rev. ed., edited by Loretto Dennis Szucs and Sandra Hargreaves Luebking (Salt Lake City: Ancestry, 1997) provides a checklist on page 208 of eighty-one different types of documents that may originate from a probate proceeding. Many of those provide valuable information for the genealogist.

Letters of Administration or Testamentary

After a death occurred the principal heirs petitioned the court for authority to begin the probate process, usually within ten to fourteen days. This petition often appeared in the legal notice section of local newspapers. Depending upon whether there was a will, either letters of administration or letters of testamentary would have been issued. With this application there was often a listing of the known heirs and their last known location. (See Figure 5-1 on page 92.)

Figure 5-1
Application for administration of the Stephen Mead estate.

To the Surrogate of the County of Greene:

THE PETITION OF William H Mead of the Town of Ashland in the County of Greene, respectfully sheweth, that Stephen Mead late of the County of Greene, in the State of New York, is dead; that he died on or about the 27th day of November in the year one thousand eight hundred and seventy seven that he was at the time of his death an inhabitant of the Town of Jewett ~~in said County, and died at his place of residence in the County of Greene~~ leaving a last Will and Testament; that the said deceased did therein and thereby appoint your petitioner & Caroline Mead Executors of the same; that the said deceased died leaving him surviving

Caroline Mead (widow), Adaline E Woodworth of Jewett Greene Co N.Y. William H Mead of Ashland Greene Co N.Y. Joel H Mead of Hunter Greene Co N.Y. Stephen M Woodworth Joseph S Woodworth whose residence is unknown & cannot after diligent search & inquiry be ascertained Ozias Hopkins & Isabella Robinson of Randolph Cattaraugus County N.Y. All of full age except Isabella Robinson who is a minor over 14 years of age

the only heirs and next of kin of said testator that the real and personal estate of said testator affected by said Will ~~does not~~ exceeds in value the sum of $ 2000.00; that as your petitioner has been informed and truly believe it belongs to the Surrogate of the said County to take the proof of the said last Will and Testament of the said deceased; that your petitioner being desirous that the said Will should be admitted to probate, and that Letters Testamentary should be granted thereon, pray a Citation issuing out of and under the seal of this Court, requiring the said widow, heirs and next of kin, personally to be and appear when and where this Court may direct, to oppose or support, as they may see fit, the probate of the said last Will and Testament. And your petitioner will ever pray, &c.

W. H. Mead

The individual requesting administration was usually the surviving spouse and/or the sons or sons-in-law of the deceased. A widow may have relinquished her right to administer the estate in favor of a son or son-in-law. This relinquishment is usually found among the loose probate papers, but it may also have been recorded in the probate court minutes book. In a case where there were no issue, the surviving father, brother, or brother-in-law may have been the petitioner. If a man died in the eighteenth or nineteenth century leaving a young widow, in all likelihood she would have asked that her father or brother be named administrator. **For the genealogist, this appointment is a wonderful clue to her maiden name.** It is the responsibility of the executor or administrator to guard the best interest of the estate, provide for the needs of the heirs, and settle the claims of the creditors.

Research Tip

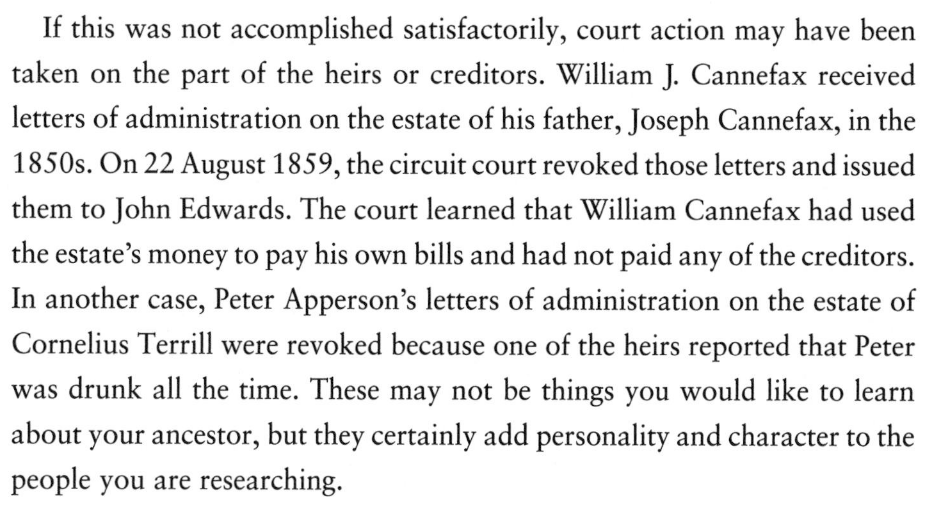

If this was not accomplished satisfactorily, court action may have been taken on the part of the heirs or creditors. William J. Cannefax received letters of administration on the estate of his father, Joseph Cannefax, in the 1850s. On 22 August 1859, the circuit court revoked those letters and issued them to John Edwards. The court learned that William Cannefax had used the estate's money to pay his own bills and had not paid any of the creditors. In another case, Peter Apperson's letters of administration on the estate of Cornelius Terrill were revoked because one of the heirs reported that Peter was drunk all the time. These may not be things you would like to learn about your ancestor, but they certainly add personality and character to the people you are researching.

The order in which a person is entitled to be appointed administrator differed from state to state, but in general the order was spouse first, then one of the children, parents, grandparents, brothers or sisters, uncles, aunts, nephews, first cousins, creditors and then public administrators. It is important to pay careful attention to those appointed administrators and executors. They were almost always members of the family, and if there were two, one *may* have been from the wife's side and the other from the husband's. This is not a rule, but a clue. Administering an estate was often time-consuming and complicated. If a public administrator was assigned to administer the case of your ancestor, it does not mean that *none* of the above people were available to perform the administration. It means none *wanted* to do it.

To illustrate the likelihood of administrators being family members, I selected at random ten people from my study of the Ozarks who left probate records. I then determined the relationship of the executors and administrators. I ignored obvious cases where the executor was the widow or one of the known sons. Here are the results: The first name is the deceased; the second, the administrator; third, his relationship to the first.

Decedent	Administration	Relationship
Benjamin U. Goodrich	Joseph Weaver	father-in-law
Felix Hoover	Spencer Clark	wives were sisters

Ann Shannon	John D. Shannon	brother-in-law
John Fitch	William Cawlfield	brother in-law
Sidney S. Ingram	Joseph Rountree	uncle
Jonathan Reno	Avenet Hollingsworth	brother-in-law
Samuel Dixon	Henry Collier	son-in-law
Townley Redfearn	Josiah Mason	brother-in-law
William Clark	Nicholas McMinn	son-in-law
Hannah Denney	James Appleby	nephew

Be sure you consider not only the administrator and securities (the individuals who supported the bond placed to administer the estate) of your ancestor's estate, but the people for whom your ancestor was the executor or administrator. If the name of the administrator is not familiar to you, check the identity of the wife of the administrator. You may find that she was a sister to your ancestor. A married woman was often not allowed to be either an administrator or a guardian, so it was likely that she would want her spouse to ensure that her brother's estate was administered properly.

As you read through the settling of an estate, you may encounter the legal term *administrator de bonis non*. This was an individual appointed by the court to administer the effects of a decedent not included in the will, or not included in a former administration of the estate. If an *administrator de bonis non* was appointed by the court, either a former administrator had died or resigned before the estate settlement was finished, or there was property not disposed of in the will. This property may have been real estate or personal property, including slaves.

Admitting the Will for Probate

Proving the will was the next step and obviously applied only to testate cases. The will was presented to the court and usually ordered recorded in the probate book. The original will was filed among the loose papers. The witnesses to the will appeared before the court and attested that the deceased individual had signed the will, was in sound mental condition, and had given the statements of his or her own free will. Sometimes one of the witnesses had died by the time the will was proved. This situation may help to establish a death date perhaps not recorded elsewhere. Someone usually attested to the signature of the witness, bringing in another associate of the ancestor. Wills judged invalid were not proved and thus not recorded in the will book. Sometimes these may still be found among loose or miscellaneous papers. Invalid wills do not appear in the probate index.

In 1693, William Robinson of Newton, Massachusetts, made a nuncupative will (verbal rather than written) but failed to name an executor. In this will he mentioned his son, William of Newton, but he left the entire estate to Elizabeth Robinson, his eldest daughter, stipulating that she care for his sons David, who was lame, and Jonathan, only thirteen years old. This did not sit well with the court. Leaving the estate to a daughter when sons were living was against the common law and custom in Massachusetts. The court refused to prove the will for the conveyance of the house and land. Two witnesses then came forward and testified that the omission of the other children from the will was "not for want of affection to them, but only out of his tender care for the providing of his lame and youngest child." They also stated that William had appointed Elizabeth to be the sole executrix, but the scribe had omitted this in haste. The purpose of this testimony is unclear, but the court refused to appoint a married woman executrix. On 21 October 1695, the court issued letters of administration to the eldest son, William. He then claimed the twelve acres of real property by birthright, and the remainder was divided into seven equal parts to be paid by William, reserving to himself a double portion. We learn from the administration, not from the will itself, that there were six living children.

Research Tip

In this case, documents regarding the entire estate gave much more insight into the life of this family, including the names and ages of all the children and the personal and economic circumstances of the father at his death, than the unrecorded will itself. Whenever a situation deviated from accepted practice, additional helpful information was often provided in the probate file or court records.

Posting a Bond

The next step in the probate process was posting a bond. The administrator and at least one other individual, usually two, posted a bond equal to the approximate worth of the estate to ensure faithful performance. Until recently, bondsmen commonly were also members of the family. If the widow was made executrix of the will or administratrix of the estate, make careful note of the bondsmen—they may have been her relatives and provide clues to her family of origin.

The law required publication of the pending probate so that creditors would know to come to court to make their claims. Debtors were also expected to come forward, but they probably were not as eager. In early times, notices were tacked on courthouses, town halls, and churches. Later, they were published in newspapers. At first glance, this would seem to have no real significance for genealogists. However, in the case of a burned courthouse, a newspaper notice may be all you have that gives the approximate date of death, the administrator, and the bondsmen or securities.

In one case, the notice added evidence to support the claim that the Samuel Strain who had administered the 1783 estate of James Strain in South Carolina was the man I was searching for, rather than a man of the same name. Within the very small estate packet, I found mention that the notice had been tacked on the door of the Long Cane Creek Church in Abbeville District, South Carolina. This was the church that "my" Samuel Strain attended and was near his residence, and thus added strength to my argument that the man who had died was indeed a relative. It is important that you carefully examine each surviving piece of paper among the loose papers and minutes, as important clues might go unnoticed if you just look for a list of heirs.

The Inventory

The next step in the probate process was to appoint two or three disinterested parties to inventory the estate. You should note these people as well, because they were likely to be neighbors and close associates who weren't entitled to direct inheritance. Both real and personal property were expected to be included in the inventory, which can provide you with an intimate look at your ancestor's life. In that inventory are clues to literacy, religious denomination, occupation, level of wealth, identity of slaves, household goods, and what was important to your ancestor during his lifetime. If there was not enough cash on hand to pay the creditors, an estate sale was held to raise the money needed. Genealogists can find clues from reading the list of buyers who attended the sale. Many of the items may have been purchased by relatives. In addition, the list can help you identify neighbors and other associates, and perhaps aid in sorting out individuals of the same name. Moreover, the estate sale may prove the existence and provide names of females who may not appear in other legal records.

Dower

If minors or other dependents survived the decedent, the court may have assigned an allowance until settlement of the estate. This allowance was exempt from creditors' claims. You will find these allowances in the court minutes. This was also the time at which the widow's dower was set off to provide for her support. Therefore, it is important that we distinguish between the terms *dower* and *dowry*, even though I have found them incorrectly used in court records themselves.

A *dowry* was the property that a woman brought to her husband at their marriage, sometimes referred to as "her portion." You may see cases in which a man willed back to his wife "her portion" as he divided his assets.

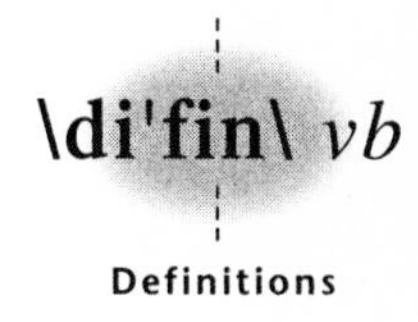

Definitions

***Dower* was the provision of the law by which the widow was entitled to a one-third life-estate in the lands and tenements of her husband at his death.** This was true if he died intestate or if she dissented from his will. By English common law, the amount was one third of the real property that her husband held at any time during the marriage. If the marriage was childless, the widow could claim one half of her husband's real property. Dower represented the minimal right of a woman to her husband's estate and was to provide for her care and that of her minor children. A man could leave his wife more than the law required, or even his entire estate, but he could not give her less. If a husband ignored the dower rule, his widow could renounce the will and demand an assignment of her thirds. This meant, however, that she could not claim part of the personal estate beyond her own "paraphernalia." In America, the usual practice was that her dower included one third of the personal estate as well as the real property. Nevertheless, the practice varied throughout the English colonies.

Under common law, the widow received a dower before payment was made to the creditors. This was to ensure that neither she nor her children would become dependents on the town or county. In Pennsylvania and Connecticut, however, a dower included a share only in what the husband owned at his death, and in Pennsylvania, the creditors were paid *before* the widow received her dower. In the South, English common law was much more closely observed. Maryland, Virginia, and South Carolina made it possible for the wife to exercise a legal right to veto her husband's land conveyances and to establish a separate estate for herself. Connecticut wives, on the other hand, possessed no property rights whatsoever until 1723. Therefore, in Connecticut and Pennsylvania, the wife had no right to influence the sale of her husband's real estate so you will find no dower releases on property. By the middle of the eighteenth century, women were beginning to participate in land sales, and in the research I have done, I usually find that the deeds in which the woman did participate had to do with the estate of her husband, father, or unmarried brother. This is not a hard and fast rule, but can be a helpful clue.

The dower right of a widow represented a life interest only. She could not sell her dower property absolutely, but she could enjoy the rent and profits from the lands during her lifetime. *If*, in the rare instance that her dower was valuable land and someone wished to take the chance that the widow would have a long life, she could sell the land temporarily. At her death, however, the dower land would return to her husband's estate. When the widow died, her dower estate descended to her husband's children in the same manner as the rest of the estate.

This was a simple process if the only children they had were with each other. If the wife had children by a prior marriage, they would *not* inherit her dower. If the husband had children by a previous marriage, the dower would go to those children. If no children survived the widow, the property descended to her husband's heirs: his siblings, parents, nephews and nieces, and so forth.

There were some peculiar laws and interpretations of laws in the South with regard to the inheritance of slaves. If you are dealing with a slave-holding family, it's wise to study the laws that applied during that time in the particular state or colony. Valuable clues to ancestry and relationships can emerge from the transfer of slaves, but the law varied to such a degree that it would be difficult to make any helpful generalizations.

Curtesy

Another important term to understand for the colonial period—especially in the South—is *curtesy*. **This was the estate that a woman may have had held either in fee simple or entail, and to which her husband was entitled at her death.** He was entitled to land held by the *curtesy* only if the couple had children born alive and capable of inheriting. Land held in curtesy was held for his natural life. It was a right not only to one third, but to the entire estate. As tenants by the curtesy, men held the real property of their wives in their role as guardian of the children of the marriage. The husband could not convey the property or devise it, but he retained all rents and profits and managed the estate. The estate would then go to their children at his death.

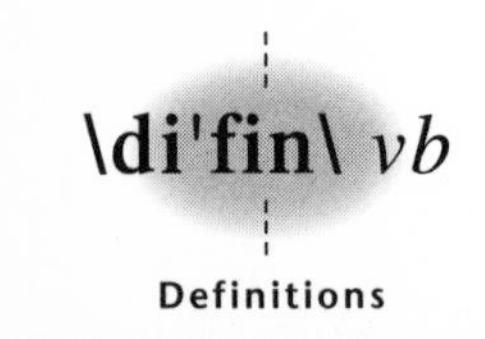

Definitions

Entail means that a piece of property has conditions or limitations set upon its inheritance.

The latest example I have seen of this practice was a deed from 1866, when Stephen H. Chism held land as "tenant by the curtesy" in Franklin County, Arkansas. In deed book C:50, he clearly stated that he had inherited this land from this third wife, Corinna J. (Rose) Quinn, and was holding the property for his stepchildren and his child by Corinna.

Distribution of Property

Moving back to the sale of the estate, if an insufficient amount of money was raised by selling the personal property, the administrator would petition the court to sell a piece of the real property. This sale was usually a private administrator's or sheriff's sale and would not name the heirs. If all the property had to be sold to pay the creditors there was nothing to be distributed to the heirs. The estate was then said to be insolvent. Unfortunately for researchers, because insolvent estates do not yield any inheritances, the documents may not yield any names of heirs.

If property did remain after the debts were paid and all the money owed the estate was collected, the court would then be ready to distribute the assets among the heirs. If the property could not be divided equally, the heirs may have filed a "friendly suit" for a land partition, in which each of the heirs would be named and an agreement made for the land to be sold. If some of the heirs did not reside on the estate, legal notice was again published in a local newspaper.

If all the persons named in the suit were residents of the estate, their

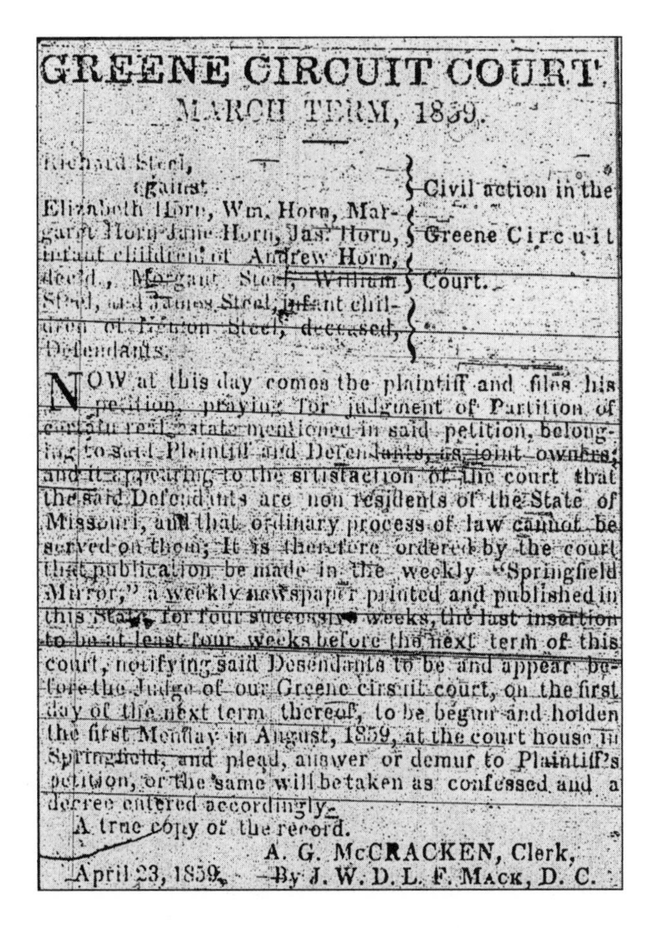

GREENE CIRCUIT COURT.

MARCH TERM, 1859.

Richard Steel, against Elizabeth Horn, Wm. Horn, Margaret Horn, Jane Horn, Jas. Horn, infant children of Andrew Horn, dec'd., Morgan Steel, William Steel, and James Steel, infant children of [illegible] Steel, deceased, Defendants. } Civil action in the Greene Circuit Court.

NOW at this day comes the plaintiff and files his petition, praying for judgment of Partition of certain real estate mentioned in said petition, belonging to said Plaintiff and Defendants, as joint owners; and it appearing to the satisfaction of the court that the said Defendants are non residents of the State of Missouri, and that ordinary process of law cannot be served on them; It is therefore ordered by the court that publication be made in the weekly "Springfield Mirror," a weekly newspaper printed and published in this State, for four successive weeks, the last insertion to be at least four weeks before the next term of this court, notifying said Defendants to be and appear before the Judge of our Greene circuit court, on the first day of the next term thereof, to be begun and holden the first Monday in August, 1859, at the court house in Springfield, and plead, answer or demur to Plaintiff's petition, or the same will be taken as confessed and a decree entered accordingly.

A true copy of the record.

A. G. McCRACKEN, Clerk,

April 23, 1859. By J. W. D. L. F. MACK, D. C.

Figure 5-2
Newspaper court reports, Steel vs. Horn.

names would usually be listed in the circuit court petition and then again in a deed when the land was sold (see Figure 5-2 on page 99).

In estates involving minors or incompetent individuals, a guardian was appointed to receive and assume stewardship over their share. Guardians were required to submit annual accounts to the court for the income received and the amount spent for care of the children. These accounts can provide a wealth of information, including locations of the children, their ages (or dates when they came of age), schools they attended, any illnesses they may have contracted, their marriages, their deaths, and other genealogical and family details. It was largely through the guardian's account of clothing purchased for an illegitimate child that I built a case for the identity of my third great-grandfather, Elijah Robinson. This article, entitled "Trousers for Elijah," was published in *The American Genealogist* in April 1988.

When there was an estate to be managed, guardians were appointed for children under the age of fourteen. Children fourteen and over could choose their own guardian. Females usually reached legal adulthood at eighteen, males at twenty-one. Most minors were eager to manage their own estates and usually went into court to release their guardians soon after reaching legal age. Knowing this can help researchers working in the colonial period, when it is often difficult to determine an individual's age.

You can get some idea of how the children lived, when they became ill, where they went to school, and so forth from reading the receipts in guardianship and curator files. In Figure 5-3 below we can see the goods bought by the guardian of Bessie Lindinbower. Items include shoelaces made from the skin of a baby goat, silk, gloves, four yards of fringe, and handker-

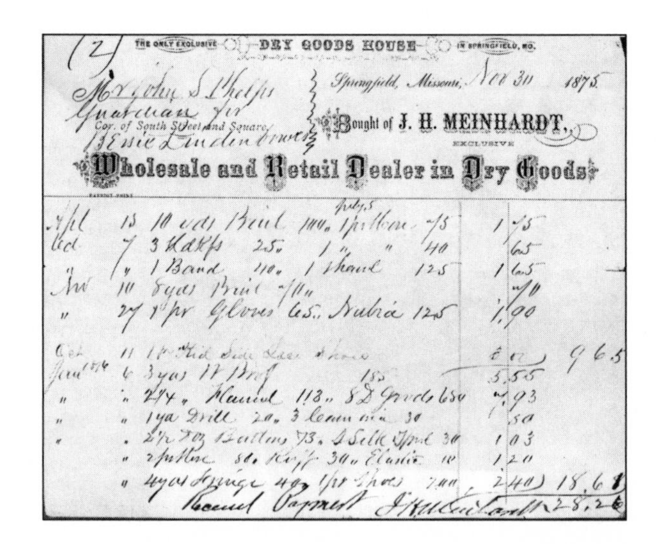
THE ONLY EXCLUSIVE DRY GOODS HOUSE IN SPRINGFIELD, MO.

Mr. John S. Phelps Guardian for Bessie Lindinbower

Springfield, Missouri, 1875

Cor. of South Street and Square.

Bought of J. H. MEINHARDT, EXCLUSIVE

Wholesale and Retail Dealer in Dry Goods

Figure 5-3
List of goods bought by guardian of Bessie Lindinbower.

chiefs. We can already tell that Bessie Lindinbower has inherited a good deal of money.

Just before final settlement, notices were published once again to give creditors and heirs a last chance to make a claim on the estate. The administrator or executor then made a final accounting to the court and the remaining property was divided in a final distribution. If one is lucky, the heirs and their residences may be listed in the court minutes. Usually, it is necessary to go through the loose papers to find receipts indicating that the heir received the amount due him from the estate. When each heir received his or her share of the distribution, they signed receipts or releases to the executor or administrator. These receipts give the name of the heir, the description or amount of property received, the name of the guardian of minor children, and usually the name of the deceased. (See Figure 5-4 below). The percentage of the estate inherited is helpful for determining the heir's relationship to the deceased, and sometimes may provide clues to the married names of the daughters. It is not unusual to find that a daughter was designated as single when the probate began, but was married by the time of final distribution.

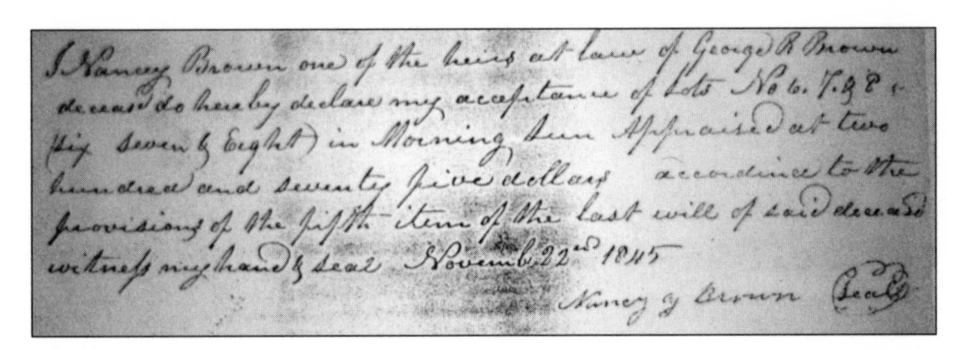
I Nancy Brown one of the heirs at law of George R Brown
deceased do hereby declare my acceptance of lots No 6. 7. & 8 (
Six Seven & Eight) in Morning Sun Appraised at two
hundred and seventy five dollars accordance to the
provisions of the fifth item of the last will of said deceased
witness my hand & seal November 22nd 1845
Nancy Y Brown (Seal)

Figure 5-4
Nancy Y. Brown and Nancy Strain deed, Cloud County, Kansas.

Colonial Law

One must be aware of two types of inheritance law in effect during colonial times that are no longer in force: the law of primogeniture and the tradition of giving a double portion to the eldest son. Before the Revolutionary War, in the New England colonies as well as in Pennsylvania and Delaware, an equal division of land and movables in the estate was granted to the children in an intestate proceeding, with a double portion to the eldest son. Remember that even when the division includes a double portion, the number of shares still reveals the number of heirs. In other words, if the records declare that there were five shares and that the eldest received a double portion, then you know that there were only four children. The double-portion rule applied only to male heirs. If the decedent had no sons, the eldest daughter did not receive an extra portion.

Primogeniture refers to the exclusive right of the eldest son, by virtue of his seniority, to succeed to the estate of his ancestor—to the exclusion of the younger sons. In other words, the eldest son inherited all real property. If there were no sons, the daughters shared equally in the real property. In cases where the decedent made a will, the eldest son may even have been omitted from that will, as his rights were clearly protected by law. The law of primogeniture affected only real estate, not personal estate; the decedent could pass on the latter in any way he saw fit. Keep in mind that many individuals did not follow the law and by practice distributed their land equally to sons, or even to all their children. This was particularly true in New York, in German families, and in parts of the country where there was great antipathy for English common law. The closer in time to the American Revolution, the more likely it was for families to ignore the common law of primogeniture.

Colonial Estate Distribution

Shammas, Carole, et al. *Inheritance in America: From Colonial Times to the Present.* New Brunswick: Rutgers University, 1987.

Connecticut	Equal distribution with double portion to eldest son
Delaware	Equal distribution with double portion to eldest son
Georgia	Primogeniture until the American Revolution
Maryland	Primogeniture until American Revolution
Massachusetts	Equal distribution with double portion to eldest son
New Hampshire	Equal distribution with double portion to eldest son
New Jersey	Primogeniture until about 1784
New York	Primogeniture until 1774 [widely ignored]
Pennsylvania	Equal distribution with double portion to eldest son
Rhode island	Primogeniture until 1770 [except 1718–1728]
North Carolina	Primogeniture until 1784
South Carolina	Primogeniture until 1791
Virginia	Primogeniture until 1785

PROBATE AND LAND RECORDS

See chapter seven on land records for in-depth coverage of this subject. I also suggest that you consult *Locating Your Roots: Discover Your Ancestor Using Land Records* by Patricia Law Hatcher, CG, FASG (Cincinnati: Betterway Books, 2003).

County land transactions are usually in the office of the recorder, although the specific title of the office may vary. The primary responsibility of those who work in the recorder's office is the handling of current land transactions. They will have neither the knowledge nor the time to help you with your land record research. It is up to you to know what you are searching for, and the most you can expect the office personnel to contribute is the location of the records.

Remember that the best evidence for proving a line of descent is through documents that track the inheritance of land. One of the most important and helpful sets of documents you can locate is a mixture of probate, circuit, and land records. Called land partitions, these documents offer a complete overview of the division of a deceased person's land. The petition for a land partition was usually filed in the circuit court or common pleas court. When the partition of the land was made, the names of those involved in the sale were also recorded in the deed books.

References to a "friendly suit" (see terms defined at the end of the chapter) might make it appear that there was some sort of family feud taking place, but this describes **the method by which the heirs reached a legal agreement regarding the division of an estate.** When I found a friendly suit initiated in Preble County, Ohio, I was able to identify the father of my third great-grandmother, Elizabeth Brown. Her father, David Pressley, lived and died in South Carolina in a county whose land records have been burned. To my knowledge, he never set foot in Ohio; yet, because he owned land in Preble County, a suit naming him was filed there at his death.

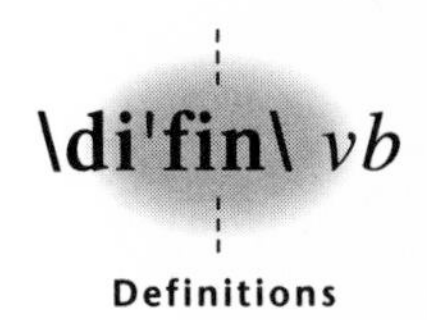

Definitions

Another listing of heirs may have occurred when a piece of real estate held by the deceased was sold. Sometimes you may find all the heirs listed together (as in Figure 5-5 on page 104), or each party may have quitclaimed their right to the parcel separately, in which case the deeds may be spread over several pages or even several deed books.

There are three great clues in the deed in Figure 5-6 on page 105. We know that a will existed in Augusta County, Virginia, for John Hamilton. We know that Andrew Hamilton was probably also connected to Samuel and Joanna Wilson, who also moved to Missouri. Because Andrew gave the share back to Joanna, we can hypothesize that he was her brother and that her maiden name was probably Hamilton (this assumption was proved correct by Augusta County, Virginia, marriages). Places of former residences are particularly important when tracing married women. One of the most common failings of genealogists is that they do not adequately search the

Figure 5-5
David Pressley deed, Preble County, Ohio.

Sheriff. Dickey. Deed to G.R. Brown & wife. Record. March 21. 1830

Whereas on the 15th day of March. A. D. 1829. a writ of partition was issued out of the court of common pleas of Preble county ohio, to Jno. L. Dickey Sheriff of said county reciting that whereas at a court of common pleas, begun and held at Eaton. on the 13th day of October A. D. 1828 Samuel Pressley, and John J. Pressley. exhibited on the chancery side of said court. their petition setting forth that David Pressley of the State of South Carolina died intestate leaving said petitioners Elizabeth Brown late Elizabeth Pressley, now the wife of George R. Brown, of this County George Pressley. Mary Lowry. late Mary Pressley, wife of Joseph Lowry and James Pressley, not residents of this State, and William Pressley. of Oxford in this State his children and heirs at law. and Jane Pressley of South Carolina his widow and dowress, and that said decedent at the time of his death was seized in fee of sixty seven acres of land, part of the N. E. Quarter of Section 9. in Township Six, of Range One, thirty three acres part of the N.W. quarter of said Section, one hundred and fifty four acres the S. E. quarter of section 19. One hundred and fifty five acres. the S.W. quarter of Section 3. and One hundred and fifty six acres the S. W. quarter of Section 32. all in Town 6. and One hundred and sixty acres the N. W. quarter of Section 28. in Town 7. all in Range one. in Preble County. and praying that said Jane Pressley. widow of decedent might have dower assigned her in said lands by metes and bounds. and that the residue. together with the remainder in the dower of said widow after her death. be partitioned among said petitioners. and the other children and heirs at law of decedent. and whereas at a court of common pleas begun and held at Eaton. On the 23rd day of February A. D. 1829. said cause came on to be heard and said court being satisfied that decedent died seized of said premises, that he died intestate. and that said defendants had had due notice of the pendency of said petition did appoint Richd. Horn, Samuel Ben, and Hugh Ramsey. Judicious and disinterested freeholders of the vicinity who are not of kin to either of the parties interested commissioners to make partition of said lands among the heirs of said decedent. after assigning to said widow her dower, therein. and commanding the said Sheriff. that by the Oaths of the afore-

brothers and sisters of their ancestors. The joint sale of real estate is one of the best ways to locate adult siblings.

Other types of land transactions found in deed books can be very helpful, such as a power of attorney, a deed of gift, a quitclaim deed, or a marital contract. It is also important to check for dower releases. Wives controlled their dower (usually a one-third lifetime estate) by controlling the sale of their husband's real estate during his lifetime. Often the law called for a private interview of the wife during a real estate transfer. This interview, legally referred to as an "examination," served as a guarantee to court officials that a woman entered into a conveyance of real estate voluntarily, and not because her husband was forcing her. By the nineteenth century, most states were requiring this release and examination. There are, however, variations among the states and colonies in earlier time periods. In fact, it is because of these variations regarding married women's property rights in early America that we must be wary of generalizations. If you are having difficulty establishing the identity of a wife within a colonial family, you should become familiar with the laws in effect in the location and period you are researching.

Research Tip

Tracking women is a great challenge in genealogy, particularly in colonies and states that did not record civil marriages. **Often, we can attempt to estab-**

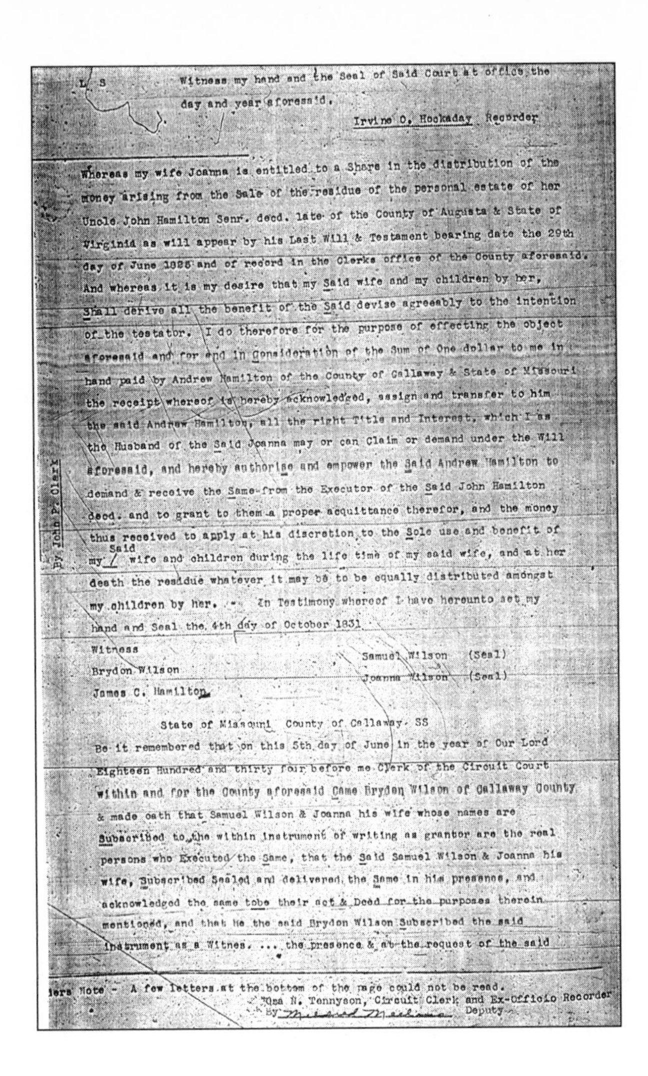
L S Witness my hand and the Seal of Said Court at office the
day and year aforesaid.
Irvine O. Hockaday Recorder

Whereas my wife Joanna is entitled to a Share in the distribution of the
money arising from the Sale of the residue of the personal estate of her
Uncle John Hamilton Senr. decd. late of the County of Augusta & State of
Virginia as will appear by his Last Will & Testament bearing date the 29th
day of June 1825 and of record in the Clerks office of the County aforesaid.
And whereas it is my desire that my Said wife and my children by her,
Shall derive all the benefit of the Said devise agreeably to the intention
of the testator. I do therefore for the purpose of effecting the object
aforesaid and for and in Consideration of the Sum of One dollar to me in
hand paid by Andrew Hamilton of the County of Callaway & State of Missouri
the receipt whereof is hereby acknowledged, assign and transfer to him
the said Andrew Hamilton, all the right Title and Interest, which I as
the Husband of the Said Joanna may or can Claim or demand under the Will
aforesaid, and hereby authorise and empower the Said Andrew Hamilton to
demand & receive the Same from the Executor of the Said John Hamilton
decd. and to grant to them a proper acquittance therefor, and the money
thus received to apply at his discretion to the Sole use and benefit of
my Said wife and children during the life time of my said wife, and at her
death the residue whatever it may be to be equally distributed amongst
my children by her. In Testimony whereof I have hereunto set my
hand and Seal the 4th day of October 1831

Witness
Brydon Wilson
James C. Hamilton
Samuel Wilson (Seal)
Joanna Wilson (Seal)

State of Missouri County of Callaway SS
Be it remembered that on this 5th day of June in the year of Our Lord
Eighteen Hundred and thirty four before me Clerk of the Circuit Court
within and for the County aforesaid Came Brydon Wilson of Callaway County
& made oath that Samuel Wilson & Joanna his wife whose names are
Subscribed to the within instrument of writing as grantor are the real
persons who Executed the Same, that the Said Samuel Wilson & Joanna his
wife, Subscribed Sealed and delivered the Same in his presence, and
acknowledged the same tobe their act & Deed for the purposes therein
mentioned, and that he the said Brydon Wilson Subscribed the said
instrument as a Witnes. ... the presence & at the request of the said

[illegible]ers Note - A few letters at the bottom of the page could not be read.
Osa N. Tennyson, Circuit Clerk and Ex-Officio Recorder
By [illegible] Deputy

By John P. Clark

Figure 5-6
Callaway County, Missouri, deed book.

lish a woman's given name and her approximate time of death by studying the deeds made by her husband. This works in the colonies and states where she had the right to control her husband's real estate transactions. In states, colonies, and territories where she did not, a researcher may presume that she had died before her time by thinking that she *should* have signed a deed when, in fact, the law did not require it. Even when a dower was required, she may not have released it (thus leaving the grantee at risk for not having a clear title) or she may have given her consent later in a separate deed.

Another type of land record that is always of great benefit to the genealogist is the conveyance that describes the chain of title. This document tracks the owners of a piece of land from the earliest owner to the present one. You rarely find these in the public land states (those formed after the American Revolution), but in state land states (the thirteen colonies or those states formed directly from them), these deeds can be of great assistance. You can find examples of deeds that describe every transaction over a period of 150 years.

Entail is another term that genealogists may encounter when searching early records, usually those before the American Revolution, and usually more often in the South than in the North. It refers to conditions or limitations placed on an inheritance by the grantor. In an entailed deed, the grantor may have specified that only his male grandchildren could finally inherit the land in fee simple, or that his land should pass only to the eldest son of the eldest son. The important thing to remember is that there were restrictions on the way land entailed could be passed by inheritance. The specific deed describes how that was to be done. Again, as we move closer to the time of the American Revolution, we are less likely to see land entailed and may begin to encounter the terms *break* or *bar an entail*, which means that the estate was to be freed from the limitations imposed by entail. This would, of course, generate a court case, which could provide even more genealogical information.

TAX RECORDS

The third set of documents, tax records, are usually found in the auditor's office. Although this is their official location, because they are not needed by current court officers, they are often stored in out-of-the-way places or even discarded. They may have been donated to a historical or genealogical society, or if the county has an archive, they may have been placed there. Tax records may also be kept at the state level; some states have microfilmed them.

The first type of tax discussed here is the poll or head tax. This tax, issued by colonial and antebellum counties and towns, was a set, uniform tax to be paid by adult males from age twenty-one (sixteen or eighteen in some areas) to age fifty-five or sixty, customarily. There was wide variation in age and other requirements, and exemptions were not uncommon. Poll tax records can be useful for identifying men with the same name, as qualifiers were often used to distinguish them. See chapter eight for examples of how men of the same name can be distinguished. Those omitted from poll tax lists usually include women (even if they owned land), indentured servants, paupers, ministers, justices of the peace, militia officers, and tax assessors; occasionally those of a particular occupation that was in demand in the community (such as ferrymen) or men with handicaps were omitted. Sometimes Kentucky communities granted exemptions to gunsmiths. In another Kentucky variation, the widow may appear on the list one year after the death of her husband, but thereafter she was exempt. Prior to 1850, one was exempt from paying taxes in Missouri on land acquired from the federal land office for five years after purchase. Local variations in tax laws can be mind-boggling; but when you become familiar with the tax laws governing an area during a particular time period, you can learn a great deal about the people who lived there. Even though these records may not seem at first glance to contain any genealogical information, they can be valuable resources.

A *quitrent* tax was a land tax typically found in New York and the colonies of the South. This tax was due the landlord or proprietor in the colony to increase his revenue. Although some quitrent lists have survived, they are difficult to locate because many remained in private hands. Quitrents were abolished during the American Revolution.

Property taxes were also levied by state and colonial governments, and the associated records can be especially helpful when tracking land transfers that were not recorded by deed. Other direct taxes by the government include an *ad valorem* tax and a *tithe*. An *ad valorem* tax was imposed on the value of the property, in contrast with a per capita tax, which was the same for everyone. A tithe was usually the tenth part of one's income contributed for charitable or religious purposes. Broadly interpreted, it can be any tax or assessment of one tenth of an individual's property. In some of the colonies, the term *titheable* may be synonymous with *taxable*. In colonial Virginia, a tithe was imposed on the personal property of males age twenty-one and older.

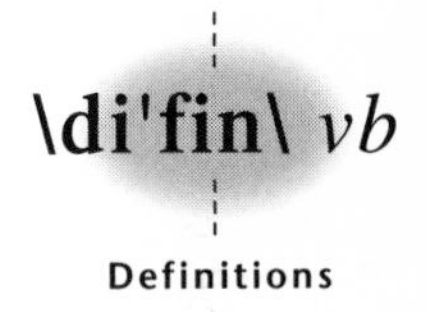

There are also other special categories of tax payers, such as inmates and freemen. The right to be called a freeman was a political right dependent upon specific qualifications imposed by law. They were not freed slaves, nor released indentured servants. They were enfranchised citizens. In New England, variations occurred throughout the colonies. A freeman was a member of the established church in Massachusetts Bay and New Haven until the Restoration in 1662. Owning property became a requirement in some colonies in the late seventeenth and eighteenth centuries, so you will need to check the exact statutes before making generalizations. In New York, New Jersey, and Delaware, there were also qualifications of age and property, but church membership was not a requirement. In Pennsylvania, a freeman was usually unmarried and thus free of family obligations. He was listed separately and sometimes at a higher rate. When he married, his name was added to the regular tax rolls. Knowing this can be extremely helpful for research in Pennsylvania, where civil marriage records were not kept until 1886. In the South, qualifications were similar to those in New England, but the church was expected to be the Church of England. Contrary to what you may suspect, an "inmate" on the tax list was not a prisoner. He was one who rented his land from a landlord and was taxed on his income.

Be aware of special taxes levied in some areas, such as an extra tax on clocks, guns, pianos, carriages, and other luxuries. Tax lists are an excellent resource for determining how your ancestor lived in relation to others in the community. For an excellent example of this methodology, see R. Martin Keen's article, "Community and Material Culture Among Lancaster Mennonites" (see the bibliography at the end of this chapter).

Tax records can also be related to deeds and conveyances, because when taxes were not paid, real estate could be sold for the taxes owed. For example, after the Civil War, the federal tax that had been levied during the 1860s was extended to the South, where many were unable to pay. The government acquired a lot of land, most of it then sold for back taxes.

Records for special taxes can be informative in others ways. In Pennsylvania in the year 1777, the colony levied a double tax on Mennonites and other Anabaptists who refused to serve in the militia. These men were called "non-associators." Professionals such as lawyers, physicians and teachers, merchants, tollgate keepers, and other groups sometimes had to pay additional taxes. Until 1829 Roman Catholics, who were regarded by some Englishmen as traitors to the Crown, were subjected to extra fines, levies, and a standard double land tax. These special taxes applied in many of the colonies until the time of the Revolution. Watch for particularly high assessments for clues to the tax status of your ancestor. Again, you must study the specific statutes of the colony or state in effect during the time you are researching. The examples above describe only a few of the special taxes that existed, but they show how much one can learn if the tax assessment qualifications and rules are understood.

CIRCUIT COURT RECORDS

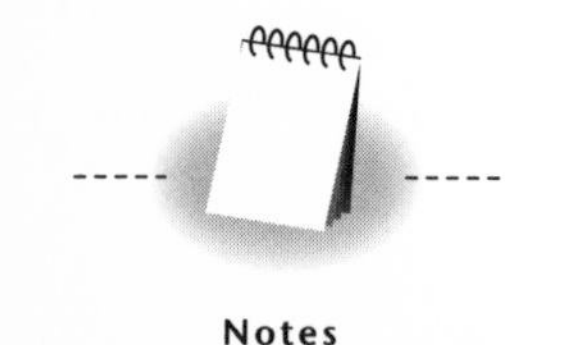

Notes

Thanks to Linda S. Myers of Nixa, Missouri, for her helpful contributions to this section.

Two types of circuit records exist at the county level: criminal and civil. Criminal records concern individuals believed to have committed crimes against the state, according to state or local statutes. Civil cases are initiated when one individual sues another. These records are officially kept in the circuit clerk's office, although storage limitations may demand that the records be kept off the premises. The terminology for these records may differ from state and state.

Two series of records are kept of the cases filed. The first are the minutes (which are indexed according to the plaintiff or defendant). These minutes record the course of the case as it proceeded from filing to disposition. Court activity such as motions filed, verdicts rendered, appeals, and judgment executions are recorded here. The second set of records is the case files, and if available, these can put a good deal of flesh on the bones of your ancestors. They contain the documents filed with the court, such as petitions and responses for divorces; suits for damages, trespassing, and slander; witness depositions; records of fees charged; and other supporting documents for the case itself.

Circuit court case files are not easy to obtain, but if they have been preserved, you should look for the following items:

- Petitions. The plaintiff states the cause for the case and the filing date and desired outcome are recorded.
- Indictments. Found in criminal cases, these state the decision of the grand jury. These can be quite detailed, describing the weapon, its weight and value, the manner in which it was used, and the exact injuries inflicted.
- Subpoenas and witness lists. These state the names of the people who have been called to testify. Obviously, these are people who have connections with either the plaintiff or defendant, and/or who were at the scene of the offense or crime.
- Depositions. Testimonies taken from those who have moved out of the court's jurisdiction. Usually depositions are written and provide extensive information. In one case I studied, the plaintiff had moved to Missouri and had purchased land. He could not sell his land, however, because his wife had to release dower in Missouri (which had not been required in Tennessee). For him to sell the land it was necessary for him to obtain a divorce. The grounds were adultery and the testimony was taken from witnesses in Tennessee, so the depositions were written rather than oral. These included the most intimate observations by those involved.
- Bonds. If money was required to ensure an individual's appearance or "keeping of the peace," securities also may have been necessary to ensure that the money would be paid. Almost always these are relatives of the individuals involved. Who else would be willing to gamble that the person would make the required court appearance?

Circuit court cases can be difficult to locate. Also remember that the index contains only the first plaintiffs and defendants. Many other names may have been recorded as the case proceeded, and there is no easy way to search records that have not been completely indexed. While not the easiest records to use, these are the very ones that may provide you with the most detailed description of your ancestor's personality.

Court records in general are detailed, complex, and numerous. They can be of tremendous value to the dedicated researcher. They often provide that very specific link between generations, or the much needed identification of a suspected ancestor. Even if they don't supply a key piece of the puzzle, they provide myriad opportunities to add to the evidence supporting a gene-

EFFECTIVE COURTHOUSE RESEARCH

A successful search of the courthouse depends on two factors: knowledge and skill. You must possess a basic understanding of the types of records kept at the county level, the terminology used in that particular state or jurisdiction, and the records which are likely to be held in that *specific* courthouse. Next, you must possess the skill needed to gain access to the records, to interpret the records accurately, and to abstract or copy those records in order to maintain orderly and complete files.

alogical hypothesis. Careful genealogists know that they must study the laws in force during the era they are researching, be familiar with the various types of court records that exist in the geographic region, and know the terms that will identify the correct records to search.

Important

Suggestions for success when researching local courthouses

1. Maintain professional dress and decorum. Your demeanor should be purposeful and businesslike. It is wise to carry a briefcase. A laptop computer also is very impressive. Everyone will think you are an attorney.
2. Be familiar with the state law regarding public access to county records. Be able to cite chapter and verse. Be courteous, but persistent.
3. Be prepared to climb ladders, venture into dusty basements, haul heavy books, and squeeze into tight spaces.
4. *Never* expect the courthouse clerk to know more about how to locate your ancestors than you do. You can expect only that he or she may know *where* the records you seek are located. Ask for assistance only when absolutely desperate.
5. Be familiar with the times the courthouse opens, closes, and breaks for lunch. Always leave *at least* ten minutes before closing time. This is very important if you expect to ever return to that courthouse and want to be treated cordially. Ask permission to work through the lunch hour

if this is your usual method. Work quietly and diligently. Hope the clerks will forget that you are there.

6. Know specifically what records and what information you are seeking. Move from the simple to the complex. Once you have located the material you set out to find, it may be possible for you to check other available sources and do some browsing.
7. Be familiar with the indexing system of that particular state or county.
8. *Always* ask to see the probate packets and loose papers, not just the record books.
9. Find out where any additional records are stored or if they have been moved to the historical society, state archives, or other repository. If stored, ask if you may see them and replace them in the exact order you found them.
10. Use the appropriate legal terminology when requesting records.

LEGAL TERMS

Administrator de bonis non: Administrator of any goods of a deceased person not already distributed by the original administrator or executor.

Ad valorem tax: A tax imposed on the value of the property; contrasted to *per capita* tax.

Administration de bonis non cum testament annexo (with will attached): Administration granted by the court when the executor of a will has died, leaving a portion of the estate not administered.

Attachment: The act or process of taking, apprehending, or seizing persons or property usually for the purpose of securing satisfaction of a debt or to guarantee appearance in court.

Chain of titles: The record of successive conveyances affecting a particular parcel of land, arranged consecutively from the government or previous owner down to present owner.

Chattel mortgage: A mortgage that involves personal, rather than real, estate.

Court of Chancery: A court administering equity proceedings.

Court of Common Pleas: The court where civil and criminal cases are begun. Most of these have been abolished, with jurisdiction transferred to district or circuit courts.

Court of the Ordinary: In Georgia, the court that formerly had exclusive and general jurisdiction over probate of wills, management of estate, and appointment of guardians.

Court of Orphans: The court in Pennsylvania or Maryland—known elsewhere as Surrogate or Probate court—with general jurisdiction over matters of probate.

Curtesy: The estate to which a man was entitled by the death of his wife that she had seized in either fee simple or entail, provided they have children born alive and capable of inheriting, i.e., not mentally incapable of managing financial affairs. It is a freehold estate for the term of his natural life. (In some states there was no requirement that issue be born of the union.)

Deed of Gift: The conveyance of land without consideration (payment).

Deposition: The testimony of a witness taken under oath from a distance, rather than in open court. A written transcript is made and becomes part of a permanent court record.

Dower: A provision by law that entitles the widow to a life-estate in the lands and tenements of her husband at his death if he dies intestate, or if she dissents from his will. Dower has been abolished in the majority of states. Although it was traditionally one third of the estate, there was wide variation among colonies and states.

Dowry: The property that a woman brings to her husband at their marriage; sometimes referred to as "her portion."

Entail: To settle or limit the succession to real property.

Entail, estate: An estate of inheritance that, instead of descending to the heirs in general, goes to the heirs of the owner's body (meaning his lawful issue), and through them to his grandchildren in a direct line. There are several variations of estate entail. (See Black and Keim in the bibliography.)

Fee simple: Refers to an estate granted to a man and his heirs with no limitations or conditions.

Freeman: An enfranchised citizen. The right to be called a freeman was a political right dependent upon specific qualifications imposed by law. A freeman was not a freed slave, nor a released indentured servant.

Friendly suit or amicable action: An action brought and carried out by the mutual consent and arrangement of the parties to obtain judgment of court on a doubtful question of law, the facts being usually settled by agreements.

Inmate: One who rented his land from a landlord.

Marital agreements: Contracts between parties who are either on the threshold of marriage or of separation. These may be premarital, antenuptial, or postnuptial agreements.

Nuncupative will: An oral will declared or dictated by the testator in his last illness before a sufficient number of witnesses.

Partition: The division of lands held by joint tenants or co-owners into distinct portions so that each is held individually.

Per capita tax: Fixed taxes, levied by head (per person). See poll tax.

Poll (or head) tax: Issued by colonial and antebellum counties and towns, this was a set, uniform amount that adult males were assessed beginning at age twenty-one (sixteen or eighteen in some areas) and continuing until they reached a set age, customarily fifty or sixty.

Power of attorney: Legal authorization for one to act as another's agent in various business matters.

Primogeniture: The exclusive right possessed by the eldest son, by virtue of his seniority, to succeed to the estate of his ancestor, to the exclusion of the younger sons.

Quitclaim: A release; an intention to pass title, interest, or claim that the grantor may have over the premises.

Quitrent: A land tax typical of the colonies of New York and the South, assessed by the ruler of the colony to increase revenue.

Tithe: The tenth part of one's income contributed for charitable or religious purposes. Broadly interpreted, any tax or assessment of one tenth. *Titheable* may be synonymous with *taxable*. A tithing man was the constable. In colonial Virginia, the tithe was imposed on the personal property of males of productive age, as established by legislative act—variously sixteen to twenty-one years of age.

COURT RECORDS: A SELECTED BIBLIOGRAPHY

Black, Henry Campbell, M.A. *Black's Law Dictionary: Definitions of the Terms and Phrases of American and English Jurisprudence, Ancient and Modern*. 5th edition. (St. Paul, Minn.: West Publishing Company, 1979.)

Glazier, Michael. *The Sessions Laws of American States and Territories Prior to 1900*. 18 vols. Available on microfiche from Redgrave Information Resources Corporation, 53 Wilton Road, Westport, CT 06880. Also available in print in many law libraries.

Keen, R. Martin. "Community and Material Culture Among Lancaster Mennonites: Hans Hess from 1717–1733." *Pennsylvania Mennonite Heritage* XIII (January 1990): 2-25.

Keim, C. Ray. "Primogeniture and Entail in Colonial Virginia." *William and Mary Quarterly* 3d series 25 (1968): 545-586.

Keyssar, Alexander. "Widowhood in Eighteenth Century Massachusetts: A

Problem in the History of the Family." *Perspectives in American History.* 8 (1974): 83-119.

Klein, Fannie J. *Federal and State Court Systems: A Guide.* (Cambridge: Ballinger Publishers, 1977.)

Salmon, Marylynn. *Women and the Law of Property in Early America.* (Chapel Hill, N.C.: University of North Carolina Press, 1986.)

Salmon, Marylynn. "Women and Property in South Carolina: The Evidence From Marriage Settlements, 1730–1830," *William and Mary Quarterly* 3d series 39 (1982): 655-659.

What to Do When the Courthouse Burned

Great emergencies and crises show us how much greater our vital resources are than we had imagined.

—William James

No, all records did not burn! Not anywhere!

—Elizabeth Shown Mills, CG, CGL, FASG

The problem of the burned courthouse is a critical one. One minute there stands a beautiful edifice undoubtedly crammed with your ancestor's records. The next moment is disaster. Solutions to the calamity of the burned courthouse are neither easy nor quick. On the other hand, the Chinese word for *crisis* is synonymous with *opportunity*, and in every crisis there is an opportunity for further growth and progress. When courthouse records are gone, one is forced to discover new records, sources, and methods. Learning these alternative strategies may be the only way to find the answers you need.

This chapter is divided into two parts. The first part will deal with the basic problem of the burned courthouse: how to find out what you should know about the county's history and records, and specific questions you should ask about your own research to narrow the field of records you need. The second half will discuss some of the records you can use that will help provide the information you need to make up for the loss at the courthouse.

To make progress despite this research problem, you will need creativity, perseverance, and a willingness to dig into the available records. Some of the records discussed here probably are not available in your public library or online. Most will not be indexed and many will not be conveniently labeled "genealogy."

However, if you enjoy the challenge of the search, think that searching is *almost* as rewarding as finding, and have the time and interest to search nonindexed and unusual records, you may solve a lineage problem others have refused to touch or considered unsolvable.

This pursuit will take work and a study of new sources. In listing these, I offer not only suggestions, but hope. In fact, I will make you a bet. I wager that you cannot find a county in which all the records were destroyed. Not just court records—but *all* the records. Some records, somewhere, still exist for that county. Finding them is up to you.

DON'T PANIC!

The first step in any crisis is not to overreact. Never make a problem bigger than it truly is. The second step is to divide the problem into parts. **When you face only one aspect of the problem at a time, the task will seem less formidable and more manageable.** Thus, when your research moves into a county that is "burned," you must begin by determining the extent and magnitude of the loss. It is possible that you were simply misinformed and there was no fire at all. Or perhaps you obtained your information from a county court clerk who said, "I am sorry we cannot help you. We have had a courthouse fire." You imagine thousands of records in a small ash heap. In reality, however, the fire occurred last Wednesday afternoon when someone threw a cigarette into a trashcan, and it burned for no more than sixty seconds. Therefore, your first question should be "Was there really a courthouse fire?" Next, if you find that a significant fire did occur, you need to determine when it happened and what it destroyed.

In some cases, only some of the documents may have been damaged. For instance, the Albany, New York, fire of 1911 burned thousands of records, but many have been salvaged. The best discussion of this disaster is in "The 1911 State Library Fire and Its Effect On New York Genealogy" by Harry Macy Jr., FASG, published in the *NYG&B Newsletter* in the Spring of 1999. We must remember that because many old documents are not readily available on the shelves, the current staff may not know or even care about where such records are stored. The vast majority of transactions conducted by county clerks concern contemporary documents, and they have neither the time nor interest to deal with older records. However, they may be able to recommend someone else who would be familiar with their holdings, such as a local researcher or historical society. Almost every community has an expert on its records, even though the position may not be an official one.

STUDY THE COUNTY

The next phase of your initial research is to study everything you can find on the county. This means county histories, Works Progress Administration inventories, and published and unpublished research guides. Look especially for well-documented county histories. A good place to start your search is P. William Filby's *Bibliography of American County Histories* (Boston: New England Historic Genealogical Society, 1983). This is a comprehensive list of five thousand county histories. Use these local histories not only for the information contained in the text, but also in the footnotes, which will tell you the sources the author used. Genealogists traditionally neglect to examine footnotes, but they are a rich source of material to broaden your research. Other good sources can be found by doing a Web search for the county itself. Often, county Web sites will list bibliographies, source material, and inventories.

My research centering on the Yocum family led me to one of the worst burned counties I have encountered, Taney County, Missouri. Taney County has experienced at least three fires and has no early newspapers or church records. I call it the graveyard of Missouri genealogy. While reading any articles I could find on the area, I came across one about an Indian trader, "William Gillis and the Delaware Migration," by Lynn Morrow, published in the *Missouri Historical Review*. Why would I read something that had neither Taney County or the Yocum family mentioned in the title? Because you must read *everything* you can find on the area that has been burned. I learned that John Campbell, who was the Indian agent, ordered two principal lawbreakers, a Mr. Denton and Solomon Yocum, off Delaware land in July 1825. Yocum had settled within the Delaware line and erected a distillery. He was making peach brandy and selling it to the Indians. This was in the area of my interest and twelve years *before* Taney County was formed. Where did the author *find* this information? The footnote referred to a letter written by John Campbell to Richard Graham. The source for the letter was the manuscript collection of Richard Graham at the Missouri Historical Society in St. Louis. This has led me to a marvelous source for information on the early white settlers of Taney County and new sources, such as Indian depredations, for further study. *Always* read the footnotes.

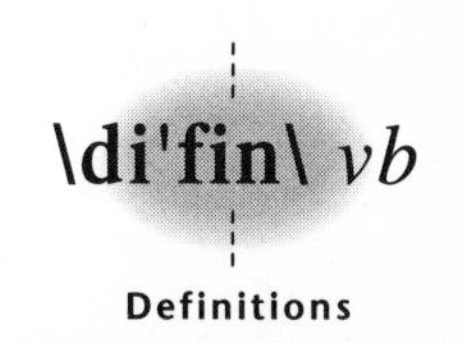

Indian depredations were claims made to the government by whites whose property had been destroyed by the Indians, and vice versa.

EIGHT IMPORTANT QUESTIONS

Ask yourself, "To what extent does this loss of records affect my personal research?" When you learn that certain records you intended to search are not available, you must consider your needs more carefully so you can narrow your search. Answering the following eight questions will help you determine your next step.

1. During what time period did your family live in that county? Narrow your range as much as possible. Did another part of the family leave at a different time than your particular branch? Could that branch have left records in another county that might relate to your family?

2. Have there been any county boundary changes that could effect your search? Surely you have discovered ancestors whose place of legal residence changed although they never moved an inch. Genealogical research often involves areas with disputed land claims, state and county boundary changes, or the formation of states from territories. The records you need might exist in the original county and not be affected by a fire in the other one, or vice versa. For example, what is now Kentucky was once Fincastle County, Virginia. The surviving records of Fincastle County are kept with the records of Montgomery County, Virginia.

John D. Shannon was another resident of Taney County, Missouri, whose records burned. I wanted to discover where he had lived before his move to Missouri, so I began by looking for connections with other individuals in the vicinity. A man named Finis W. Shannon died before Taney County was formed from the parent county of Greene. This was early in the region's history, when there were few people in the area, so perhaps these two men were related. Finis's probate file was remarkable. It not only showed that he was a brother of John D. Shannon, but gave the origin of the brothers as Williamson County, Tennessee. In addition, it contained records of both their father (for whom Finis had been executor in Tennessee) and their grandfather in North Carolina!

Important

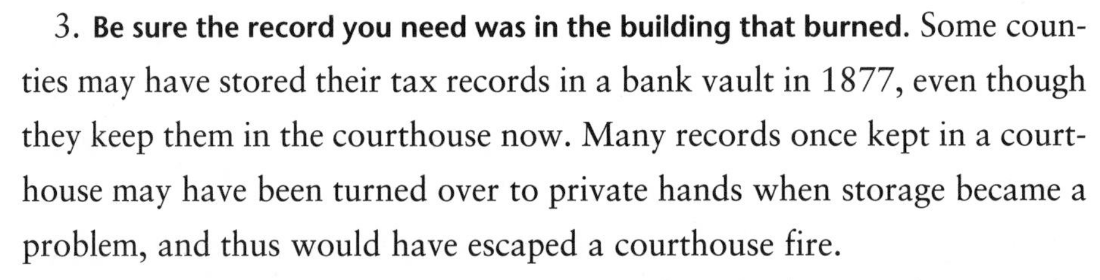
3. **Be sure the record you need was in the building that burned.** Some counties may have stored their tax records in a bank vault in 1877, even though they keep them in the courthouse now. Many records once kept in a courthouse may have been turned over to private hands when storage became a problem, and thus would have escaped a courthouse fire.

The records of Vernon County, Missouri, have had quite a history. The courthouse there was burned in 1863 during the Civil War. When a Civil

War widow attempted to obtain a pension record after the war, she was told the marriage records were not available. But from the county history we learn:

> The courthouse records had a remarkable experience. Col. Hunter took them to Springfield. When General Price fell back into Arkansas they were taken along and stored for a time at Bentonville, then, as the Federals advanced along, they were moved hither and thither. On one occasion they were deposited in an empty building and in the hurry of leaving, would have been abandoned but for Major Prewitt, who placed them in his wagon and hauled them away. At last the confederates abandoned them for good and they fell into the hands of a federal regiment—a Kansas Regiment. So intense was the hatred for the people of Vernon County for Kansans, and so bitter the prejudice against them, that few would have believed any report other than they were burned. On the contrary, they took the greatest care of them. The records books were placed in one strong box, the papers in another and each box guarded carefully. From far down in Arkansas, the records were brought by gradual journey from post to post until at last they reached Fort Scott, Ks where they were kept until the close of the war and the reconstruction of the county. They were then restored to the county authorities at Nevada, with only one book, Deed Book B, and a few unimportant papers missing.

4. Be sure you understand the legal jurisdiction for the time period and records you are searching. Which court had authority over the matter in which you are interested? For instance, many divorce records you would expect to be in the courthouse may be found in legislative journals during the early, formative period of a state.

Prior to 1774, probate records for Suffield, Connecticut, were within the jurisdiction of Hampshire County, Massachusetts. In South Carolina, the equity courts had different jurisdictions than the counties. Therefore, it's possible that the courthouse records completely burned while the equity cases survived. That is exactly the case for Lexington District, South Carolina; indeed, the equity is all that survived for that county. Tax records for many burned counties in Kentucky are held at the state level and have been microfilmed. Remember, records are not always where you would expect them to be. Moreover, you may be able to locate copies of burned documents that were stored elsewhere.

5. Did your family live near a county boundary? Be sure to search adjacent counties just in case the record you need was never touched by the fire. People often took out marriage licenses in the most convenient courthouse, not necessarily in the one of legal residence. If you are researching an early period when boundaries were not well defined, people may have thought they lived in one county when they actually lived in another. One of my ancestor's lands is now quite clearly in Laurens County, South Carolina, but he believed it to be in Newberry, so he recorded deeds there—as did several subsequent individuals.

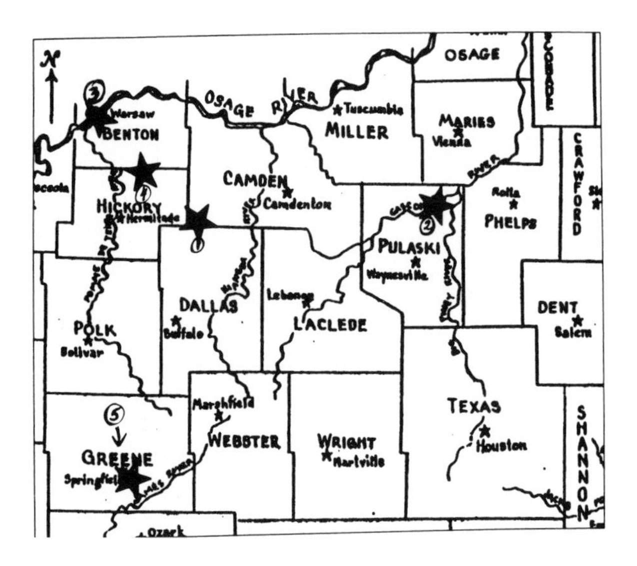

Figure 6-1
Map of Southwest Missouri—William Montgomery and daughter.

In 1833, William Montgomery lived in the sparsely settled region of Southwest Missouri shown in the area marked (1) in Figure 6-1 above. His sixteen-year-old daughter wanted to marry a boy she had met while they had been living on the Gasconade River (2). The justice of the peace in Gasconade County would not marry them there, since the father of the bride was not present and she was underage. The family then sent for the justice of the peace who was the closest in Benton County (3), but he would not marry them either since they were not in his geographical jurisdiction. So the couple and relatives traveled over the county line to his area, called "Pippin Hollow," where the wedding took place. At the time, the hollow was located in Benton County, which became Hickory County in 1848 (4). The marriage, however, occurred before either Hickory or Polk County was formed. Thus, that marriage was recorded in Springfield, the county seat of the parent county of Greene (5). Records are not always where you expect them to be!

6. What specific records did you expect to search and why? If you own

a family Bible that gives contemporary information for all births to a couple, and this information is confirmed by the federal census, why did you need to search the probate records? Learning all you can about your ancestor is important, but if your ancestor's records were victims of a courthouse fire you may not have that luxury. You may have to accept that you will never know as much about this family as you would like to know.

7. What information did you hope to gain? What did you wish to learn that you don't already know? You may have to focus on exactly what you *need* to know and where to obtain that piece of information. It may be that the most important thing you need to know is the link that will get your research out of that particular location.

8. How was the information going to affect your line of descent? This is, after all, the critical factor.

THE COURT RECORDS ARE GONE!

The next step is to envision the worst possible scenario and determine how to deal with it. Let us now assume that the record you desperately need was the victim of two conflagrations of immense proportions, one that occurred thirty years after your family moved to the county and one that happened three days after they left.

We must now narrow our task and focus our search. We must try to find either a *duplicate*, a *substitute*, or a *replacement* for the lost record. And then we must use that document to the greatest extent possible.

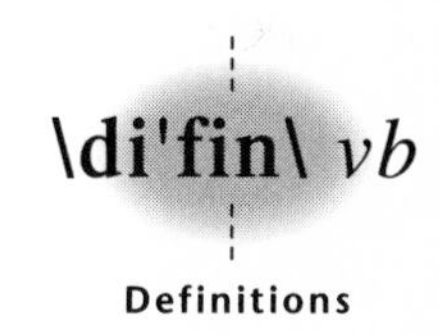

A duplicate is a copy of the original record. A duplicate may exist because the original record was copied when a new boundary or jurisdiction was formed, or because your ancestor moved and wanted to establish a previous legal relationship. A duplicate may have been required by law, such as in the case of probate. A will is usually recorded in every county in which the individual owned land. Often, duplicates of marriage records exist in the home and church as well as in the courthouse. Or there may be a duplicate because your ancestor chose to submit a document as evidence for a completely different purpose, such as a pension or land warrant.

Records can be filed in the strangest of places. I found a will for Jonathan Hopkins in the Revolutionary War pension application of Elijah Curtis of Massachusetts. I haven't the foggiest idea what it was doing there. It is not at all unusual to find Bible records in Revolutionary War pension applications or marriage licenses and death certificates in Civil War pension records.

Virgil White's 4,014 indexed pages of Revolutionary War abstracts has opened a number of these misplaced or misfiled records.

For More Info

Virgil D. White, *Genealogical Abstracts of Revolutionary War Pension Files*, 4 vols. (Waynesboro, Tenn.: The National Historical Publishing Co., 1990).

Published records (provided they are complete transcripts, such as *Suffolk Deeds, Public Records of the Colony of Connecticut, Records of the Massachusetts Bay*, and *Records of the Colony of New Plymouth*) are examples. These records were reproduced in their entirety. Microfilmed records would also fall in this category. It is possible that a courthouse lost records *after* microfilming was done.

A *substitute* is a document that contains exactly the same or similar information as the one you are searching for, but which is produced for another reason. Examples of substitutes include pension affidavits, newspapers, church records, court cases, land plats, and tax records.

Copies of tax records often were sent to the state auditor, so they may be one of the few types of records to survive a courthouse fire. They can give clues to descent (by following the land transactions), migrations (when people dropped off the rolls or were first assessed), and even ages (there was usually a defined age at which men began to pay taxes, and often an older age when they became exempt).

You can find marriage records or affidavits concerning them in federal pension records. Pulaski County, Missouri, has lost most of its records from before the late nineteenth century, but I was able to find documentation for a marriage that took place there in a pension application. Rachel Jones, widowed during the War of 1812, reported in her application that she had married William McLaughlin in Pulaski County, Missouri, on 21 September 1850, and that he died 21 December of the same year. Reports of marriages are also found in Oregon Donation Land applications. Isaac Cook reported in application #388 that he had married his wife, Sarah, on 8 September 1815, in the burned county of Burke, North Carolina. Unfortunately, he didn't give her maiden name. In addition, divorce records often give the exact date of marriage and the wife's maiden name.

A *replacement* is a record filed to replace a lost one. Examples include affidavits attesting to the lost facts, refiled deeds or wills, and chaining of destroyed titles by land title companies—tracing the titles from the original owner to the current one. For instance, the Hamilton County, Ohio, courthouse burned 28–29 March 1884, during a riot that ensued after a jury returned a verdict of manslaughter for a person city residents believed to be guilty of first-degree murder. Many records went up in flames. The county commission decided to reconstruct marriage records by calling in original documents and copying them at taxpayer expense.

Deeds are the records that are replaced most often because people are anxious to have a clear title to land they own and may some day want to sell. William Turner filed a deed in the burned county of Taney, Missouri, on 21 July 1886, telling how on 27 March 1861, *twenty-five years earlier*, he had purchased the SW ¼ of section 18, township 26, range 16. I was able to solve one genealogical problem using a combination of information from a case file for a federal land entry and rerecorded deeds. The case involved a land entry made in 1836, an attempt to clear title to the land in 1921, and a deed from 1876 that was rerecorded in 1917.

Court actions can occur long after the event. Jeremiah Cheek left a will in Bedford County, Tennessee, in 1823, but it did not survive the courthouse fire there. When the heirs quarreled in 1834, a suit was brought in chancery court. The will was produced and recorded in minutes for the proceeding, which did survive the fire. The will was a detailed one, naming each heir. This example involved a relatively short time between court events, but cases may extend over a long period of time. One such case involved a land claim made in 1768 by Thomas Manning of Moreland, Philadelphia County, Pennsylvania, that was filed in Suffolk County, Massachusetts, involving a parcel of land near the Sheepscott River in Maine that was bought by John Mason 20 January 1652. Your ancestor also may have been involved in a court case long after he left the county.

Look for the many substitutes that exist for courthouse records. **Listed below are sixteen major genealogical sources that are not located in courthouses:**

Idea Generator

1. Home and family sources
2. Town and state vital records
3. Census records (all types)
4. Bounty land records
5. Military records
6. Pension records (state and federal)
7. Church records
8. Newspapers
9. Manuscripts and diaries
10. Cemetery records
11. Business and employment records
12. Federal land records
13. Compiled biographies
14. School and college records
15. Court of Appeals records
16. Records of lodges, fraternal orders, and other societies

Following is a review of some common records we would expect to find in a courthouse, and suggestions for identifying a duplicate, substitute, or replacement for the lost document. Remember, what we need is not the record itself, but the information it contains. When a courthouse has burned, obtaining that information becomes more difficult, but it's not impossible. We just need to be absolutely clear about what it is we seek. The list below is not exhaustive, but it offers suggestions as to where you might look and how you might think about your problem. The examples merely scratch the surface of what is available.

Probate Records

If your ancestor owned property in a different state or county from the one in which he died, the land cannot be sold until a copy of the will or administration is recorded in the county where the land was held. I have found several probate proceedings and/or wills from Kentucky in the land records of Greene County, Missouri. Brent Holcomb, a professional researcher, found several wills from the burned county of Hanover, Virginia, in South Carolina records. Therefore, you might try to locate land records of the county where your ancestor came from in the records of the area where he might have planned to settle later, to see if his probate record was recorded or duplicated there. If the person you seek was a man of means or married a woman whose family may have left her land in a different county, search the surrounding counties. This is particularly true if your ancestor lived on the frontier and a new area opened up near his place of residence. He may have purchased land there very cheaply with no intention of living there, but with the hope of making money from it. A will was often copied into a deed book in the area into which the settler moved, or sent back to the original county where he may have still owned land. Two such wills found in Miller County, Missouri, are Philmon French's will of 1859, stating that he was of Onondaga, New York, and the 1869 will of Andrew Estes. The latter was recorded in Crawford County, Arkansas, but a courthouse fire in 1877 destroyed all probate records there.

You may be able to find a substitute or replacement for your ancestor's will by finding the will of a relative who lived in a different area. Records of the estates of single persons or those who died without children are especially good at naming large numbers of relatives. Burditt Sams died at age seventy-five in St. Clair County, Missouri, in 1846, leaving no children. The courthouse in St. Clair was burned during the Civil War, destroying probate and marriage records. The circuit court minute book survived. In that minute book is the division of Burditt's estate among his twenty-one heirs—most of whom did *not* live in St. Clair County, and some not even in the state of Missouri. Joseph G.E. Baynham's will is recorded in St. Clair County Deed Book C:92 and refers to another will that was still in force in Halifax County, Virginia.

Another substitute for an intestate proceeding is a land partition among the heirs. These partitions and other circuit court proceedings often were published in the legal notice section of local newspapers. For instance, on 5 June 1858, the *Springfield Mirror* contained a notice from the adjoining county of Webster, Missouri:

> Phebe Hyden, Simon Lakey, John Pock and Ruth Pock, his wife, Jackson Hodges and Anna Hodges, his wife vs. Jacob Lakey, Levi Davis and Rebecca Davis his wife, John Lakey, Andrew Lakey, Lewis Lakey, Sissial Lakey, Phebe Lakey & Lidia Lakey. Petition to assign the dower of Phebe Hyden and to divide the real estate among the above named plaintiffs and defendants, heirs of Jacob Lakey, deceased.

This legal notice names eleven children, three spouses, and the name of the remarried widow. Although one cannot find legal notices for every probate that may have been lost to fire, you would be surprised at the number that were published naming at least the administrator and securities, and sometimes heirs as well.

Newspaper legal notices may not include all the probate information that you would like, but they do provide the date that letters of administration or testamentary were issued. Experience indicates that these were first issued within fourteen days of the decedent's death. This at least tells you that the man died in that county and didn't move away. From legal notices that appeared in the newspapers of Greene County, Missouri, I was able to document over seventy-five deaths that occurred in surrounding counties between 1844 and 1850, even though the original probate records had burned. It's worth the effort to locate any surviving newspapers in an area where other records were destroyed. The best source for eighteenth-century newspapers is the Web site for the Library of Congress: <www.loc.gov/rr/news/18th>. Printed sources include Clarence Brigham's *History and Bibliography of American Newspapers 1690–1920*, Winifred Gregory's *American Newspapers 1921–1936, Newspapers in Microform 1848–1983*, and the United States Newspaper Program Union List from 1690 to the present.

Probate proceedings may be appealed to an appellate or supreme court, where they are often published. The decennial digest indexes for each state publish appeals to state and federal courts; these are located in law libraries, state libraries, and some university libraries. Completed federal court case files (1790–1930) are usually deposited in the regional federal archives and records centers. Following is one from my own family.

> Cases in the supreme court of the state of Vermont: Moses Robinson, Aaron Robinson, Samuel Robinson, Elijah Robinson, and Fay Robinson, John S. Robinson, only son and heir of Nathan Robinson, deceased, heirs of Moses Robinson, late of Bennington deceased, appellants from a decree of the judge of probate for a distribution of the estate of said deceased.

Marriage Records

When you are looking for a substitute or replacement for a marriage record, the best places to look are within home sources such as letters, diaries, and Bibles. Most of us consider marriage to be one of the most important events of a lifetime, so these records frequently remain in the family. When reporting events to relatives far away, marriages are among the first communicated. The following letter was dated 3 February 1869 from Monmouth, Illinois: "Kate Wallace and her new husband are here also. Perhaps you don't know who her new husband is. Well, it's Joe Brown, half-brother to Aunt Liz and they were married Christmas Eve." I have searched Warren County (where Monmouth is located) and three adjoining counties for that marriage record, but have not found it. This is the only source I have.

One of my luckiest encounters while searching for family sources in unusual places involves a Bible record for a Kansas family that had been submitted to the Kansas State Historical Society. A loose sheet of paper that did not appear to pertain to the family inexplicably had been stuck within that record. It said: "Francis Berry and Esther Day were married 29 January 1812 by Tidence Lane, J.P. in East Tennessee." The archivists at the Kansas Historical Society sent it to the Tennessee Genealogical Society, which published it in *An'Searchin* in the July–September 1972 issue. It was relatively simple for me to locate the residence of Tidence Lane. Although Hawkins County, Tennessee, is not a burned county, the marriage for Berry and Day was not recorded there. Genealogical journals often publish unusual and obscure family material. If you consult the Periodical Source Index (PERSI), something about your own family may surface.

In the January 1983 issue of *The Virginia Genealogist*, Elizabeth Shown Mills, CG, CGL, FASG, who often lectures on the subject of burned counties, described finding marriage information hidden within a survey book from the badly burned county of Buckingham County, Virginia. The entry read, "Capt. Thomas Anderson, deceased . . . willed to his late wife, now Mrs. Birks."

Another substitute for a marriage record is a divorce record. Although later ones are filed in the courthouse, divorces that occurred early in a state's history were recorded in published journals of the statehouse or senate. You wouldn't bother getting a divorce if you were never married, so if there was a divorce, *ipso facto* there was a marriage. In fact, the marriage date and place often are part of the divorce record. It's also possible that, even if the divorce was never completed, a petition may have survived. Petitions far outnumber divorces granted. A divorce also may have been appealed to a superior or supreme court.

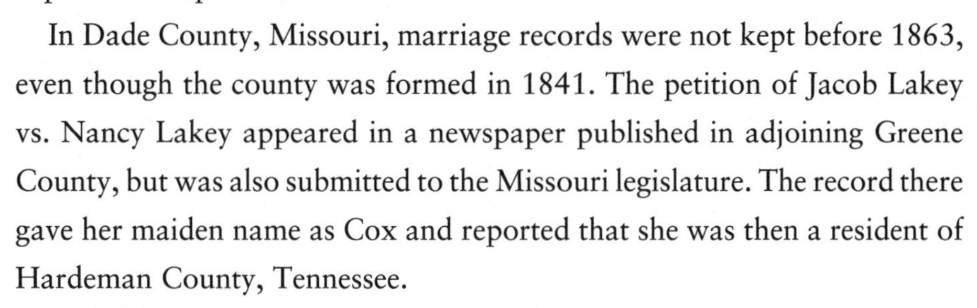

In Dade County, Missouri, marriage records were not kept before 1863, even though the county was formed in 1841. The petition of Jacob Lakey vs. Nancy Lakey appeared in a newspaper published in adjoining Greene County, but was also submitted to the Missouri legislature. The record there gave her maiden name as Cox and reported that she was then a resident of Hardeman County, Tennessee.

Newspaper divorce petitions may also be helpful. On 7 January 1845, the *Springfield Advertiser* posted the following notice: "Stephen D. Sutton vs. Susannah Sutton. Married in 1831 in Jackson, County, Alabama. Defendant deserted plaintiff in 1833 and is a nonresident of the State of Missouri." Divorces were more common than you might believe, and they could be heard in various courts. Read the chapter on "Divorce and Separation" in Marylynn Salmon's book, *Women and the Law of Property in America* (Chapel Hill: University of North Carolina Press, 1986) and Glenda Riley's *Divorce American Style* (Oxford: Oxford University Press, 1991) for more information on this American tradition.

In addition to legal notices reporting petitions for divorces, newspapers also printed warnings to the public, such as this one published in January 1857: "Warning not to trade with my wife Nancy Ann Critcher. Signed C.D. Critcher of Wright County [Missouri]." Wright County is a partially burned county. The surname Critcher does not appear in either the 1850 or the 1860 census there. This type of notice, indicating probable separation even when a divorce did not occur, appeared in even the earliest newspapers. They at least state the given name of the wife and a date by which the marriage must have occurred. The *Vermont Gazette* began publishing in

June 1783; by November of that year, Samuel Herrick of Bennington was complaining about his wife, Lydia, leaving his bed and board.

Churches also provide substitutes for county marriage records. Although church records can be hard to locate, they are often still available at the local level. Check local libraries, historical societies, and archives, then move to state and national repositories. Examine church newspapers, as well as the records of church historical societies and church-supported colleges and universities. Church records frequently are turned over to such institutions and may be stored in unexpected places. For instance, the Baptist church records for Middletown, Orange County, New York, are housed at the Southern Baptist Theological Seminary in Louisville, Kentucky. The National Union Catalog of Manuscript Collections (NUCMC) may help you locate church records.

The documents citizens most often attempt to save from fire, flood, and other destructive events are land records. These are also the records most likely to be rerecorded after the disaster. When looking for replacement documents, don't neglect deed books that may have been created long after the originals were destroyed. It is not uncommon for a father to make a deed of gift to his daughter at her marriage. If the family was a slave-holding one, the gift may have been a slave rather than real property. As any real property would automatically go to the husband, sometimes the bride's father would sell her share to his new son-in-law for an unusually low sum of money. If the father was concerned about his son-in-law's profligate ways, he may have made his daughter a deed of gift to be held in trust and not subject to her husband's controls. The following deed illustrates that situation.

> On July 9, 1836, Benjamin Porter of Robertson County, Tennessee, for love and affection for daughter Mary Thompson, wife of Thomas G. Thompson, now resident of Cooper County, Missouri, gave to her and the legal heirs of her body a negro woman slave Philes, about 18 years of age, and her boy child, Henry, aged about 7 months. These slaves are not to be subject in any way to pay her husband's debts (Cooper County, Missouri, Deed Book E:117).

This marriage is recorded neither in Missouri nor Tennessee.

In the genealogy *The Sims Brown Family* [of South Carolina], James Alvan Brown writes, "Richard S. Brown m. (2) Elizabeth Parham. Richard d. 16 March 1841. Nothing is further known about Elizabeth Parham Brown. A supposition is that she remarried and moved west." South Carolina did not begin to record marriages until 1911, but a deed dated 24 May 1852 recorded in Newberry County, South Carolina, Deed Book EE:117-118, states that: "Eliza Tranum of Macon County, Alabama, sold land which had belonged to the estate of her husband R.S. Brown, deceased, and that she had since intermarried with Joseph Tranum, who has also died." Thus we have record of the residence of Richard Brown's widow and her subsequent marriage.

A deed may also contain a record of a marriage contract. One such contract was recorded 16 October 1812, in Newberry Deed Book N:209 between Charles Thompson of Newberry District, South Carolina, and Nancy Gray, widow, of Abbeville District, South Carolina, stipulating certain financial conditions.

Always check cemetery records and tombstones, where you can find "wife of" and sometimes "daughter of."

Marriage records can be difficult to locate in New York. The state censuses of 1865 and 1875 give the dates of marriage for a couple from the preceding year.

If county land records have been destroyed, don't neglect the federal land entries for those states defined as "federal land states" rather than "state land states." All of the land records I have obtained for Pulaski and Taney counties in Missouri have come from the federal records. Yet, I know exactly what parcel each early settler owned. Microfilmed copies of all federal land states (except Missouri and Alaska) are available at the Family History Library. Once you have an approximate land description for the parcel of your interest, the tract books will provide you with the number of the case entry file, which may include additional information. Also see Patricia Law Hatcher's *Locating Your Roots: Discover Your Ancestors Using Land Records* (Cincinnati: Betterway Books, 2003), pages 79-95.

Although some counties have lost all public records to fire, in most cases, at least a few remain. It is important to examine all extant records to glean any available clue.

CASE STUDIES

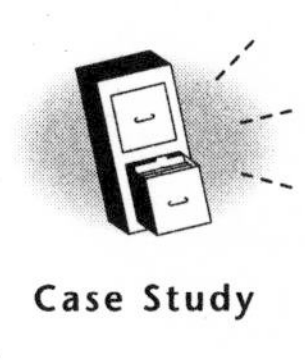

1. I was working on a Butler family from Missouri whom I traced to Overton County, Tennessee—a partially burned county. Neither marriage nor probate records from before the 1860s still exist. Some circuit court minutes, however, have survived. Filled with foreclosures, debt notices, and jury lists, these may also contain items of more interest to a genealogist. The minutes of the October 1843 term of the Overton County circuit court

gave me the name of Thomas Butler's wife as well as those of her brothers and sisters, her father's name and when he died, and the death date for his widow, possibly Jane Butler's mother. There was only one way I could have found this information: by reading every page of the minutes that survived.

2. Isaac Clark settled in the burned county of Pulaski, Missouri, but he also purchased federal land in Miller County, though he did not live there. The only Pulaski County records that have survived are two probate books: wills and administrator's bonds.

Isaac Clark did not leave a will, but he was living in Pulaski County in 1840, and the configuration of his family on the 1840 census gave me an approximate date for his marriage. His household consisted of one male age five to ten, one male age ten to fifteen, one male age thirty to forty, two females under age five, one female age five to ten, one female age ten to fifteen, and one female age thirty to forty. Assuming that those listed include Isaac himself, his wife, and their children, the eldest children were born between 1825 and 1830, thus placing a marriage about 1824 or 1825, and Isaac's birth year probably between 1800 and 1802, because in his culture, males usually married at about the age of twenty-one. He did not survive until the 1850 census.

I checked Miller County for the sale of his land there. As Missouri required a dower release on land sales, I hoped to find the given name for Isaac's wife. In 1838, Isaac and his wife, Mary, sold to Peter Miller their forty-acre federal land entry in Miller County for $150. The witnesses were Miller Wilson and John Wilson.

No marriage for Isaac Clark and Mary [—?—] was found in Missouri records.

I turned to the two surviving probate books in Pulaski County. I knew there was no estate for Isaac Clark, but I wanted to check for estates in which he might have been involved. Isaac Clark was the executor for the will of Cary Boyd of Crawford County in 1832 (Crawford was the parent county of Pulaski). Lydia Boyd was the widow and received all of the estate. A nephew, Francis Boyd, was mentioned. John Laughlin and William Clark were securities for the estate on 20 August 1833 in Pulaski County. As two men named *Clark* were involved in Cary's estate and no one named *Boyd*, was it possible that the widow Lydia Boyd had been a Clark?

Although Isaac Clark chose to live in Pulaski County, his first land entries were in Miller County. Rarely does an individual move to a new area and buy land where he is a complete stranger. Who else bought land in Miller

County at the same time? Among others was a man named Robert Boyd. A local history informed me that he moved to Missouri from Greenup County, Kentucky, and that his wife was Susanna Clark. A search of Greenup County, Kentucky, records revealed that Cary Boyd of Pulaski County, Missouri, was the son of Robert Boyd of Greenup County, Kentucky (Cary was named in Robert's will). Marriages in Greenup County also revealed the marriage between Cary Boyd and Lydia Clark. In the 1830 census, Robert Boyd was listed next to John Clark. On 8 April 1823, Isaac Clark married Mary Horsley, and his father, John Clark, gave permission. Some of my assumptions had been wrong: Isaac had married earlier than I had thought, by a year. That was, however, fortunate for me, because he was underage and had to get permission to marry. I was now working in a county with *records!*

Important

It is important when working in a burned county that you consider your ancestors' neighbors and try to rebuild their community. What were their naming patterns, migrations, birth patterns, church affiliations? By studying the community as a whole, you may be able to locate information about neighbors that provides clues to finding similar information for your own family. All serious genealogists know that you cannot study your family as though they lived on an island. Examining records for the entire community is even more crucial when you are working in a burned county.

3. John Birchfield bought land in 1836 from the Springfield [Missouri] Land Office in the area that became Taney County in 1836. Taney County has lost all public records before the 1890s. The county had no newspaper until the 1880s. John Birchfield died about 1844, as the final settlement of his estate was announced in the newspaper of adjoining Greene County in 1847. The administrator had been James Birchfield. I had found James and John Birchfield mentioned in an 1834 estate record, which stated that they had replaced fences and corralled hogs. I was guessing that James was a son, but he had died before the 1850 census, leaving a young widow. Research on the Birchfields went nowhere. At the same time, in the section of land where John Birchfield entered his federal land, an entry was made by Felix Enloe. So I traced Felix. He appeared on the 1835 tax list of Greene County, before Taney County was formed, but didn't appear on the 1840 census, just four years later. As no county land records survived, I sent for the federal land entry files. I learned from case file #10 from the Springfield Land Office that on 25 January 1838, Felix Enloe, then of Franklin County, Missouri, assigned his parcel of land to John Birchfield.

The 1840 Missouri census index showed Felix Enloe living in Franklin County, Missouri, about 130 miles to the east. Moving my research to that area, in the adjoining county of Washington, I learned that in 1825, Felix Enloe had married Nancy "Burchfield." The 1830 census of Washington County, Missouri, showed John Birchfield. Further research in Washington County, which still has its county records, confirmed he was the man who later settled in Taney County. With more family information gathered in Washington County, I easily traced him back to Franklin County, Kentucky.

4. Seth Moore and Isaac W.R. Moore took out adjoining federal land in Camden County, Missouri, a county that has no surviving public records before 1900. Isaac had disappeared by the 1840 census, but Seth remained; his entry in the 1850 census showed that he had children born in Tennessee in the early 1830s. Only one household showed the proper configuration in the 1830 Tennessee census, but it was in another badly burned county: Cocke County. With an Internet search, I was lucky to find Isaac W.R. Moore on the 1870 mortality schedule of Independence County, Arkansas. Research in that county showed him there in the 1860 and 1870 censuses, with children born in Tennessee. A man listed as "I.W.R. Moore" was head of household in Jefferson County, Tennessee, in 1850. Further research there uncovered Isaac White Rogers Moore's father, Jesse, who left a will in Jefferson County dated 1849 in which he named not only his son Isaac, but his son "Seth, now in Missouri."

As you can see, a burned courthouse offers a great opportunity to explore heretofore unknown genealogical regions. Creativity, persistence, and endless optimism are the keys to this type of research. I cannot guarantee you success, but I can guarantee that you will learn more about genealogical sources in this pursuit than you ever dreamed existed.

Give Me Land—Lots of Land

Considering the entire spectrum of American genealogy, land and property records have probably helped solve more difficult problems than any other single source.

—NORMAN E. WRIGHT, *BUILDING AN AMERICAN PEDIGREE*

Acknowledging that land records are among the most valuable records produced for genealogical research is simply *not* enough—you have to *use* them. Many researchers simply ignore them. Why? Although it is hard for me to imagine, Pat Hatcher states in her book, *Locating Your Roots: Discover Your Ancestors Using Land Records* (Cincinnati, Oh.: Betterway Books, 2003), that genealogists avoid land records because (1) they may be confusing, (2) they can be difficult to locate, and (3) they contain both valuable information and routine data, and one never knows which will be uncovered. If you have not already read a good deal about land records and worked with deeds, I recommend that you read Hatcher's book for definitions of terms commonly used in land records.

Take the following exam to see how much you already know about using land records. **This will not only test your current knowledge, but the answers on pages 134-135 will point to some of the valuable items found in deeds and other types of land transfers.**

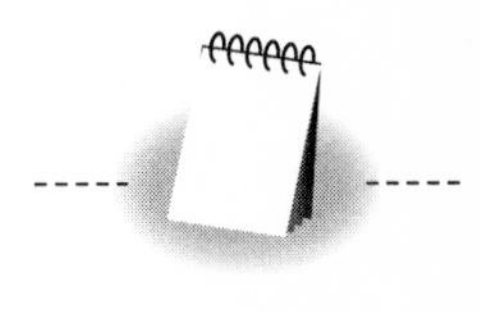

Notes

True or False

1. If you want to learn when your ancestor sold his farm, the best method is to check the grantee index book.

2. For a land transaction to be valid, the deed had to be recorded at the county courthouse.
3. Virtually all the land acquired by the United States after the American Revolution is surveyed on the rectangular survey system.
4. When an individual obtained a parcel of land from the government rather than from another private party, it is called a patent or grant.
5. If a man died after 1800, intestate, but still retaining a parcel of land, each heir had a claim on that land.
6. If several individuals together sell a parcel of land owned previously by a deceased individual, most likely they (or their spouses) are related to that man.
7. In the states that originally made up the Northwest Territory, a wife must release her dower privately at each land sale made by her husband.
8. Under the law of primogeniture, which was in effect in some areas during the colonial period, the eldest son was entitled to a double portion of the estate.
9. One of the advantages of the rectangular survey system is that neighbors are usually listed in the deed.
10. You know how to locate section, township, and range on a map. If I tell you that Farmer Lemuel Seed lived in the NW ¼ of section 20, township 28 north, range 22 west of the 5th principal meridian, you can locate his farm on a map.
11. In the lower-left corner of most deeds, the signatures of witnesses will be found. The first is from the husband's side; the next from the wife's side. Those signatures are to protect her one-third dower right.
12. During the colonial period, all thirteen colonies assured a female her dower right before creditors could make claims on the estate.
13. The federal government has mandated that all states use the same type of indexes to land transfers.

Answers

1. **False.** The grantor (or direct) index gives the buyer. The grantee (or indirect) index gives the seller.
2. **False.** If only it were true! Deeds need not be recorded to be valid. Moreover, because there was usually a fee connected with recording a deed, some people, particularly family members, might not have been able or willing to pay. Many land transfers went unrecorded, or were recorded *many* years and several transfers later.

3. **True.** It is important to know the difference between "federal land states" and "state land states." The primary difference is whether the state (or colony) was the first to distribute the land, or whether it was initially distributed by the federal government.
4. **True.** Becoming familiar with the terms used in the transfer of land will make your research easier and the data you find easier to analyze. Become familiar with terms such as *patents*, *fee simple*, *abstract of title*, *acknowledgment*, *deed of gift*, *trust deed*, *land partition*, *mortgage*, *quitclaim*, *power of attorney*, and *warranty deed*.
5. **True.**
6. **True.** This will be discussed in more detail later in this chapter.
7. **True.** Colonies and the lands formed from them varied in whether they required a dower at particular periods. Be familiar with dower policies in the area and the time period you are researching; release of dower rights is among the few types of records created by married women.
8. **False.** Primogeniture, which was in effect in some of the southern states until after the American Revolution, meant that the eldest son inherited all the real property. In colonial New England, the eldest son was entitled to a double portion.
9. **False.** In the *metes and bounds* survey system the neighbors are often listed in the deed, referred to as the "bounders" or "abutters." This does not mean that it is impossible to determine neighbors in the rectangular survey system, but usually they are not listed within the deed.
10. **True.** I hope.
11. **False, false, false.** This legend continues to make its rounds in genealogical newsletters, but it has no bearing in reality.

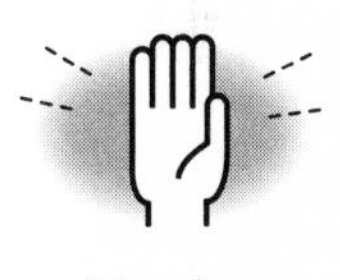

Warning

12. **False.** Dower release was not common in the New England colonies.
13. **False.** We can only wish it were true. There are many types of land indexes, and a careful study of how an index works in a particular state will help ensure that you do not miss valuable records.

Ninety percent of all white males in this country owned land at some point in their lives. This is just one of the factors that makes land records so important to genealogists. Land endures. After the wars, the courthouse fires, the family migrations, the boundary changes, and the economic declines, the land endures. Because ownership of land has been so important, people are careful about maintaining good land records. They try to make sure their names are spelled correctly, and they distinguish themselves from others of the same name in the community by using a middle initial or an individual designation, such as "Abraham Myer, the blacksmith," or the terms Sr. and Jr. Landowners strive to make sure the titles are clear so that they can sell or pass the land to others without entanglements. If there is a courthouse fire, the land records are the first to be saved, and if they are lost, they are the first to be replaced. All of these factors aid the genealogist. This does not mean that you will find every title cleared, or that you won't find mistakes in deeds, including creatively spelled names. It means that these records are the most *likely* to be correct of all those we use in our research.

In addition, by knowing exactly where a piece of land is located and tracking its transfer, the genealogist is less likely to fall into the common trap of following someone of the same name rather than the correct ancestor. I come from a long line of farmers, and one thing can be said for farmers: Nothing, with the possible exception of family, is more important to them than their land. In fact, most of my immigrant ancestors, whether they came in 1870 or 1630, came to this country for an opportunity they did not have in Europe: they came to own land. Many of my ancestors did not leave wills or probate records. Many of them were not regular church members, and if family Bibles existed, they have long since gone by the wayside. But my forebears left land records, and it is through those records that I have solved some of my most difficult genealogical problems.

Following are some of the items that you can find within land records. These provide direct evidence for the information sought. Later in the chapter, I will show how you can gain genealogical information from indirect evidence in deeds.

DIRECT EVIDENCE FROM DEEDS

You can learn an ancestor's earlier place of residence.

The initial rule of thumb is to locate the first land purchase your ancestor made in a given location. Obviously, the first place to look for that deed is the grantee deed index. The first entry may have been made before he moved, or before he established his residence in the new county. In a Georgia deed dated 4 September 1836, George B. Wardlaugh of Bibb County, Georgia, sold to James Brown of Newberry District, South Carolina, 202½ acres in the first district of Coweta County, Georgia (Coweta County, Georgia, Deed Book E:150).

Or, on 15 May 1830, Robert and Mary Rabe, formerly of Scott County, Kentucky, now of Marion County, Missouri, for $200 sold to Levi Barkley of Marion County 80 acres in Marion County. (Marion County, Missouri, Deed Book A:29).

If you cannot locate that first land purchase in the grantee books, your ancestor may have obtained his land by military warrant. The bounty land warrant index for the American Revolution and some of the warrants issued for the War of 1812 have been microfilmed by the National Archives. The bounty land warrants that are not indexed are at the National Archives. For the American Revolution, the bounty land records have also been filmed. There are many other reasons individuals could have received bounty land (see Patricia Law Hatcher's, *Locating Your Roots*, pages 76-77).

Perhaps your ancestor obtained his land from the federal land office in a sale of public land. Sometimes duplicates of those land records are in the county offices, but more likely they will be found only at the federal level, especially for the eastern states. These patents have remained in local offices in the western states. To learn how to obtain the land records for an individual who acquired federal land, see the "Public Lands" chapter in Hatcher's *Locating Your Roots*. Another excellent source for this information is Ken Hawkins's online guide to using Record Group 49, Land Entry Files of the General Land Office, which can be found at <www.archives.gov/publications/general_infomation-leaflets/67.html>.

It is important to note the people who bought land at the same time as your ancestor. Even when entering federal land, people could choose where they wanted to live, and they may have lived in a certain location for a number of years before they actually completed the land entry process. Watch for individuals who purchased land in the same area as your ancestor. Their names may be easier to trace than the one you are searching, or perhaps that family left better records in the community. Cheap land in a new area attracted family groups, and not just those who were closely related. Within a frontier community, it is almost always possible to link early settlers together—if you have the patience and the desire to do it. **Finding a cluster of names in one community may lead to that same cluster of names in an earlier place of residence.**

Research Tip

For example, Joseph Miller and Benjamin U. Goodrich bought land the same day in adjoining sections. If you were looking for their origins, which surname would you try to trace—Miller or Goodrich? In this case, Miller was the easier to track because he became an important member of the community, living to a ripe old age and leaving many descendants. Benjamin Goodrich was only about thirty years old when he bought land, but he died the same year, leaving just one child. Because of their land purchases, I surmised that Benjamin was some relation to Joseph. Sure enough, when I found Joseph Miller in Maury County, Tennessee, I also found a record of Benjamin's marriage to Joseph's daughter.

Do not despair if the first land purchase does not pinpoint where your ancestor came from. Check all of the deeds he created. Sometimes a later deed will give you that information. In 1845 Richard Brown recorded a deed of gift in Polk County, Missouri, that he had written in 1828, when he lived in White County, Tennessee. In another example, Samuel Moore of Polk County, Missouri, fell on hard times in 1838. He took out a mortgage on the money he expected to receive from the estate of William Lamm in Harrison County, Kentucky. Those deeds would have been much easier to locate if an index for the early land records of Polk County, Missouri, existed. Instead, I read the deeds page by page. This is much easier when your ancestor is settling in a newly formed county, but you should consider reading all deeds page by page even if they're from a long-established county because no index is perfect, no matter when it was compiled.

You can find an individual's destination

Always read the last grantor entry for a man in a given location. That deed may tell you where he went. People were reluctant to burn all of their bridges behind them and may not have wanted to sell that last remaining piece of property until they were sure that they wanted to stay in the new area. Genealogists often become frustrated when they encounter the problem of an individual who lived in a community for a long time and then suddenly—just when the researcher expects to find a will—disappeared. It was not uncommon for a man, particularly a widower, to spend his last few years with a child, often a daughter. That last deed may tell you where he went to spend those remaining years as he concluded the business of a lifetime.

Sometimes the individual returned to sell his last piece of property, but more often he issued a power of attorney to a friend or relative still residing in that community to sell his land for him.

> On 7 November 1833, Benjamin Coats of Polk County, Missouri, gave power of attorney . . . to sell land in Bedford County that formerly belonged to Baily W. Coats, deceased, and now owned by his heirs (Bedford County, Tennessee, Deed Book H:284).

Although not as common as a deed made after someone has moved to an area, sometimes a deed stating where the grantor planned to go was made before he left the county.

> John Hendricks, Nathan Witt and Nancy, his wife, of Estill County, Kentucky, being about ready to remove to the state of Missouri appointed Robert Clark to transact all business needed to settle the estate of James Hendricks, deceased (Estill County, Kentucky, Deed Book E:196). (Note: this deed not only tells you the destination of Nathan and Nancy Witt, but her probable maiden name as well.)

From deeds, you find an individual's heirs

When you find a group of individuals who sold land together, and that land belonged to an individual who had died, you can assume that these people are probably his heirs, even if it is not stated.

Important

If a man died still owning property, there must be some disposition made by the heirs. One of the ways land was sold was an administrator's sale. The administrator of the estate petitioned the court to sell the land to raise money to pay the debts of the estate. Unfortunately, these petitions did not provide the names of the heirs. In another unhelpful situation, the administrator sold the land and the court ordered him to divide the money obtained among the living heirs, but did not name them. If land was left in the estate after all the debts were paid, it must be divided among the heirs. If there was a great deal of property, there may have been enough to allocate a share or "lot" to each of the heirs. Commissioners (usually three) were appointed by the court to evaluate the land and determine the best way to divide it so that each piece would be of equal value. That recommendation was returned to the court, which determined who received which lot. The deed book may include a helpful map showing how that land was divided (see Figure 7-1 on page 140).

After Thomas Toler Jr. died in Wayne County, North Carolina, the land was divided in August 1821:

> In obedience to an order from the county court, the subscribers divided the land of Thomas Toler Jr. between the heirs of said deceased as the above plan shows. This division was completed October 27, 1821 (Wayne County, North Carolina, Deed Book 12:20).
>
> Lot no. 1 was to Jesse Toler for four acres on the edge of Sawpit swamp.
>
> Lot no. 2 was to John Toler for four acres adjoining Jesse Toler's.

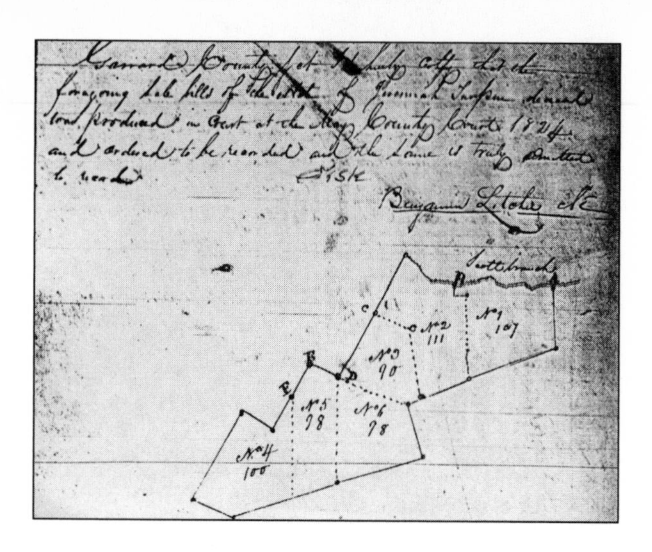

Figure 7-1
Estate division of Jeremiah Turpin, Garrard County, Kentucky. Probate Book A:384.

Lot no. 3 was to Richard Toler for four acres adjoining John Toler's land.

Lot no. 4 was to Dixon Toler for four acres adjoining Richard's tract.

If one or several of the heirs petitioned the court to partition the land, but the court determined that the land could not be divided without causing a loss of value to everyone concerned, the land was put up for auction. Sometimes one of the heirs would be the highest bidder, and then he would pay the others in cash, keeping the real property for himself. On other occasions, an outside party bought the land and the cash was divided among the heirs, depending on what portion of the estate they were entitled.

Another possibility is that the heirs may have decided to sell the land to one of the siblings for a small amount of money. Perhaps the others had received money from their parents over the years, while the younger one stayed at home and cared for the aging parents. Or some of the heirs may have moved away and were no longer interested in the land that remained. In that case, each heir had to sell his or her share to the sibling who wanted to gain all shares in order to have clear title. You may find all of the heirs listed in one deed of sale to their sibling, two or three selling together, or each selling individually. The deeds may be scattered throughout the deed books over several years of records. Some deeds may actually tell you the number of undivided shares in the land, which indicates the number of heirs and the portion each inherited.

Following are some examples of these types of deeds, what we can learn from them, and the steps we must take to gain more information.

In the deed abstracted below from Boone County, Missouri, the heirs are carefully outlined.

> On August 25, 1829, heirs of John Robinett Jr., who died intestate, as a co-partner of Pleasant Robinett, left a parcel of land in Boone County that was sold by his heirs to Pleasant Robinett. John Robinett Jr.'s heirs were father, John Robinett, and brothers and sisters Joseph Robinett, David Robinett, Moses Robinett, Pleasant Robinett, William C. Robinett and Sarah Robinett, Mary Robinett, who had intermarried with John A. Cotton, Rebecca Vivion, who had intermarried with John G. Vivion, and Rachel Pemberton, who had intermarried with Lewis H. Pemberton. (Boone County, Missouri, Deed Book C:217).

Another set of deeds illustrates another type of recorded distribution.

> On August 24, 1841, John Keller and wife, Nancy, sold to George Zumwalt all their right, title and interest in real property which descended to Nancy as one of the heirs of George Zumwalt, deceased (Franklin County, Missouri Deed Book D:449).

From this deed, we can assume that a younger George Zumwalt bought the shares of the deceased George Zumwalt. Was Nancy a daughter of the elder George, and therefore a Zumwalt? We can't make that assumption yet, but it's likely. Our next step is to see if we can find other heirs of George Zumwalt Sr. selling land to the living George Zumwalt. Check the grantee index.

> On August 24, 1841, David Crow and wife, Elizabeth, sold George C. Zumwalt their one-seventh part of the estate of George Zumwalt Senr., deceased, that descended to Elizabeth as one of the heirs (Franklin County, Missouri, Deed Book D:448).

We now have identified another heir, Elizabeth, perhaps George Sr.'s daughter or sister, and we know that there are seven parts to the estate of George Zumwalt Sr. If we looked only for people named Zumwalt who were selling land to George Zumwalt, we would not find the married women who were also heirs. Continue to check the grantee index to find additional heirs.

> On August 16, 1841, William Coshow and his wife, Elizabeth, sold to George C. Zumwalt their right, title and interest, it being one undivided seventh part, which descended to John Zumwalt as heir and was sold to William Coshow (Franklin County, Missouri, D:448).

Watch out for the red herrings! Some deeds are not as explicit as this one. They may report the sale of a one-seventh share without explaining that the land was acquired by *purchase, not by inheritance*. The heir here is John Zumwalt, not Elizabeth Coshow. Continued research in the grantee deed books eventually showed all seven children of George Zumwalt Sr.

Remember that indexes do not always lead to the list of heirs you are looking for. Some of the land partitions to which I have referred are indexed under the name of the executor or administrator of the estate. You can find this individual's name in the books containing letters of administrations or testamentary, the probate minute books or the bond books. Some counties may have all these records; some may have retained only one of them. It's also possible to find some of these records indexed under Sheriff's Deeds or under the name of the sheriff himself. That makes it more difficult for you, but it's still worth it if the deed contains the names of all the heirs. So keep looking.

You can find an individual's spouse

Prenuptial agreements are often recorded in deed books. This type of agreement is usually found when a man and woman have been married previously and are both bringing property to the marriage.

> On November 13, 1775, Vincent Mayer and Elizabeth Neukommer of Lancaster County, Pennsylvania became engaged and formed a prenuptial agreement. She was bringing £116, 9s. 7p to the marriage, and Vincent Mayer promised that if Elizabeth died before him he would pay back the sum to her children (Lancaster County, Pennsylvania, Deed Book GAG:143).

Such an arrangement may have been made in a first marriage if the woman was bringing property that she had inherited and wanted to keep as her own. This was more common with personal property than with real estate.

> On December 19, 1835, whereas a marriage is intended between John W. and Priscilla and whereas Priscilla is possessed of personal estate she inherited from her father, William Price, deceased, to wit; two negro slaves named Malinda and Dan, and a share of money . . . such property will be held in trust and she may at any time during her lifetime devise such property (Barry County, Missouri, Deed Book A:20).

Standard dower was a one-third interest in the husband's real estate for the wife's lifetime only. Upon the death of the widow, her dower lands were divided among her husband's heirs. Note that it was only *his* heirs; any children she might have had in a previous or subsequent marriage were not included in the division of the dower. **Please be sure that you do not write a woman off as dead before her time.** Clerks were not always as careful as they should have been in obtaining a wife's dower. Rarely did a wife have to sign a dower release on a mortgage, even though that land was subsequently lost because the mortgage was not paid. Or perhaps the wife was not able to be present at the time the deed was made. Sometimes the wife would not release her dower until much later. In some instances, the male grantor would post a bond to ensure his wife's release of dower. In the following example, the fact that the release was not made until later was extremely helpful because it revealed where the family was living.

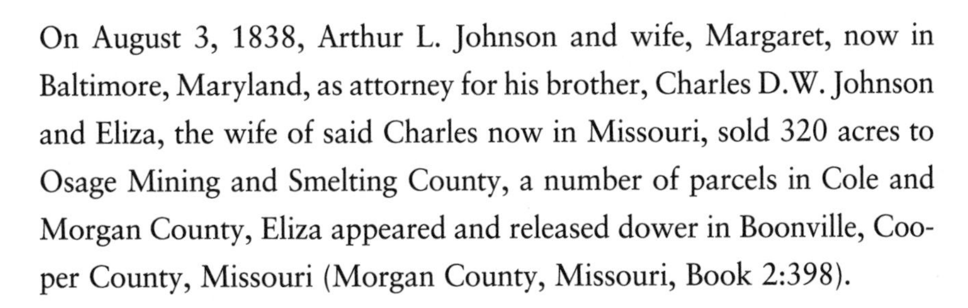
On August 3, 1838, Arthur L. Johnson and wife, Margaret, now in Baltimore, Maryland, as attorney for his brother, Charles D.W. Johnson and Eliza, the wife of said Charles now in Missouri, sold 320 acres to Osage Mining and Smelting County, a number of parcels in Cole and Morgan County, Eliza appeared and released dower in Boonville, Cooper County, Missouri (Morgan County, Missouri, Book 2:398).

Let's say that you know your ancestor died in 1852, and that he owned a farm at his death, but you can't find any deed executed by the heirs. Your problem may be that the deed was not recorded until much later. Perhaps after their father died, the children let their mother or stepmother live on that land for the rest of her life. Then they sold it after she died, which may have been twenty years later. Or maybe they gave it to one of their younger brothers who had been taking care of their mother, and after he died, his youngest son needed a place to farm. In that case, the actual heirs might not sell the land for another thirty-five years. Or, in another scenario, the children gave the land to their saintly sister, Susan, who had taken such good care of their mother in her later years. After her parents' deaths, Susan married Timothy Timberbottom. So now, the land either passed to the Timberbottom children or was sold to benefit all the heirs, but was indexed under the name Timberbottom. For every piece of land purchased, there must be some disposition of that land or the title is not clear. You simply have to keep looking.

If the title is not cleared at the time the individual who owned the property died, there may be a suit in circuit court later. Charles Rountree of Polk County, Missouri, died in 1851 and left no issue. The land title was not cleared and a suit was instigated in 1874. Seventy-five people were named in the suit as having title to the parcel of land. Their relationship to the deceased was not listed. I did, however, finally identify those heirs and published the results in the Fall 2002 issue of *Ozar'kin*.

If you know the land description, your search to chain the title may be easier if you use the tract books. These books list land sales by land description, section, township, and range, rather than by grantor or grantee. They then guide you to the deed book that describes the sale. In some states these tract books are in private land abstract offices; in others, such as Ohio, Illinois, and Kansas, they are located in the deed office. Even though tract books may be in private rather than public hands, I have never been charged to look at older records, but no doubt some holders may charge a fee.

I was researching the family of Caroline Elliott, who supposedly had lived in Greene County, Missouri, in the mid-nineteenth century. I wasn't having a great deal of success in the standard sources. I did find that a man named Thomas F. Elliott, supposedly Caroline's husband, had purchased a small parcel of land. On 26 July 1844, Jacob H. Smith and his wife, Mary Catharine Smith, of Greene County, sold to Thomas F. Elliott of the same location, for $290, the fractional NW ¼ of section 5, Township 29N, Range 20W containing 80 acres more or less (Greene County, Missouri, Deed Book C:303).

Thomas F. Elliott did not appear on any of the extant tax rolls, including the one for 1843. He did not appear in the census of 1840 or 1850. There was no record that he had sold the land. What had happened to it? It was obviously still sitting there and someone owned it. How had it been transferred?

From the map pictured in Figure 7-2 on page 145, I discovered that by 1876, the parcel in question was owned by Abner McGinty. I tried tracking the deed back by finding who McGinty purchased the land from, and where that man had purchased the land and so on, but I hit a dead end at a man named Edmund Turner. I could not determine how Edmund had obtained the land. So, I went to the tract books at the Hogan Land Title Company. At the place in the transactions where the deed book and page should have been listed, there was a notation: "cc 1875-165." The man at the abstract office had no idea what the notation meant, and said that he had asked at the courthouse, and they had no suggestions, either. I decided I would try the circuit court records for the year 1875 and look on page 165.

"On 22 May 1875, the circuit court of Greene County rendered a decision in the case of *Abner C. McGinty vs. the unknown heirs of Thomas F. Elliott, deceased*." The suit was over the parcel of land I was researching, "which

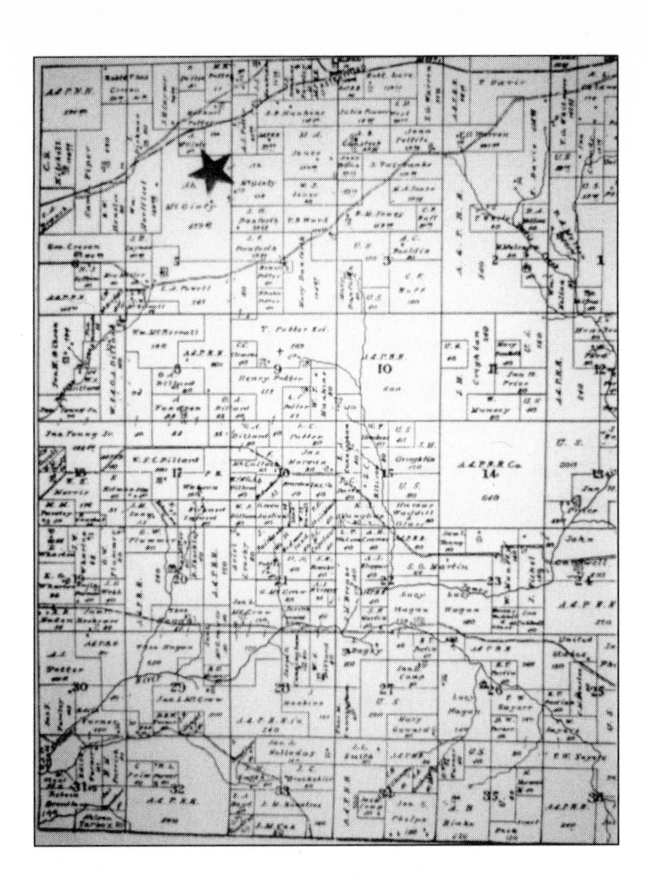

Figure 7-2
Map of Greene County, Missouri, from the *Illustrated Historical Atlas of Greene County, Missouri.*

Thomas F. Elliott allegedly sold on 26 July 1844 to Edmund Turner, but failed to make him a deed." The suit then told me that Edmund Turner had sold the land to Bedford Henslee, who in turn sold it to William A. Norfleet, who deeded it to the plaintiff. The court agreed to clear the title and removed any right, title, and interest the unknown heirs of Thomas F. Elliott might have. I was back to square one as far as Thomas's heirs and his wife, Caroline, were concerned, but I had disposed of the elusive piece of property and knew Thomas was dead by 1875. In addition, I had made an important friend at the land title company. My next step would have been to check the actual case file for the suit, but unfortunately, it was destroyed when the courthouse basement flooded.

Reminder

Remember that you need to track down every piece of property owned by your ancestors and determine its disposition. As you can see from the example of Caroline Elliott's family, there is the problem of the unrecorded deed. Unfortunately, there was no law stating that a deed must be recorded for it to be valid and, in fact, a fee was required to record a deed. Eventually, people found that they should record deeds for their own protection, but in the early history of the country, it was common to simply hand over your land without making any record of the transaction. As long as someone had the original deed and it was made over to the grantee, he could sell the property. This is the reason we find holes when attempting to chain a title of land back to its original owner. I have given you a method for chaining titles in federal land states using the tract, or abstract, books. In a state land state, which was surveyed on metes and bounds, you must try other methods, such as platting the land. For an excellent lesson on platting land see chapter eleven of Hatcher's *Locating Your Roots: Discover Your Ancestors Using Land Records*.

You may discover the parents of a man's wife in land records

On 29 July 1728, William Upham, who married Thankful "which is said daughter and co-heir of Joseph Dana, late of Concord," quitclaimed his right to eight acres in Concord (Middlesex County, Massachusetts, Land Records 28:243). All printed genealogical works have Thankful incorrectly listed as the daughter of Daniel Dana. This deed proves she was the daughter of Joseph.

By the time a man moved into his fifties, his children would have been starting their own families. Many fathers bought their sons or sons-in-law parcels of land, or divided some of the acreage they already possessed. We all know to look for deeds of gift from a man to his son or son-in-law that say "for love and affection." But you also should know the usual price of land during the period you are searching. Some young men did not want an outright gift, so if the land was sold for much less than the going rate, you may have a clue to a relationship.

Bird and Nancy Estes sold 180 acres to Garret McDowell for just $50, when the going rate was $125 per acre. Further research showed why. On 19 February 1830 in St. Clair County, Illinois, Garret McDowell married Nancy Estes.

By the time a man entered his sixties, he would likely begin making some final plans, and may have made deeds of gift to his younger sons, perhaps with a provision that they would allow him to remain in the home and take care of him in his later years. He may also have chosen to distribute his land to his children, one deed at a time. In that case, he wouldn't have to make a will and could avoid probate.

To find all of these treasures, you must be able to account for every piece of property purchased by your ancestor. I make a table such as the one in Figure 7-3 on page 147 to help me keep track.

Land records are an underutilized resource. To gain the most from them, they must be examined in their primary form, which is not easily available.

NAME	DATE	ACRES		SEC	TWP	RANGE	REFERENCE
James & Elizabeth Brown	7 Jan 1814	160	SE ¼	1	6	23	Book B, p 3
sold to son, James	15 Sep 1829						Book 10, p. 196
James Brown	4 Jan 1814	160	NW ¼	1	6	23	Book 2, p. 3
willed to son, John C.	1822						W.B. A, p. 133
James & Elizabeth Brown	15 Apr 1822	80	NE ¼ S ½	1	6	23	Book 6, p. 43
sold to son, Nathan	15 Sep 1829						Book 8, p. 432

Figure 7-3
In and Out Land Table for property owned by James and Elizabeth Brown.

Even if you order microfilm from the Family History Library, researching deeds may require you to check ten to fifteen reels, or even more, to find all the land transactions made by your ancestors. Many researchers may not understand the jargon used in deeds and may decide that searching land records is more complex than it truly is. Yes, working in them can be tedious, time-consuming, and downright boring. After reading all the legal verbiage four hundred times, you may wonder why they couldn't have found an easier way to transfer land from one person to another. Soon, however, you will learn how to ignore the nonessential parts and find the nuggets of valuable information. There are hidden treasures in those deed books, and you will be well rewarded if you don't give up the hunt.

Land records are among the most valuable of all sources genealogists use. Land provides a tangible connection between the past and present. Documents arising from land transfers record transactions involving our ancestors and one of their most precious possessions. Those records provide us with a multitude of clues and evidence for the genealogical connections we seek.

CASE STUDIES

Case Study

Case I

James Brown lived in Newberry District, South Carolina, when his father's estate was settled in 1830, but his later residence was unknown. The Newberry County local history said, "James Brown married Melvina Haynes and moved to Georgia." James had a brother, Robert, for whom I was also searching. His wife, Ann, was mentioned in her father's 1852 will, which said she also resided in Georgia.

I read every entry in the 1850 Georgia census, looking for a James Brown with wife, Melvina, who was born in South Carolina. There were at least fifty entries for men named James Brown, but I found nothing. I checked all the 1850 census entries for a man named Robert Brown, born in South Carolina, married to Ann. Still nothing. I had been so sure the two brothers would be living close to one another. Now what?

I found the answer in a deed executed back in South Carolina more than fifteen years after James and Robert had left. "On 17 February 1852, Nancy Brown, Abram Moore and Elizabeth, his wife, of the state of South Carolina, with James Brown and Robert Brown of Coweta County Georgia, in consideration of $1500 to be paid by George Brown of Newberry District, did convey 170 acres on Timothy Creek" (Newberry County, South Carolina, Deed Book EE:106-107).

But where was James in the 1850 census? Right in Coweta County, age forty-four, born in South Carolina—but my other clue, wife Melvina, had not helped at all. The James listed in Coweta County was married to Lavinia, so I hadn't picked up on him. When I visited the cemetery in Coweta County, I found James buried next to his wife: Lavinia Melvina Brown. Where was Robert on the 1850 census? He must have been on vacation; he was missed by the census taker even though he appeared as a slave owner on the slave schedule. Thus, he was living near his brother, just as I had originally suspected. I found him buried in the same cemetery with wife, Margaret Ann. One deed had solved the problem.

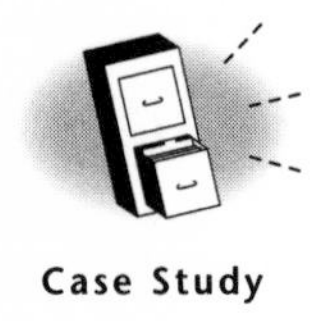

Case Study

Case II

Too often New England researchers build imaginary stone walls around towns and assume that everyone with the same name who appeared in the vital records of a specific town was somehow related. This was the case with David Robinson. David Robinson married Mercy Segur in 1726 in Newton, Massachusetts. It had been assumed that there was only one Robinson family living in Newton, so David was assigned to that family in several publications. When researching that family I discovered that David was not named in the probate of either his alleged father, William, or an alleged brother, Jeremiah, who died without children. If David were a son of William Robinson, he would have been the only child whose birth was not recorded in the town records. Neither was the name David found among any of the family's descendants. To which Robinson family did David truly belong?

It was easy to learn that a man named David Robinson had been born to George and Sarah Robinson in Watertown, Massachusetts, but there was no further printed information on that line, and there was nothing to connect George Robinson to the town of Newton. While it is true that Watertown and Newton were not far apart—just across the Charles River from one another—why would David marry a girl from Newton if his family was in Watertown? No children of Mercy and David were mentioned in the town records of either Newton or Watertown, and there were no other stray families named Robinson in Newton.

On 1 June 1728, David Robinson produced his only deed in Middlesex County: David Robinson of Needham sold to John Taylor of Newton, a tract of land lying in Weston, consisting of forty-one acres bounded by land of Joseph Whitney, westerly by John Kimball and southerly by his own land. Sarah Robinson, "the mother of the said David Robinson," and "Mercy Robinson, the wife of said David yielded up all their right of dower" (Middlesex County, Massachusetts, Land Records 27:422).

We find a David Robinson who lived in Needham (Suffolk County) and sold land in Weston (Middlesex County), which bordered his own land, but we have no idea how he acquired either parcel. This is the only land record for David Robinson in Middlesex County. Since this man had a wife named Mercy, it seemed possible he was the man who married in Newton. Since he had a mother named Sarah, it is possible that he was the son of George of Watertown. A George Robinson died in Weston, Middlesex County, in 1726, but he left no probate records.

Eventually, the case was established through land records, but it was not easy. To help you see how the connections were made, we will move backward (instead of in circles as I did for a considerable length of time). This is an approximation of George Robinson's land transaction as it was finally constructed. There was only one deed recorded for George Robinson Sr. in Middlesex County.

On 10 January 1721/22 George Robinson of Weston, yeoman, and his wife, Sarah, sold a mansion house and fifteen acres to Samuel Jennison of Watertown. That acreage was bounded on the southwest by the Weston line (bordering the town of Sudbury), on the southeast by land of George Robinson, on the northeast by land of John Kimball, which formerly had been owned by Caleb Green, and on the northwest by land of Samuel Jennison.

Returning to the crucial deed executed by David Robinson in 1728, we are reminded that the land he conveyed was abutted on the west by John Kimball and on the south by land he retained. A description of that parcel would place the land of John Kimball to the northwest, the exact same relationship to the land held by George Robinson Sr. seven years previously. Therefore, David Robinson and his wife, Mercy, were in possession of the land held by George Robinson before his death and probably where the widow, Sarah, still resided.

The locations of these men in the various towns—Watertown, Newton, Weston, and Needham—gave the impression that George and David Robinson were constantly moving. It fact, it was the *boundaries* that were changing. The map in Figure 7-4 below, drawn in 1831, is available from the Massachusetts State Archives. It shows both contemporary town boundaries in 1831 and the original town lines.

Over and over you will find that land records untie the knotty problems that other records cannot untangle. *Never* overlook their value when reconstructing your own family's history.

Figure 7-4
New England town map.

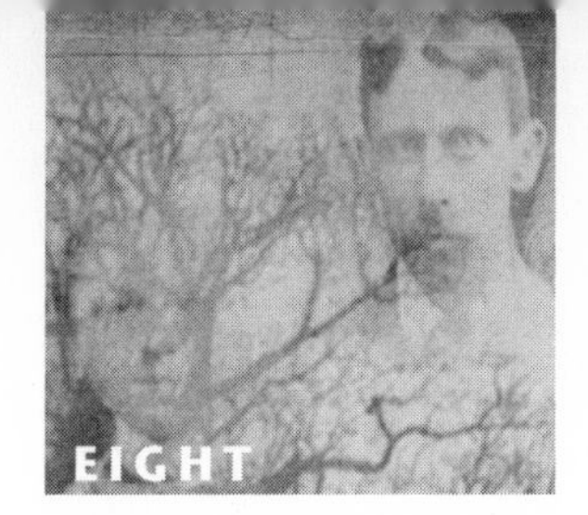

Sorting Individuals of the Same Name

People are part of something greater than themselves: family, neighborhood, ethnic, economic, social group, legal system, religious organization, historical era. Sharing a name does not mean sharing an identity.

—Helen F.M. Leary, CG, FASG

Two men named James Harvey Glenn, one born in 1846, the other in 1848, were buried in Monmouth City Cemetery, Warren County, Illinois, a town currently of only ten thousand people. One survived the Civil War and had several children; the other died at age eighteen from an illness while serving in the Union Army. He neither married nor had children. One of them is my cousin. Which one?

Two men named Michael Hoffman lived in Butler County, Pennsylvania, in 1850; each was born in 1836 and each married a woman named Mary. One is the son of Jacob, and one the son of Casper—but which is which and which is my great-grandfather? Two men named George R. Brown, three named Nathan Brown, three named John Brown, and four named James Brown all lived in Israel Township, Preble County, Ohio, in the 1820s and 1830s. They were all members of the same Presbyterian Church. Are they members of the same family? If so, how are they related, and which one is my ancestor?

These are just a few of the problems of sorting individuals of the same name I have encountered in my genealogical research. Working on each of these problems, I have become intrigued by the difficulty of establishing identities for two or more individuals living in the same place at the same time. I have found it to be a difficult but very common problem.

The first time I fell into one of these genealogical pits occurred early in my research, while I was looking for the father of Michael Hoffman, my paternal great-grandfather. It was only after a trip to the county of his residence that was I able to identify my Michael Hoffman as the son of Casper Hoffman rather than Jacob Hoffman, to whom I had originally assigned him. In the process of sorting them out, I obtained a considerable amount of information on the *other* Hoffman family, including locating their ancestral home in Germany and identifying the maiden name of Michael's immigrant mother—no small task, I assure you. I truly thought I had the right family, but because there were confusing contradictions, I kept wondering, "Is this right? It doesn't *quite* fit." Finally, nagging questions forced me to admit that I was just trying to explain *too* much. I had found a lot of blue pieces of my jigsaw puzzle, so to speak, but what looked to me like sky turned out to be ocean instead.

So, I convinced my husband that the garden spot of the western world was located just north of Pittsburgh in Butler County, Pennsylvania, and that *that* was where we should spend our next vacation. I learned two very significant things on that trip. First, I learned that more productive research can be accomplished when you have personal access to a wide range of primary records. By looking at signatures on documents in the Butler County courthouse examining church records, and locating family groups in cemeteries, I was able—without much difficulty—to establish that my great-grandfather was the son of Casper rather than Jacob Hoffman.

The other important thing I learned on that trip was the value of researching communities rather than just individuals. I had become so enmeshed in the problem of identical names—especially since Hoffman is such a common German name, and there were so many families in that area who shared it—that I had not looked at the bigger picture. **I had not placed each man in his own community and culture to learn about him as a person.** I had not studied the geography well enough. I had not studied the history of churches the families belonged to. I had not studied how their different communities developed. If I had, I do not think I would have stayed confused for so long.

Important

The communities where Jacob and Casper Hoffman lived were on opposite ends of the county: one in Cranberry Township on the west, the other straddling the townships of Summit and Clearfield on the east. One church was Roman Catholic with typical architecture, a cloister, and a cemetery with typically Catholic tombstones; the other was Lutheran Reformed and considerably different in form and appearance. One community had been

Figure 8-1
Map of Butler County, Pennsylvania. The stars indicate where the two Michael Hoffmans resided.

settled in the 1830s, primarily by immigrants from Baden, the other in the late 1840s by immigrants from Hesse and Alsace-Lorraine. The houses looked different, the surnames of the neighbors were different, even the contemporary restaurant food was different! The two Michael Hoffmans shared nothing but a common name. This was my introduction to the genealogical dilemma of the name is the same.

The problem of sorting out people with identical names plagues every genealogist at some time. No matter how unusual the name, it seems that more than one person always bears it. Yet, the problem can be solved more easily than you might think if you examine enough records and do not jump to conclusions before the evidence warrants it.

Ralph Waldo Emerson said: "Nature never rhymes her children, nor does she make two men alike." No individual wants to be confused with another. All of us want the world to recognize our uniqueness, so we do our best to let others know exactly who we are. Our ancestors felt the same way, and found various means of distinguishing themselves in their communities. To sort out individuals of the same name, we must study the traces that each left behind. By carefully analyzing each clue we find in documents, cemeteries, published histories, and other sources, we can reconstruct the lives of the people who created them, and glean enough information to separate those with identical names.

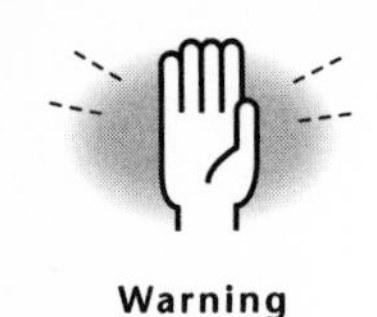

FIVE COMMON ERRORS

Below are five common mistakes made by genealogists attempting to sort out individuals with the same name.

1. *Connecting an event or relationship (such as birth, marriage, death, or military service) to an individual for no reason except that the name is the same.* This is the pit we fall into most often and with the most serious consequences. Many genealogists do not seem to realize that our hardest task is to be *absolutely sure* that a particular document or event pertains to the specific individual we are researching.

A common example is linking a certain man and woman because you have found a marriage record showing his name and her given name. For many years, published secondary sources held that William Upham, born 1747, of Newton, Massachusetts, was married to Lydia Jackson, born 1756. A marriage did occur between *a* William Upham and *a* Lydia Jackson in 1774, but the man involved was William Upham, born 1723—the other William Upham's father. In other words, the published genealogies had the younger William Upham married to his stepmother, his father's second wife.

It's easy to see how the confusion occurred. William Upham III (the man born in 1747) was closer to Lydia Jackson's age than his father was, but primary documents show that the son's first wife, Ann, had not died, and that she continued to release her dower on deeds long after the elder William Upham was creating deeds with a wife named Lydia. Obviously, the compilers of those published genealogies made assumptions without examining enough crucial documents.

Another problem that entered into this situation was the use of the terms *senior* and *junior*, which in colonial times referred to any elder and younger men of the same name rather than father and son. In this case, there were three generations of men named William Upham. Each of the elder two had changed his name from junior to senior when the older man died. This confounded researchers, who prolonged the confusion by failing to check when the deeds were *created* rather than when they were *recorded*. From the records, it would appear that William Upham Sr. was making deeds after he had died, because by the time the deeds were recorded, the younger William Upham had assumed that title and was creating his own records.

2. *Neglecting to search records thoroughly and systematically.* The differ-

ence between ordinary researchers and excellent researchers is not in the records they locate, but in how they use them. Examine each record for the details it contains and assimilate those details *completely*. It is not enough just to extract names and dates. If you are already having problems with too many people of the same name, you must develop different strategies to distinguish those individuals. Learning to recognize those scraps of valuable information that can be pieced together to form a meaningful whole takes a critical eye and a patient mind. Too often researchers look only for obvious genealogical markers such as "my son" or "my dearest daughter, Susan, wife of Jesse Snopdewox" to establish a relationship. Even when you can find such phrases in a historical document, you must be sure they apply to the person you think they do.

3. *Moving too eagerly to a preceding generation before the latest generation has been fully explored.* It is an axiom in genealogy that ancestry is too quickly sought; offspring not thoroughly studied. Whenever people ask me how to locate an ancestor's parents, the first question I ask them is, "Do you know who his brothers and sisters were?" Ninety-nine times out of a hundred, the answer is no. Identifying the siblings, or at least some of them, is the first step in tracking backwards, and is crucial when dealing with individuals of the same name. How do you find those brothers and sisters? By studying your ancestor's associates, friends, and neighbors. The people with whom he is most likely to be involved throughout his lifetime are his extended family members.

4. *Relying on secondary sources.* They are probably more confused than you are! Don't attempt to make conflicting data fit something that is already in print, or you may be making your job more difficult than it should be. Do your own work. Printed sources may lead you to some records, but when dealing with people whose names are the same, it is crucial to examine the primary documents yourself. Others may have missed valuable clues that could solve your particular mysteries.

5. *Drawing hasty conclusions based on insufficient evidence.* All of us are eager to solve our genealogical dilemmas. Too often, however, we do not examine enough sources to make absolutely certain that our conclusions are justified. It is unlikely that any one or two documents will provide enough evidence for a conclusion to be reached. This is particularly true when there is more than one person living in a given neighborhood at a given time bearing the same name.

Now that we have defined the errors we must avoid when dealing with identical names, let's look at the methodology for sorting out the individuals involved.

STEP ONE: To resolve the problem of distinguishing between individuals with the same name, you must know *your* ancestor.

Before you go looking for his parents or place of origin, be certain that you have identified the person from whom you descend. If you discover several men of the same name in the next area of your search, stop! Go back to the previous community where you can positively place him, or move your research to a more recent time period when you are sure you can identify him in the records, then study him thoroughly. One of the red flags I should have suspected as I researched my Hoffman ancestors was that I *knew* how my grandparents felt about the Roman Catholic church. When the man I believed to be my ancestor only two generations before them turned out to be Roman Catholic, I should have suspected that he didn't belong to our family. Now, after twenty-five years of research experience, I would certainly recognize something like that as a red flag.

Too often, genealogists study names, not people. They collect reams of material on the births, marriages, and deaths of people with the same surname from every conceivable geographic location. But in order for that data to be meaningful, the names must be seen as representing *people*, and those people must be studied within their social context. Researchers must get to know the socioeconomic status, culture, lifestyle, religion, and political beliefs of their subjects to the greatest extent possible.

Once you are sure that you have found the man from whom you descend, look for his distinguishing characteristics: his brothers and sisters, his wife, his children, his in-laws, his age, his occupation, and his level of wealth and

RISING'S RULE

Always assume that there is at least one other person with the same name as the individual you are searching living in that community. If you do so, you will never automatically attach a piece of data to a specific individual. Instead, you will reserve judgment until you have determined that no other individual by that name existed at that place at that time. If exhaustive study supports your conclusion, you have not lost a thing. If you find that there *is* more than one person by that name, you will not have to redo your work.

education. What did he tell you about himself? His name may be the same as someone else's, but he wasn't the same person.

STEP TWO: Pinpoint his location.

It's amazing how quickly things can fall into place once you make that simple determination. If you just pull names from records and then try to fit them into family patterns, your research can become more confusing than it should be. Be sure you know the genealogy and formation of the counties you are researching, as well as any significant geographical features that might affect settlement patterns. I was amazed at how easy it was to distinguish between the various Franklin lines in Amherst County, Virginia, once I knew that a mountain separated several of the families.

When you know where each man of the same name lived, you will find different neighbors listed in the census, different people witnessing their wills and pension applications, different executors of their estates, different buyers of their land, and so forth. The wives they chose, the ministers who married them, their children, and their children's spouses all will be different, even though their names are the same. Once you know the neighbors, it becomes easier to determine which man in the census is the one you seek, and this census entry will give you a pattern of ages and dependents, especially with those difficult census records before 1850. The census information also gives you clues regarding his livelihood and lifestyle.

The first example is a simple one. We need to determine how many men named George W. Kelley lived in a small community in Missouri. Look at the five recorded land purchases, all made within a year of one another. *Hint:* If you do not know how to read the following land descriptions, see Hatcher's *Locating Your Roots* or a good beginning genealogical reference on land records.

George W. Kelley bought land in section 25, township 31, range 24, west of the 5th Principal Meridian.

George W. Kelley bought land in section 25, township 35, range 23, west of the 5th Principal Meridian.

George W. Kelley bought land in section 35, township 35, range 23, west of the 5th Principal Meridian.

George W. Kelley bought land in section 36, township 35, range 23, west of the 5th Principal Meridian.

George W. Kelley bought land in section 36, township 35, range 23, west of the 5th Principal Meridian.

What we can't help but notice is that four of these parcels were in approximately the same location, while one was several miles away, in an adjoining county. Does this mean there were two men involved? That would be a hasty conclusion, although it does appear that way. Were there *only* two? That would be another hasty conclusion, as two or more men may have been relatives choosing to live close to one another.

Figure 8-2 below shows the locations of the parcels.

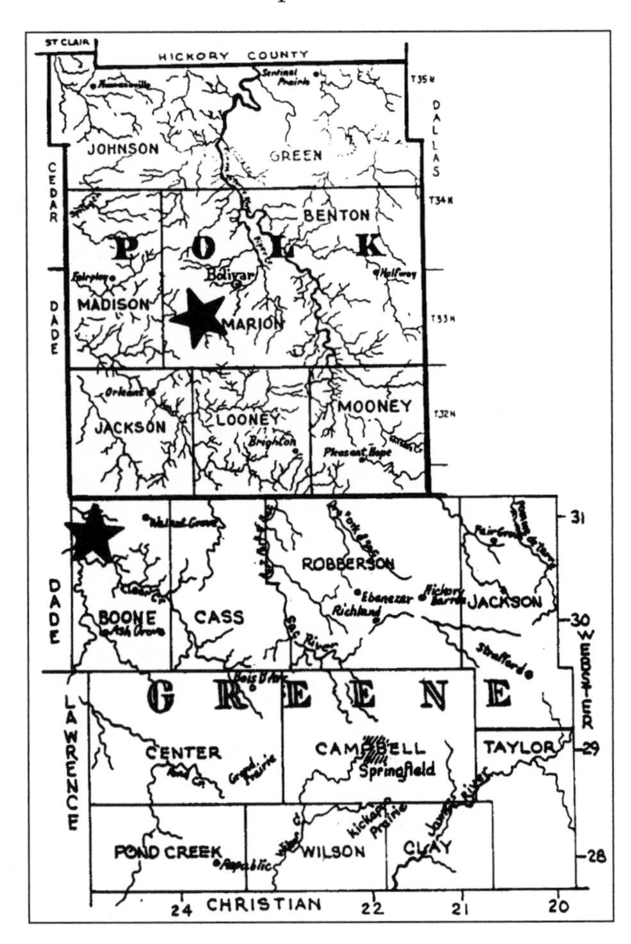

Figure 8-2
Location of George W. Kelley's land.

Only the most important information located after extensive research is presented here.

1. Jesse Kelley told a local historian that his father purchased land near Walnut Grove.
2. George W. Kelley was born July 1789; he died June 1869 and was buried in the Kelley Cemetery located in section 12, township 34, range 23. In which county is the Kelley Cemetery?
3. In 1850, George W. Kelley was enumerated in Greene County, dwelling #1251. His occupation was sheriff. He was age forty-one, born in Tennessee. With him were Sarah, age forty, born in Tennessee, Jesse M., age

twenty, Ellen, age eighteen, Harrison, age sixteen, Sarah E., age fourteen, all born in Tennessee. The rest of the children were born in Missouri.

4. In 1850, George W. Kelley was listed in Polk County, dwelling #651, age sixty, born in North Carolina, a farmer. With him were Elizabeth, age forty-eight, born in South Carolina, as well as Henry M., age twenty-seven, Russell W., age nineteen, and Amanda, age twenty-one, all born in Illinois, and younger children, all born in Missouri.
5. George W. Kelley was said to have lived in Logan County, Illinois (Goodspeed's *History of Polk County*, p. 661).
6. Jesse M. Kelley appeared at the Old Settler Dinner in 1906 and stated that his father had come to Missouri in 1837. "I was born in Greene County, Tennessee, in 1830. My father represented this county in the State Legislature for one term and was twice sheriff of this county."[1]

The information here points to two men of the same name. That conclusion can be drawn not only from the land descriptions and how they align with the census records, but from the age given on the tombstone and its correlation to the census, the occupations of the two men, the names of the wives, the statement of one of the men's son, and their different origins.

This simple example merely sets the stage for examining cases that are much more complicated. The steps the researcher must take are the same no matter how complex the problem is; the clues, however, may be much more subtle and difficult to locate.

Reminder

Remember, the second step is to pinpoint the location.

STEP THREE: Determine the ages (or approximate ages) of the people involved.

The census, of course, is one of the best resources for searches after 1850. Before that period, affidavits, taxation, and life events will aid in this search. (See chapter two, "Finding Births, Deaths, and Marriages Before Civil Registration.") The importance of knowing an individual's age is that it will help you decide which life events pertain to which person. As our task is to determine which record belongs to which person, recognizing normal age-related behavior or knowing how laws may affect people at certain stages of their lives will help distinguish those of the same name.

STEP FOUR: Enlarge the circle.

Move outside the records that the men of the same name created in order to obtain more surnames to work with. Get to know your ancestor's children, his siblings, his in-laws, and, of course, his neighbors. This can help you determine how many men there are and which record belongs to whom. Let's look at John T. Williams as an example. One of the ways we determined that there were two men named George W. Kelley was the two census listings. What about this case, in which there were again two census listings in two counties?

John T. Williams
One Man or Two?

August 28, 1850	*October 26, 1850*
Polk County, Missouri, no township	Greene County, Missouri
#209-209	#1276-1276
James H.M. Smith, age 44, born Kentucky	Allen Williams, age 52, born Kentucky
Martha, age 38, born Kentucky	Anna, age 47, born Tennessee
Lennah H., age 14, born Missouri	Angeline, age 19, born Missouri
John M., age 12, born Missouri	Jasper, age 18, born Missouri
Ephraim G., age 11, born Missouri	Elizabeth, age 15, born Missouri
Annis J., age 9, born Missouri	Redmon, age 12, born Missouri
James F, age 4, born Missouri	Mary J., age 10, born Missouri
Hue L. age 2 b. Missouri	John N., age 6, born Missouri
Duly A. Davis, age 14, born Illinois	Benj. F, age 4, born Missouri
John T. Williams, age 75, born Virginia	Francis M., age 4, born Missouri
	#1277-#1277
	John T. Williams, age 76, born Virginia
	Mary, age 72, born Virginia

In this case not only are the names the same, but the ages are very close and the places of birth are the same. In the first listing, however, the elderly man is living with another family, perhaps that of a daughter and son-in-law. In the second listing, he is a married man maintaining his own household. Could he have both married and moved and thus be enumerated on both censuses? Clearly we need more information. There were no probate or land records for John T. Williams in either county. There was no newspaper notice of either marriage or death. No marriage was recorded in either county for John T. Williams. How would you *enlarge the circle*?

We need more information for James H.M. Smith and his wife, and for

Allen Williams—men with common names who lived in different counties. Unfortunately, onomastic evidence (from child-naming patterns) lends little help here. Both families include a son named John, but that name is too common for us to make any assumptions from it, and none of the others correlate. A local history of Polk County, however, does tell us that Martha Smith was the child of John T. Williams and his wife, Mary Russell. But no one named Mary was living in Polk County with Martha and James Smith, and that census was taken in August, earlier than the one in Greene County, which was taken in October. Mary was in Greene County with John T. and a possible son Allen Williams. Therefore, we must have two men, right?

The answer to this problem lies in the dates when the enumerations were taken. Neither was taken on the official date of the census, June 1. What rules were given to the enumerators? They were to count the people living in the household as of June 1. The enumerator in Greene County followed the rules. Mary Smith was still living on June 1, 1850. By the time a different census taker visited the Smith home in Polk County in August, Mary had died, and so he did not report her within the household. Someone in the household, however, must have told him that she had recently died because he put her on the mortality schedule even though she did not *officially* belong there. Only one man was represented in these two census listings. (There *was* another man named John T. Williams living in Polk County at the time, but that's *another* story!)

STEP FIVE: Gather as many records as possible.

Study the details. **Don't just write down the names—they've been causing us enough trouble already!** Be sure to note locations, associates, witnesses, and neighbors. Place the records in chronological order rather than attaching them to individuals and families. The more records you are able to find that pertain to the people you are researching, the easier your task will be.

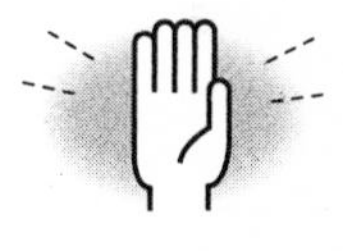

Warning

Tax records are one of my favorite means of distinguishing individuals from one another because they reflect shorter periods of time. People could easily come and go during the decade between census reports, but taxes were taken at least once a year and many years of those rolls may have survived. Correlated with land records and census data, they can prove invaluable. They sometimes contain designations the tax collector used to be sure that he had taxed the right man for the correct amount. Some of the designations I have found jotted next to men named *Newcomer* in the tax rolls of Lancaster County, Pennsylvania include "thick" (which meant "fat"), "poor," "renter," "red," "gentleman," "tenant," and "inmate." Sometimes the tax collector designated the men named Newcomer by where they lived—"John Newcomer, half-way," "John Newcomer, Ulrich Road" and "John Newcomer, Bainbridge"—or by their occupation, such as farmer, blacksmith, innkeeper, miller, turner, stiller, shoemaker, and gunsmith.

You also need to watch for the confusing terms *senior* and *junior*. These terms do not necessarily imply any sort of relationship. *Senior* merely referred to the eldest man of that name in the community, *junior* the younger, and *third* the next. If the elder man died or moved away, everyone moved up a notch, so "junior" became "senior," "third" became "junior," and so forth. This practice was most common during the colonial period, although in many instances it persisted into the nineteenth century. Of course, *senior* and *junior* may refer to father and son—and then again, they may not. To summarize, you cannot rely on these terms alone to differentiate between individuals or confirm a relationship.

Records associated with your ancestor's church affiliation are also helpful. Membership and other church records can help you find names and dates, of course, but learning about the tenets and doctrines of that church will help you better understand the individual and the community. What was acceptable behavior, and what wasn't? Was your ancestor a conformist or a rebel? People did not always remain within the same church all their lives. If someone changed affiliation, there may be a notation that will help you differentiate between him and the man of the same name. Examples might include a marriage outside of the Quaker meeting, or the marriage of a man of the Dunkard faith in a German Reformed Church.

Many researchers have had difficulty sorting out the Newcomer family in Lancaster County, Pennsylvania. This family group, persecuted Mennonites from Switzerland and the Palatinate, arrived in America about 1722. The Mennonites, often called "the plain people," were Anabaptists and pacifists who believed in living as close to God as possible, and spent most of their energies preparing for the next life rather than recording the events of this one. As may be expected, they left few records.

During the latter half of the eighteenth century, there were at least ten men named Christian Newcomer living in the western half of Lancaster County, at least nine men named John Newcomer, and four named Abraham Newcomer.

One of the early problems I encountered was identifying the parents of Christian Newcomer, a man born about 1793 who married Elizabeth Hartman in the Lutheran church in the village of Lancaster. Because he served in the War of 1812, I learned a lot from his military pension record about the events of his life after he left Lancaster County in the 1820s. But who were his parents?

Researchers initially assigned him to the family of an older man named Christian Newcomer and his wife, Anna Witmer of Manor Township, Lancaster County. But when I pointed out that Anna Witmer Newcomer would have been about fifty-two years old at the time of this Christian Newcomer's birth, and that this Christian was ten years younger than Anna's youngest child, a new set of parents was sought. This time the selected father was another Christian Newcomer, a man who lived in Hempfield Township. In the 1800 census, however, there were two men named Christian Newcomer listed as living in Hempfield Township. One of these men had three males under the age of ten in his household, so he appeared to be the best prospect. This Christian Newcomer was believed to be the brother of the John Newcomer of Hempfield Township, who left a will in which he named each of the eight children of his deceased brother, Christian. Those children were John, Christian, Abraham, Jacob, Elizabeth, Henry, Mary, and Barbara—all very common names among the families in the area. The testator was born about 1760 and lived until 1848, approximately eighty-eight years. He and his wife had no surviving children when he made his will in 1822. Most researchers had written down the names of the eight children named in that will and let it go at that. On this basis alone, the Christian Newcomer who married Elizabeth Hartman was assigned to this family. The names fit, so the pieces fit, right?

This example provides an excellent case for "letting the record speak to you." John Newcomer's will tells us more than just the facts written there; it tells us about the values and beliefs of the individual who made it. Let's review what it says. In addition to naming his deceased brother's children, John Newcomer gave $100 to another man named John Newcomer, whom he called "an elder in our Mennonist Society in trust to the poor." Obviously, the testator was still an active Mennonite. The discrepancy between this John Newcomer's religious beliefs and the actions of his supposed son, Christian Newcomer, the husband of Elizabeth Hartman, should provoke some questions. Would John Newcomer, the active Mennonite, have given an inheritance to a man who married in the *Lutheran* church and took up arms in the War of 1812?

Further research proved that Christian and Elizabeth Hartman were living in Hamilton County, Indiana, when the nephew of John Newcomer, the Mennonite of Hempfield Township, signed the receipt for his inheritance. That nephew, Christian Newcomer, was living in Ashland, Ohio—not Indiana. The discrepancy in values, however, was the first red flag that should have told the researcher that this is likely not the same family.

Signatures can also be extremely helpful when sorting out individuals of the same name because each is unique. Military records and probate packets are good original sources for signatures. Other sources include petitions for roads, for the laying out of a county boundary, or for the formation of a militia company. If your ancestor did not leave probate records himself, he may have been a witness or deponent for one of his neighbors. He may have signed a receipt for work done for a deceased neighbor, or he may have signed a variety of documents as the attending physician, the mortician, the carpenter who built the coffin, the crop harvester, the fence mender, or the wood chopper. Try to find those signatures, because comparing them can help you sort out individuals. (Of course, if your ancestors could do nothing more than sign with an *X*, this may not be particularly helpful!)

Deeds and other land records are invaluable. When you gather information, note the exact description of the land owned by each man, how he acquired it, and how he disposed of it. If he made a will, pay particular attention to how he refers to the land containing "the dwelling house." Who is living there now? Will the widow retain the house until her death? Which land goes to which son? How is that land described on the tax list? Follow that land through the years, even after the man you are seeking has left it.

STEP SIX: Remain alert to inconsistencies and contradictions.

Don't manipulate the data to fit a highly desirable hypothesis. Remember to do your math so you don't have sixty-year-old women giving birth and seventeen-year-old boys having their fourth child. Contradictions or inconsistencies should raise red flags to warn you that more than one person probably generated the records.

STEP SEVEN: Place the records in chronological order, not in families.

This is a truly essential step. When you gather a lot of data, it is easy to become overwhelmed. However, when you place the records you have gathered in chronological order and make note of the ages of the individuals involved, you probably can eliminate many names from further consideration. Perhaps documents from the same time period appear to name different spouses for the same person. In other cases, the man you seek may seem to be in two different locations simultaneously. Or perhaps the individual seems to be doing contradictory things—making a major land purchase while experiencing the foreclosure of his farm. Chronology is said to be the spine of history; this is also true for genealogy. The facts must fit a logical order and usually correlate with normal behavior for a person of his age, marital status, and socioeconomic level.

STEP EIGHT: Analyze your findings and put the pieces together slowly, logically, and consistently.

Do the pieces fit together? Has the picture of a unique person emerged? Can you include all the facts you have uncovered? If not, you need more information.

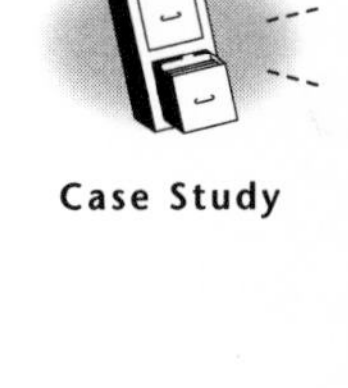

Case Study

Let's go through another case illustrating the steps involved in sorting out individuals. In this situation, we will try to find the origins of a man named Benjamin Johnson. We know nothing about this man except that he purchased forty acres of federal land in Greene County, Missouri, on 25 January 1838. Since we know nothing else at this point, we will move to the second step in the process: pinpoint his location. Figure 8-3 shows the location of the land.

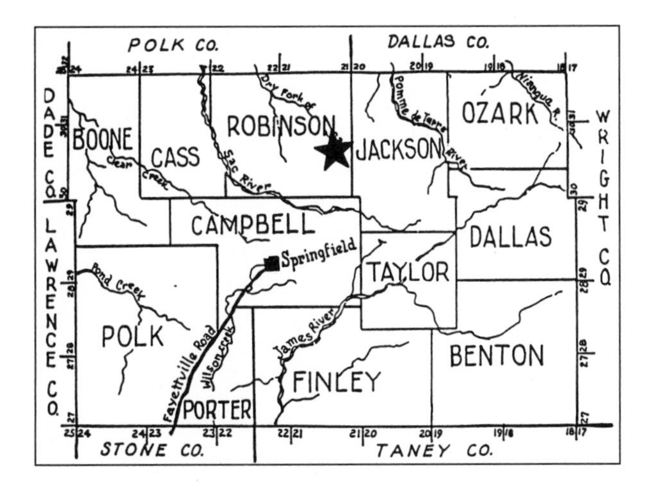

Figure 8-3
Location of Benjamin Johnson's land.

The next step is to *enlarge his circle*. As this land is on the rectangular (or section, township and range) survey system, we can correlate his neighbors on the land with the listing in the 1840 census rather easily. Fortunately, there was only one man in Greene County named Benjamin Johnson who was head of household in 1840. His household consisted of one male under five, one male age ten to fifteen, one male age fifteen to twenty, one male age forty to fifty, two females age five to ten, two females age ten to fifteen, two females fifteen to twenty, and one female age forty to fifty. Thus, we know we have a middle-aged man who appears to be married and who has a number of dependents, some of whom may be his children. We are fortunate that the census taker did not alphabetize this census. Enumerated on the same page were Joseph Headlee, William Dysart, Robert W. Sims, William Jenkins, Columbus Williamson, Archibald Adams, John Headlee, and Jeptha Wallace. By checking the land purchases of these men, we know that the Benjamin Johnson listed in the 1840 census is the man who bought the land.

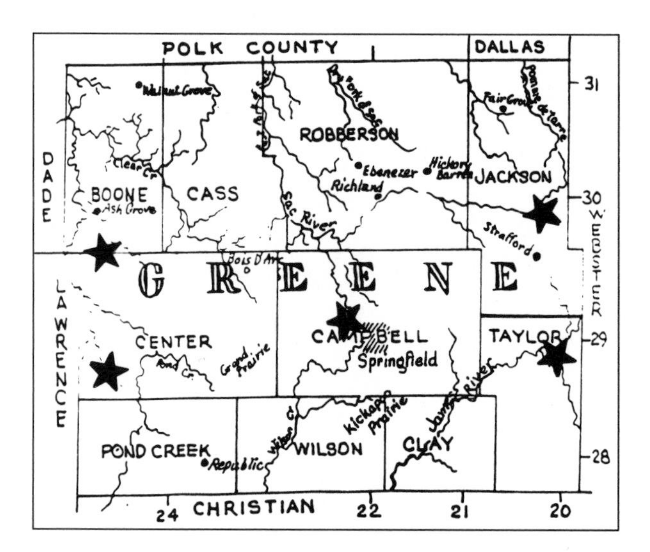

Figure 8-4
By 1850 there were five men named Benjamin Johnson.

Of course, the 1850 census will give us more specific information. Oops! By 1850, there were five men named Benjamin Johnson living in Greene County. None were living near the town of Ebenezer and none were the right age with the right family configuration to match the man who was head of household in 1840. I examined the records for each one and had to eliminate all of them as the Benjamin Johnson who purchased the land. For now, we had better confine our search to the years between 1840 and 1850, when *our* Benjamin Johnson was likely to be generating records that will tell us more about him.

I checked all available records: marriages, county histories, circuit court minutes, probate, and tax records. I took careful notes and placed every piece of information that I found in chronological order. Of course, you always collect more information than you need, but you never know which piece of data is the crucial one until the problem is solved. The more information you gather, the more likely it is that you will have the critical pieces.

1832 John Headlee settled on the Sac River followed by two brothers-in-law Benjamin Johnson and James Dryden. The county history stated John Headlee was the son-in-law of Fanny Sims (Holcombe, *History of Greene County, Missouri,* 1883, p. 148).

1833 First Greene County, Missouri, tax list. No Benjamin Johnson listed.

1834 Benjamin John*st*on was listed on the unalphabetized Greene County tax list. He was two doors from John Headlee and next to Harris G. Joplin, Fanny Sims, and Henry C. Morrison. He was the only one of the surname. He was taxed for one cow and one poll.

1835 Benjamin Johnson paid a tax for one horse, one cow, one poll. He was listed between Daniel Johnson and Wm. Johnson, the only ones of that surname on the list. This tax list was alphabetized.

1835 No James Dryden on the tax rolls. Instead, in 1835 Frankey Dryden, a widow, paid a tax on one horse and one cow, but no poll. On 30 April 1837 Frances Dryden married Andrew Guinn. They were married by Harris G. Joplin.

1840 Only one Benjamin Johnson was head of household in the Greene County census. The household included one male under five, one male age ten to fifteen, one male age fifteen to twenty, one male age forty to fifty; two females age five to ten, two females age ten to fifteen, two females age fifteen to twenty, and one female age forty to fifty. The next heads of household on the list were Joseph Headlee, Wm. Dysert, Thos. J. Whitlock, Robert W. Sims, Columbus Williamson, Archibald Adams, and John Headlee. From the position of the neighbors, this Benjamin Johnson appeared to be living on the above tract.

1841 Benjamin Johnson purchased 160 acres in Section 4, Twp. 29, Range 24.

1842 Benjamin Johnson purchased 160 acres in Section 9, Twp. 29, Range 24.

15 January 1842
Benjamin C. Johnson mortgaged "land which had not been entered, but where he now resides" in Section 19, Township 30N, Range 20W of preemption land, one bay mare, one brown cow, and one common

clock for $150, payable in twelve months to Zachariah Sims. Signed Benjamin C. Johnson. Wit: T.M. and Henry C. Morrison (Greene County Deed Book B:245). There was no release.

25 January 1842

John O. Sheppard and wife, Sarah Jane, sold to Benjamin Johnson for $534.00 the SE ¼ of Section 4, Township 29N, Range 24W and the E ½ of the NE ¼ of Section 8, Township 29N, Range 24W consisting of 240 acres. Witnesses were James H. and Joel H. Haden (Greene Co. Deed Book C:941).

1843 Three men named Benjamin Johnson paid taxes in Greene County. None were paying taxes on land, so they may have been exempt by purchasing federal parcels. The list was alphabetized.

a. One was between J.C. Johnson and Joseph Johnson. This man paid taxes on seven horses, two cows, and one timepiece, but no poll.
b. One was between H.G. Joplin and Emily Jarrett, Napoleon Jarrett, and William Johnson. He paid taxes on one horse and six cows, and a poll.
c. The next Benjamin Johnson was listed very close—just three names from the Benjamin Johnson in section "b," above—and was between William Johnson and C.A. Jameson. This Benjamin was paying taxes on one horse, two cows, one timepiece, and a poll.

Biography: Benjamin R. Johnson was born in Greene County, Tennessee on 1 September 1824. His parents were Benjamin and Mary Johnson, the former a native of South Carolina, the latter of Virginia. Benjamin's father came to Greene County in 1841 and settled where the subject still resides in Center Twp. and lived there until his death in 1867 (Holcombe, page 654). (*Note*: In 1883 Center Township included the land in Twp. 29, Range 24.)

1850 Five men named Benjamin Johnson. None fit the man under study. All were studied and eliminated. The man in Boone Township was sixty-four years of age. A Benjamin N. Johnson, age twenty-two, born in Tennessee, was living in Robinson Township. He was next door to William Johnson, age fifty-two, born in North Carolina. No other clues emerged.

There were forty-two marriages in Greene County before 1850 for people named Johnson. None were named Benjamin.

Remember that the county history gave a relationship for Benjamin Johnson. The history stated that in "1832 John Headlee settled on the Little Sac River followed by two brothers-in-law Benjamin Johnson and James Dryden." That sentence is not completely clear. Did the history mean Benjamin and James Dryden were in-laws just to each other, or to John Headlee as well? Also remember that the county history related that John Headlee's mother-in-law was Fanny Sims. You may recall that Robert W. Sims and John Headlee were listed on the same page as Benjamin Johnson in the 1840 census. We have made only two attempts thus far to enlarge the circle for Benjamin Johnson. We have not started looking for other men named Johnson. We have started looking for people who may be connected to a *specific* man named Benjamin Johnson, and we already have three: John Headlee, James Dryden, and Fanny Sims.

The nonalphabetized tax record of 1834 gave him more associates: John Sims, Fanny Sims, John Headlee, Henry C. Morrison, Zachariah Sims, Harris Joplin, and James K. Alsup.

In 1835 he paid taxes for one horse, one cow, and a poll. What does this tell us? This man was *not* King Midas. We know he was in his forties and had a large family, but he owned only two animals. He would undoubtedly fit today's poverty guidelines.

Let's look again at the 1840 census and note that other now-familiar names appear on page 254: Fanny Sims, Zachariah Sims, Joseph Headlee, L.H. Sims, James K. Alsup, Andrew B. Guinn, and Elisha Headlee.

Now what? **Let's check some other records commonly used by genealogists.**

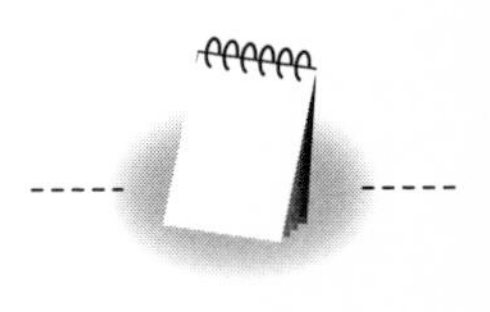

Notes

1. Not surprisingly, there was no probate for our Benjamin Johnson—nor for anyone of that name. What about his associates? In November 1835, John Headlee became administrator for the estate of James Dryden, deceased. In 1839, widow Franky Guinn signed a receipt for her dower, so we know that Franky, James Dryden's widow, had remarried.
2. No one named James Dryden was listed in the census or on tax rolls. In 1835, widow Franky Dryden paid taxes, and in 1837, she married Andrew Guinn. They were married by Harris G. Joplin.
3. Now we go to the land records. I found four deeds made between 1841 and January 1842 for men named Benjamin Johnson. Three were purchases and one was a mortgage. Let's return to our chronological list.

A man named Benjamin Johnson was making significant purchases of land, all located in township 29, range 24. This was not the same location where the first Benjamin Johnson had lived.

On 15 January 1842, Benjamin C. Johnson mortgaged "land which has not been entered, but where he now resides" located in section 19, township 30, range 20 of preemption land, one bay mare, one brown cow, and one common clock for $150, payable in twelve months to Zachariah Sims. Signed Benjamin C. Johnson. The witnesses were T.M. and Henry C. Morrison. There was no release to the mortgage.

A number of significant items are apparent here. One man named Benjamin Johnson was making large purchases, while the other was mortgaging everything he owned. Thus, we know that as of January 1842, we have two men. Two other significant facts emerge from this mortgage. First, this Benjamin Johnson was now using the middle initial C. Second, we have a new man who is willing to loan *our* Benjamin C. Johnson money—Zachariah Sims.

Let's now look at the only surviving tax record of the 1840s. Three men named Benjamin Johnson were paying taxes in Greene County. None were paying taxes on land, so they were either squatting, renting, or were exempt from taxes because they had recently entered federal land. The tax list was alphabetized.

a. One Benjamin Johnson was listed between J.C. Johnson and Joseph Johnson. This man paid taxes on seven horses, two cows, and one timepiece, but no poll.

b. One Benjamin Johnson turns up between H.G. Joplin and Napoleon Jarrett. He paid taxes on one horse and six cattle, but no poll.

c. The next Benjamin Johnson was listed very close to the man named Benjamin Johnson in section "b," above, and was between William Johnson and C.A. Jameson. This Benjamin Johnson was paying taxes on one horse, two cattle, a timepiece, and one poll.

Can we make any guesses here as to which one of the three *might* be the man we seek? Clearly, he wasn't the man who owned seven horses. We know *our* Benjamin Johnson lived near Harris G. Joplin, but this man owned six cows and he didn't pay a poll, which *our* Benjamin probably should have done, given what we believe to have been his age. The livestock and one other possession, a timepiece, fit most closely with the third man.

We learned from the county history that Benjamin R. Johnson was born in Greene County, Tennessee, on 1 September 1824. His parents were Benjamin and Mary Johnson, the former a native of South Carolina, the latter of

Virginia. Benjamin's father came to Greene County in 1841 and settled in Center Township, where the subject still resided, and lived there until his death in 1867. Note: *When this local history was published in 1883, Center Township included the land in Township 29, Range 24.* Who is this guy? Benjamin *R.* Johnson was the man who purchased the land in 1841.

In the 1850 census, five men named Benjamin Johnson were listed. All were studied and eliminated.

What should we do now to find *our* Benjamin Johnson? Notice that a pattern of names has emerged around our subject—Dryden, Headlee, Sims, and Joplin—suggesting a web of relationships. So, we put aside our study of the name *Johnson* and look at the names of the other individuals. It was easy to learn that Fanny Sims and her son-in-law, John Headlee, came from Bedford County, Tennessee. In that county, the following document was uncovered.

> On 26 July 1832, Fanny Sims, widow and relict of Briggs Sims, deceased, of Bedford County, Washington Sims, Briggs Sims, Zachariah Sims, John Sims, Burwell Sims, Holly Sims, Delphia Sims, James Dryden and wife Frances, formerly Frances Sims, John H[e]adley and wife Polly, formerly Polly Sims, Benjamin Johnson and wife Sally Johnson, formerly Sally Sims, Bennet Robertson and wife Elva D. Robertson, formerly Elva D. Sims, Clinton Morrison and wife Nancy, formerly Nancy Sims, all heirs and legatees of Briggs Sims, deceased, sold to Robert W. Sims 196 acres in Bedford County on Rock Creek. The witnesses were Briggs G. Sims, Zachariah Sims, Benjamin Johnson and Burwell Sims. The deed was registered 14 March 1833.

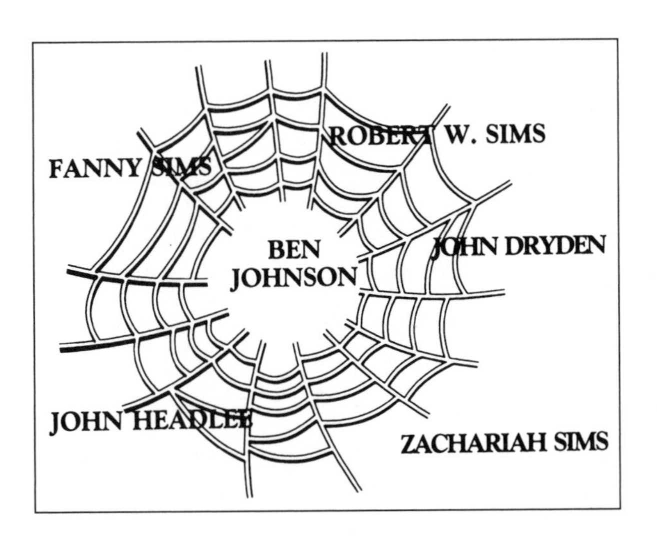

Figure 8-5
Web of Benjamin Johnson's connections.

Benjamin Johnson had indeed moved to Greene County, Missouri, with relatives. None of them, however, were named Johnson. This deed shows how the various people with whom he interacted were related. They were his in-laws and descendants of Fanny Sims. Notice how much more you can discover when you think of people as connected by webs rather than by the straight lines and boxes you see on pedigree charts and family group sheets.

Sorting out individuals with identical names can be a frustrating challenge, but it's not as hopeless as it may sometimes seem. In fact, if you follow the eight steps outlined in this chapter, it may be a lot easier than you think.

Whenever you research a name, remember that you are seeking a person, a real human being, one just like you and me—not just a person who may share a name with someone completely different.

---

[1] *Personal Reminiscences and Fragments of the Early History of Springfield Greene County Missouri Related by Pioneers and Their Descendants.* (Springfield, Mo.: Springfield Printing Company, 1979.)

The Critical Connection: Finding Ancestors Who Lived Before 1850

The period between the Revolution and the Civil War, when most of the westward migration occurred, is the most difficult period of all in which to trace ancestors.

—DAVID CURTIS DEARBORN, FASG *REFERENCE LIBRARIAN, NEW ENGLAND HISTORIC GENEALOGICAL SOCIETY*

Genealogists often have difficulty tracking their ancestors in the years between 1790 and 1850. Many give up. The most obvious reason is that the requirements for the federal census changed radically between 1840 and 1850. I have heard some genealogists tell others that the censuses taken before 1850 are of little value for family research. How wrong they are! Another factor adding to the difficulty of tracking ancestors during this period is the huge migration that took place between 1795 and 1812—the greatest movement of peoples America had known. Overcrowding in New England, soil depletion in the South, and the pioneer spirit of those in the Mid-Atlantic States pushed people westward to the Appalachians until the War of 1812. Scarcely was the last shot fired in that war when the movement began again, this time on an even grander scale. The lake plains of Indiana, Illinois, and Michigan; the Gulf Plains of Western Georgia, Alabama, and Mississippi; and the trans-Mississippi frontier all experienced immense growth from 1814 to 1839. The people were restless, always looking for greener grass and new opportunities. Unfortunately, keeping accurate records for future genealogists was not a priority for them.

John Wilkinson was a typical pioneer of this period. He was a jack-of-all-trades of Ulster Scot heritage, with a limited education and even more limited aspirations. He was unusual, however, in that he wrote an autobiography in his old age. He began writing in 1861, tracing the nineteen moves he made from his birth in 1793 in Greene County, North Carolina (now Tennessee), to his Missouri residence in 1867. Figure 9-1 illustrates the relocations of just this one man. Some of your ancestors may have been as restless as John. The surprising thing is that other than in 1800 and 1810, when John lived in eastern Tennessee, where census records have been lost, he can be found in every census from 1820 through 1860—if you know where to look!

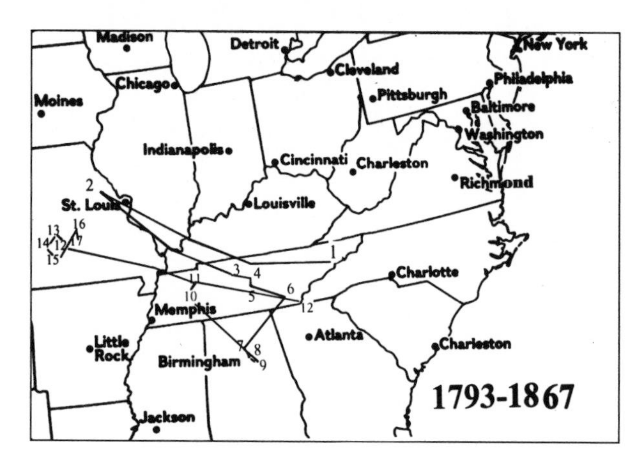

Figure 9-1
John Wilkinson's migration.

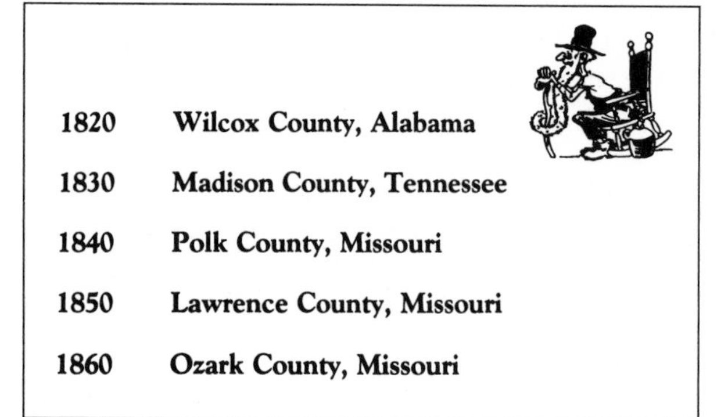

1820	Wilcox County, Alabama
1830	Madison County, Tennessee
1840	Polk County, Missouri
1850	Lawrence County, Missouri
1860	Ozark County, Missouri

Figure 9-2
John Wilkinson's census listings.

FUNDAMENTALS OF FRONTIER STUDY

1. The first element one must consider when tracking westward migration is geography. Figure 9-3 on page 175 is a "hardiness" map from a gardening book that shows shaded bands running somewhat parallel across the country.[1] The bands mark zones that indicate temperature variations, especially the expected highs and lows, so that the farmer or gardener can determine what kinds of flowers, vegetables, and crops are likely to best grow there. These bands are called *life zones*. **Demographers have found that before 1850, people seldom moved more than two life zones from their original location.** In

Important

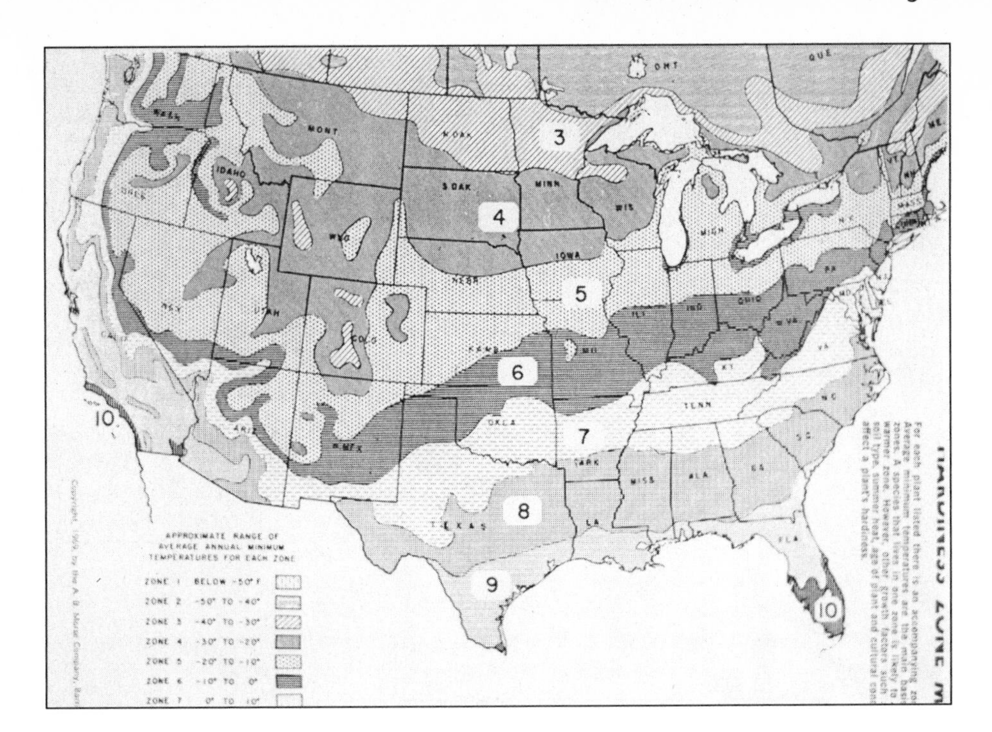

Figure 9-3
Hardiness Zone map.

other words, someone living in upstate New York probably would not move to southern Missouri. Who is most likely to move to southern Missouri and northern Arkansas? People from Tennessee, Kentucky, western Virginia, and western North Carolina. The reasons are logical. Farmers from those areas would know how to make a living in southwest Missouri. They could expect the same climate, so they could bring seeds to grow the same plants and use the same tools. Where did the people from upstate New York move? This map makes it clear: northern Ohio, Indiana, Illinois, and Michigan. Where did those from South Carolina and Georgia move? Into the opening territories of Alabama, Mississippi, and Louisiana.

I found the theory that people geographically stick to what they know fascinating; but being from Missouri, the "show me" state, I couldn't just take the demographers' word for it, so I performed two tests. First, I surveyed the three volumes of Virgil D. White's *Genealogical Abstracts of Revolutionary War Pension Files* (Waynesboro, Tennessee: National Historical Publishing Company, 1990–1992). I randomly selected fifty pensioners to determine where they served during the war, and where they applied for their pensions. Figure 9-4 on page 176 shows a map detailing their migration patterns.

Next, I surveyed 838 pioneers of Southwest Missouri. In their move to Missouri, only two men moved more than just one life zone from where they previously lived. One was a doctor who had been born in Massachusetts; he migrated first to Vermont and then to Ohio before coming to Missouri.

Figure 9-4
Migration of Revolutionary War soldiers.

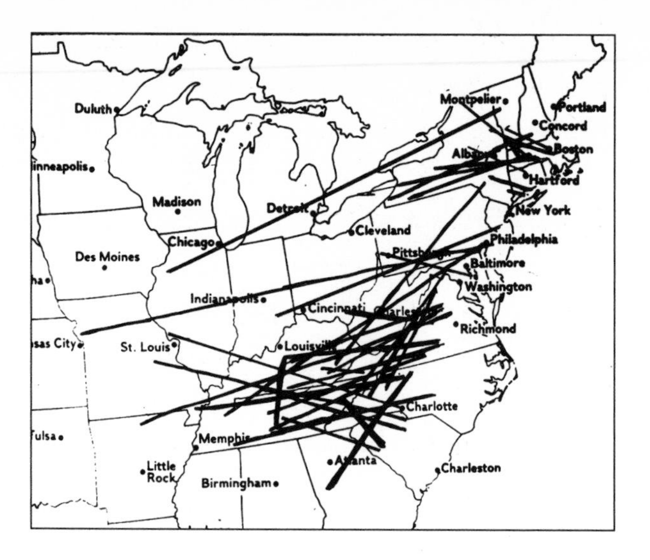

The second was a lawyer from Hartford, Connecticut. The reason for these deviations from the norm is simple: neither man depended on the land for his source of income. Three people came from more than two life zones away, but one was from Ireland, one from Canada, and one from southern Alabama. Interestingly, the family from southern Alabama did not fare well in Missouri. After the deaths of several family members, they moved to southern Arkansas and northern Texas.

2. The second element to consider is the prevalent economic conditions at the time your ancestors moved. Few job opportunities, exhausted soil, the breakup of large land holdings, and overextended credit all were economic conditions that could push our ancestors from their communities. Land available on credit or for low capital investment, the need for extra hands on frontier farms, and the need for blacksmiths, tanners, merchants, and wheelwrights in new towns were conditions that could pull people who were economically strapped toward a new community. Become familiar with the history of major economic "booms" and "busts" on both the national and local levels. Although the Panic of 1837 created major problems in the east during the late 1830s, the resulting hard times did not reach some areas in the middle of the country until the early 1840s.

3. The third element to consider in studying frontier migrations is the distance between the old location and the new. One example involves the opening of what previously had been Cherokee territories until after the treaties of 1817 and 1819. People who lived in central Tennessee and western North Carolina flocked to the southwest section of Tennessee and the northern part of Alabama. It was new, virgin territory, often only a short

distance from where they had lived. The opening of the Chickasaw territory in western Tennessee provides another example. Migration into Iowa from Illinois and northern Missouri when the Iowa Territory opened constitutes a third example. The period between the War of 1812 and 1850 involves dozens of such examples. From what region did many of the people who lived in the newly opened area come?

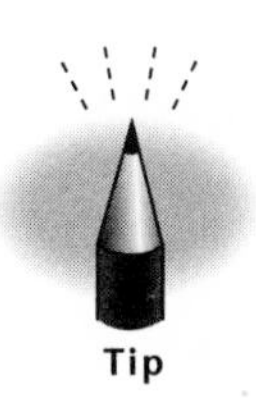

In the vast majority of cases, you can find an individual's origins by tracking the origins of his neighbors and associates. Sometimes that's the only way you can track them, because some individuals simply do not create enough records in their lifetime in either community to definitely identify them. But, by placing one person within a community of others who have recently moved into a pioneer neighborhood, you can usually find enough records produced by the others to identify the individual that you seek. Sometimes it takes the identification of a number of connected individuals before you can find the one with records that can provide the information you need. You probably won't encounter anyone who jumps out of the records and hollers, "Here I am, the one individual out of the thirty who is going to prove significant to you as you try to find the home of Andrew Hayes." Instead, you must patiently review, analyze, and distill the data until that pivotal individual or record appears. You may have to stop and turn around on a number of paths before you finally see a signpost that will point you in the right direction.

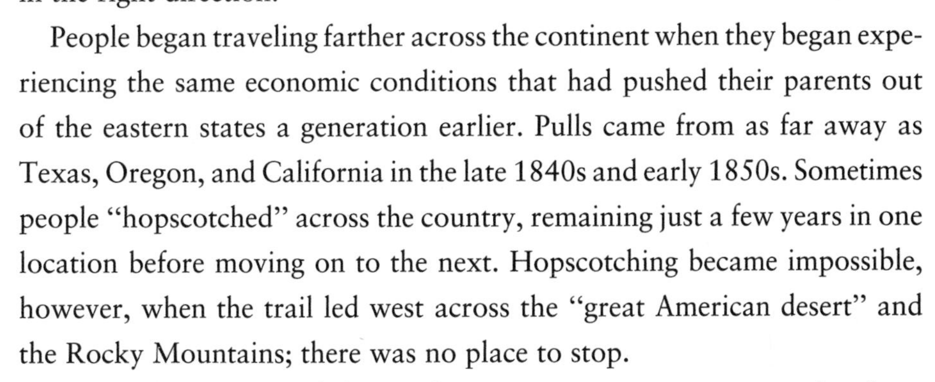

People began traveling farther across the continent when they began experiencing the same economic conditions that had pushed their parents out of the eastern states a generation earlier. Pulls came from as far away as Texas, Oregon, and California in the late 1840s and early 1850s. Sometimes people "hopscotched" across the country, remaining just a few years in one location before moving on to the next. Hopscotching became impossible, however, when the trail led west across the "great American desert" and the Rocky Mountains; there was no place to stop.

How did people travel during the time your ancestor was moving from one place to another? Become familiar with both land and water routes, and the geographic barriers your ancestor would have had to overcome. Study the modes of transportation that would have been available to him.

4. The fourth element to consider in examining migrations is the personal and social motivations behind them. These might include the death of parents and subsequent division of property, the "honeymoon migrations" of young people wanting to start off on their own, or the desire to maintain

the "clan" system by keeping a family together. Sometimes entire church congregations moved together. Debt, personal obligations, and legal entanglements motivated many individuals to leave their homes, and more than a few unhappy marriages ended by desertion.

LAND POLICIES

Although there were many reasons for people to risk the move into new territories and communities, one of the strongest was the possibility of acquiring land. In the process of transferring land from the Indians to the federal government to individual landowners, many records were created that can benefit genealogists. Although land documents vary according to the area and time period, there are some general principles you can follow to locate the records you need.

From the time of the American Revolution until after the Civil War, the federal government followed the same basic procedures. First, the Indian title had to be cleared. Sometimes this involved working with a number of tribes, which could take extended periods of time. If you are interested in Indian ancestors, records documenting the agreements between the federal government and the tribes—as well as their individual members—can reveal a great deal of information about both the Indians and the "intruders." In theory, white settlers were not to move into an area before the title was cleared, but seldom did they wait until all the arrangements had been formalized—they simply intruded and squatted. Next, surveyors went into the area and laid out the land. After the War of 1812, they used the rectangular survey system, dividing the land into sections, townships, and ranges.

Second, a land office was opened. The earliest such office opened in 1800 in eastern Ohio, and the land was offered at public auction. Although the federal government initially offered credit, it was a paperwork nightmare. By 1820, land was offered for cash only, and payment was required the day the purchase was made. If land remained unsold after public auction, it was then opened to private entry in unlimited amounts at $1.25 per acre. If two applicants sought the same tract of land that had been opened to private entry, it was sold to the highest bidder.

Land transactions generated at least two types of records that are available to modern researchers. The receiver made one entry into a *tract book*, recording the date; the parcel description by section, township, and range; the certificate number; and the date the patent was issued. Those tract books have been microfilmed and are available for all states except Missouri and

Alaska through the Family History Library, or through private purchase. One may also examine the originals at the National Archives. The other type of record, *cash entry files*, contain receipts. Originals also are stored at the National Archives.

This receipt includes name, residence, date, location of purchase, price, and amount of land purchased. There may be other papers in the cash entry files, particularly if there were later disputes over the land, but most packets are pretty slim. To find the cash entry number, go to <www.glorecords.blm/gov> and search the land patents. Enter as much information as you can about your ancestor. When the record appears, go to the tab labeled "Patent Description" for the land description, land office, and cash file number.

Land transfers made after the initial purchase are recorded in the county recorder's office. This all seems fairly straightforward, doesn't it? The reality, however, may prove to be quite different.

Researchers will probably encounter two major problems. First, because the federal government of the nineteenth century didn't move a lot faster than it does now, most land patents were not issued until several years after the purchases were made. Many individuals wanted to move on before they received their patents. Sometimes they went ahead and sold their land and recorded the transaction in the county deed book, only occasionally stating that the patent had not yet arrived. Often, you must return to the federal cash entry file to follow the chain. In that file you may find the assignment of the land entry to another individual and a request that the patent be issued to him. Sometimes this assignment was made within months of the original purchase. The first buyer may have remained in the area, or he may have left immediately—often for parts unknown. With the passing of time, federal paper work fell further behind. Sometimes people simply abandoned their land; sometimes entries were not completed, or certificates did not find their way to legitimate owners. Sometimes titles were not cleared for decades. One parcel I studied had a title entered in 1836 that was not cleared until 1934!

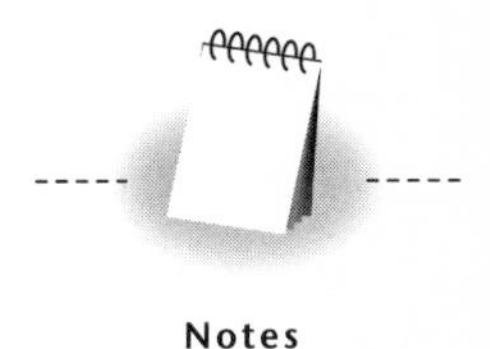

The second problem you may encounter is preemption. As I mentioned, a lot of people already lived on the land by the time the Indian titles were settled and the federal government got around to selling it. Many farmers had improved and cultivated their land, and they were not eager to see someone else snatch it. They wanted preferential rights to purchase the land, and they wanted a reasonable price. Settlers had long been in the habit of preceding a surveyor and a legitimate sale. They moved into an area, selected the land they wanted (contrary to the intrusion laws), and then demanded the right of preemption. Preemption began as early as 1814 for territorial settlers, but general preemption legislation was not approved by Congress until 1830. Under the Act of 1830, which was extended with minor revisions until 1862, every settler or occupant on public land who had been in possession of that claim for a designated time could purchase 40 to 160 acres for $1.25 per acre. Affidavits were required to support those claims, and these often may be found in the individual cash entry files. Such affidavits provide original signatures and establish those critical neighbors that are so helpful to genealogists.

The cash entry files, which are shaped like the loose probate packets, vary greatly in size and content. They often contain just the application and the receipt. If a controversy developed, however, they can be quite extensive. Only rarely do you find critically important documents within cash entry files, but in one instance, I was able to find mention of a man's prior county of residence in Virginia; in another, I found a crucial clue to the identity of a man who lived in a county where records had been destroyed by fire.

FINDING RESTLESS PIONEERS

Although a genealogist may begin by following general search principles, in order to find your particular needle in that vast haystack of frontier settlers, you will have to employ some more specific techniques.

There is no single, sure-fire method for locating ancestors from the early 1800s. What may work beautifully in one case might fail miserably in another. In his will, Archibald C. Adams left land in Bedford County, Tennessee, to his daughter, Mary Ann Sims. Thomas James paid a stud fee on 9 April 1835 in Madison County, Tennessee, for breeding his mare to a local stallion. The receipt was in his probate packet. But I have examined hundreds of other probate records that don't give the slightest clues as to origins. Two probate records helped me locate the prior origins of frontier settlers.

Some deeds are wonderful. Richard Brown made a deed of gift to his children in White County, Tennessee, in 1828, and then recorded it in Missouri in 1843. David Stockton didn't sell his land in Meigs County, Tennessee, until after his arrival in Missouri in 1839. It's exciting to find one of these deeds. On the other hand, I have examined literally thousands of deeds in the past fourteen years and only a few have provided these keystones to prior origins. There are no shortcuts, no magic documents. You find clues; then like Hansel and Gretel, you follow the crumbs down the forest path. Following are five methods that have worked well for me.

1. Pinpoint patriarchs
2. Reconstruct relationships
3. Focus on families, not on names
4. Find friends
5. Follow the trail

PINPOINT PATRIARCHS

The most difficult people to locate before 1850 are those born between 1800 and 1820. If they moved west as young men, you are unlikely to find them listed as heads of households in an earlier census in their previous community. **When you are looking for the origins of a young adult who was new to the frontier, you must connect him to an older person living in the same frontier community.** It doesn't have to be a father; it can be a mother (beware: sometimes this may be a remarried mother with a new surname), father-in-law, mother-in-law, uncle, brother, brother-in-law, or minister. Older adults tend to create more records than younger ones. In addition to being listed as heads of households in censuses, older people were more likely to buy and sell land, more likely to be administrators and executors of estates, more likely to be involved in court actions as witnesses or bondsmen, and more likely to have participated in some event that makes them eligible for federal benefits.

Research Tip

One of the best methods of finding connections to older individuals is to study the probate records of the community in which your young ancestor was living. For whom was your ancestor the executor, administrator, or guardian? Read the probate minutes and loose probate files for the earliest time period in which your ancestor lived in a community. This will reveal those connections that can yield valuable clues.

Another method is to study deeds—not just for obvious clues like the ones I mentioned above, but for more subtle ones. If your ancestor purchased land from someone, did he buy at the going rate, or did he seem to get a particularly good deal? In other words, could the transaction have been more like a gift from a relative?

If your ancestor fell into debt, who stood as security on his note? Older people usually had more money than younger people, and usually were considered more reliable and responsible. Who would trust your ancestor enough to lend him money or agree to make good on his debts?

After you make a connection to an older person, try tracking that man. Three situations in my research can serve as examples. Joseph Akard and James M. Pike of Missouri were the administrators for their fathers, who were heads of households in 1830 in Tennessee. Henry Collier administered the estate of his father-in-law, Samuel Dixon. In Samuel's probate packet was an unpaid bill from a merchant in Perry County, Illinois. Anthony Ayres was located because he administered the estate of Mary Bewley. That probate file revealed that Catharine Bewley had relinquished her right to administer the estate of her daughter, Mary, "in favor of her son-in-law, Anthony Ayres." Many researchers study only the probate records of their ancestors. Ignoring the probate records created by others in the community can be a fatal error.

Sometimes the clues to relationships with older individuals are more subtle. For example, Jacob Alderman bought forty acres in 1838 in Polk County, Missouri. In the 1840 census, he was listed as head of a household with one male under age five, two males age five to ten, two males age ten to fifteen, one male age forty to fifty, one female age five to ten, and one female age twenty to thirty. He was the only man of that surname living in the county. In 1845 Jacob and his wife, Lucy, sold this forty acres to Richard Brown. Jacob Alderman paid taxes in Polk County in 1841, 1844, and 1848. Charles and Hiram Alderman were taxed in 1844. Hiram was underage at that time. By 1848, Jacob was over fifty-five years of age. From all this information, we can deduce that he must have been born about 1792. No probate or marriages under the name of Alderman were located in Polk County. By the 1850 census, Jacob Alderman must have left the community, although I cannot find him in the 1850 census indexes for Missouri, Oregon, California, Arkansas, or Texas (all likely migration spots), nor does he appear on any Internet databases.

However, there was a significant deed recorded on the page following the record of Jacob's sale to Richard Brown. It was made on the same day for an adjoining parcel, forty acres sold by Charles Bolt Sr. He was listed next to Jacob Alderman in the 1840 census. Was he still in Polk County for the 1850 census? No, but Charles Bolt *Jr.* was. He was listed as age fifty-five, born in Virginia. It is difficult to tell when Charles Bolt Jr. left Virginia because the oldest child in his home, age fourteen, was born in Illinois. Although there were no marriages in Polk County for anyone named Alderman, a Mary Bolt had married Thomas E. Wright there in 1839. In 1850, she was recorded as living in adjoining Dallas County, age twenty-eight, born in Virginia.

My next step was to check the 1830 Virginia census, combining the names *Bolt* and *Alderman.* I found both in the record for Montgomery County, which listed the following as heads of households on p. 51: Charles Bolt Sr., Charles Bolt Jr. and Jacob Alderman. Marriage records clinched it: Jacob Alderman married 25 April 1822 Lucy Bott [*sic*], daughter of Charles Bott.

RECONSTRUCT RELATIONSHIPS

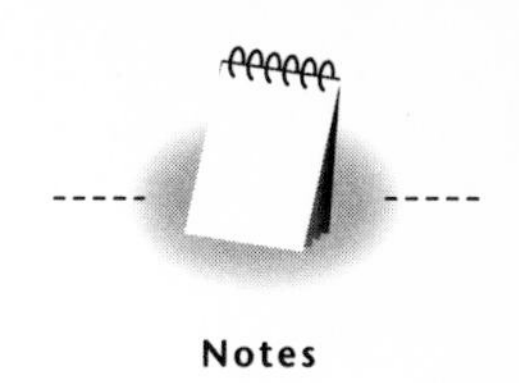

Notes

How do you find your ancestor's relatives? **You reconstruct relationships by looking for the people your ancestor cared about during his lifetime, those on whom he depended and who depended upon him.** Start by looking for connections in the community where the individual lived. Study all the records that he produced and write down the names of the people with whom he associated. At first, it may appear that these names represent many unrelated individuals, but a pattern will eventually emerge. Then find the records that those people created, and search them carefully for the tiny breadcrumbs that will lead you through the forest.

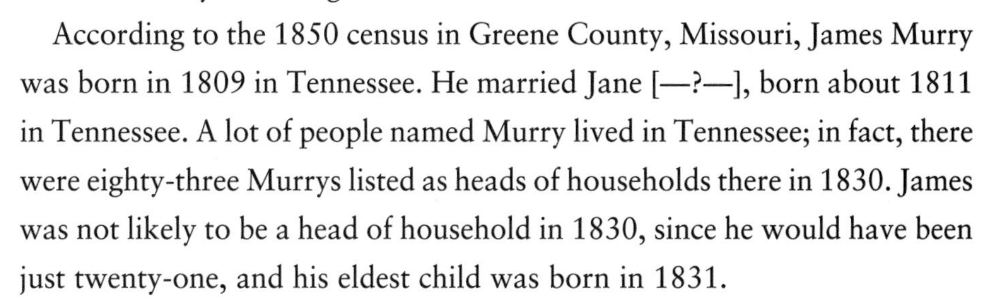

According to the 1850 census in Greene County, Missouri, James Murry was born in 1809 in Tennessee. He married Jane [—?—], born about 1811 in Tennessee. A lot of people named Murry lived in Tennessee; in fact, there were eighty-three Murrys listed as heads of households there in 1830. James was not likely to be a head of household in 1830, since he would have been just twenty-one, and his eldest child was born in 1831.

I looked a long time for James Murry's origins outside of Missouri, examining a lot of the records he created as well as records for all the other Murry families in Greene County, Missouri. The key to James's origin was a very small one. On the 1843 Greene County tax list, James Murry was administrator of the estate of Jonathan Douglas, holding $1,100 at interest for which he had to pay a tax. Who was Jonathan Douglas? He did not appear in the census or any other earlier records I located. I had never seen the name in connection with any other family I studied in Greene County.

I examined Douglas's probate file—a very small packet. It revealed that Jonathan Douglas was planning to move to Missouri but became ill while on a scouting trip. James Murry cared for Jonathan from the time of his illness until his burial. Upon submitting his bill for this responsibility to the court in 1842, James Murry applied for administration of Jonathan Douglas's estate. Those papers stated that administration also was granted for Jonathan's estate in Monroe County, Tennessee.

I immediately went to the Monroe County census for 1830. There was Jonathan Douglas—and several households away, James Murry. All kinds of new records subsequently opened up, including a trail leading toward James's parents. So, James Murry *was* head of household in 1830. Yes, I know now that I could have examined just the census records of the five men named James Murry in the 1830 Tennessee index, and I might have found the one I wanted. But without his connection to Jonathan Douglas, how could I have been certain that I had found *my* James Murry?

Usually the clues to reconstructing relationships are not as subtle as in this case. Other questions you might ask include: Who were the sponsors at family baptisms? Who helped establish the local church at the same time as your ancestor? Who were the guardians for his children? Who did his daughters marry? Who supported his pension or bounty land application?

FOCUS ON FAMILIES, NOT ON NAMES

You may find it necessary to reconstruct a whole family before you can find its origins in a prior community. In the process of reconstruction, you probably will find names of associates that can help you identify a former residence. By reconstructing families, you can learn the relative ages of its members and determine how the dependents should fall into the age categories of various census records. If you reconstruct the family in a later time period and determine all the children who survived to adulthood, those same children should appear in the parent's household in earlier decades.

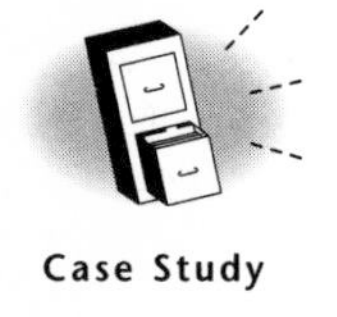

Case Study

William Jenkins Family

Let's look at the family of William Jenkins. In 1837, William Jenkins purchased 160 acres in Section 21, Township 30, Range 21 of Greene County, Missouri. After pinpointing his location, we need to get an idea of his age. William Jenkins appeared as head of household in the 1840 federal census, listed between Thomas J. Whitlock and Columbus Williamson. His household consisted of two males age five to ten, one male age ten to fifteen, one male age fifteen to twenty, one male age twenty to thirty, one male age fifty to sixty, one female age ten to fifteen, one female age fifteen to twenty, one female age twenty to thirty, and one female age forty to fifty.

What do we now know about this family? That it included an older man who apparently had a living wife and several children. Because of the ages of the children, we can surmise that William was nearer the age of fifty than forty. We know the names of two neighbors, Whitlock and Williamson.

At the time of the 1850 census, William Jenkins was still in Greene County, listed in dwelling #551. He was sixty-six years old, born in Georgia; his wife Susan, age sixty-one, was born in North Carolina. The children then living with them had been born in Kentucky: William W., age twenty-seven, Willfred, age twenty-five, Edward, age twenty-one, James W. and Irvin W., both age nineteen.

From this information, we deduce that the family should have been living in Kentucky in 1830, and at least three of their children should be on that census. But because there was more than one Jenkins family who met the criteria, it would be quicker and more reliable for us to reconstruct the family in Missouri before we move our search back into Kentucky.

I used the following sources to reconstruct the family: marriage records, cemetery inscriptions, probate records, deeds, local histories, and newspapers.

A family for William Jenkins

Let's look at each family member and see what the records tell us that can help us determine their origins. William's wife was Susan [—?—]. (We're lucky that Susan is an easier name to search than Sarah or Mary!) We know Susan's approximate age and her birthplace. From her age, we know that she could have been the mother of all the children. Because the family was from Kentucky, she should have signed deeds releasing her dower. Now let's look at the children.

i. Dominick Jenkins was living in 1863 when his father made a will naming him as the eldest, but we have no additional information for him. He did not appear in any records in Greene County. As the eldest child, he may have established connections in a prior community; perhaps he had married and did not want to migrate with the family.

ii. Caroline Jenkins was named in her father's will by first name only, and no marriage record was located for her in Greene County. She was not living with her parents in 1850, so perhaps she had married before the family left Kentucky. It's probable that she would have been in the fifteen-to-twenty age category in 1830; therefore, we will place her birth around 1813.

iii. According to the 1850 census, John H. Jenkins was born ca. 1815 in Kentucky; therefore he should have been about fifteen years old in 1830, falling into either the ten-to-fifteen or the fifteen-to-twenty age category.

iv. Elisabeth C. Jenkins was born 17 September 1816 and died 13 March 1845. She was buried at Mt. Comfort Cemetery and her gravestone reads "d/o W. & S. Jenkins." Since she was alive in 1830, she should fall into the female ten-to-fifteen age category.

v. Williford Jenkins was born 24 February 1821 in Kentucky and died 18 November 1898. He, too, was buried at Mt. Comfort Cemetery. Since we know his death date, we could look for an obituary. He would have been nine years old in 1830, falling into the age five-to-ten category in the census.

vi. William W. Jenkins was born in 1823 in Kentucky, according to the 1850 census. He would have been about seven years old in 1830, and therefore in the five-to-ten age category—but look at the age of his sister, Sarah, listed below. William's age may be wrong, or he could have been a twin.

vii. Sarah Jenkins was born 17 February 1823; she died 26 February 1845, "d/o W. & S. Jenkins," and was buried in Mt. Comfort Cemetery. She would have been about seven years old in 1830.

viii. Susan Jenkins was born ca. 1825 in Kentucky; she married William Whitlock 1 January 1846 in Greene County, Missouri. They were married by C.C. Williamson (Greene County, Missouri, Marriage Book A:140). What can we learn here? That Susan would have been five in 1830, and that because she married a Whitlock and was married by Christopher C. Williamson, she connects with both neighbors listed in the 1840 census.

ix. Edward Jenkins was born ca. 1829 in Kentucky. He should have been the one male under five listed in 1830.

The last two children were born after 1830, so they would not figure in our reconstruction.

Let's recheck the 1840 census and see if the ages are consistent with what we have learned to be *sure* we have the right family. Have we accounted for the all dependents? Census ages are rarely exact from decade to decade, so we must make *some* allowances; except for William Jr., everyone fits in the category where they should.

1840 Greene County, Missouri, p. 254
William Jenkins

2 males 5-10 [too young for the 1830]	1 female 10-15 [Susan]
1 male 10-15 [Edward]	1 female 15-20 [Sarah]
1 male 15-20 [Williford]	1 female 20-30 [Elizabeth]
1 male 20-30 [John H.]	1 female 40-50 [Susan]
1 male 50-60 [William]	

Now, instead of searching the 1830 census for a William Jenkins with three known dependents, we are looking for a man with seven dependents—possibly eight, if we count Dominick, who was said to be the oldest.

There were five men who were head of household in Kentucky in 1830 named William Jenkins, but now only one Jenkins household fits the proper configuration; it was in Caldwell County.

William Jenkins—1830 Caldwell
County, Kentucky, p. 170

1 male under 5 [Edward]	2 females 5-10 [Susan, Sarah]
2 males 5-10 [William W., Williford]	1 female 10-15 [Elizabeth C.]
1 male 10-15 [?]	1 female 15-20 [Caroline]
1 male 15-20, [John H.]	1 female 40-50 [Susan]
1 male 20-30 [Dominick]	
1 male 40-50 [William]	

Clinchers!

On 12 May 1836 William and *Susanna* Jenkins sold to James L. Priest land on Eddy Creek for $1000. The marriage book recorded that Caroline Jenkins married C.C. Williamson 4 March 1834 in Caldwell County. Additional deeds led to William's father, John Jenkins, and all of William's brothers and sisters. Not only did I find William, but C.C. Williamson as well (Caldwell County Kentucky Deed Book H:185).

FIND FRIENDS

More than any other method, identifying and locating my ancestor's associates led me to the correct origins of the families that I was researching. Associates often turn out to be family, but even if they do not, they may lead you to the people and the places you seek.

Important

***No* record is too obscure or insignificant to offer a vital clue.** Ordinary researchers scan records looking for the genealogical "headlines"—the big nuggets rather than the tiny kernels—and in doing so, they often miss important details. Excellent researchers, on the other hand, never let a clue slip through their fingers. Let's look at an example.

Greenberry Adams was an ordinary man, one who created very few records in the fifteen years he lived in Greene County, Missouri. I will not list all the records that I checked where he did *not* appear. All I knew was that according to the 1850 census, he was born in 1803 in Tennessee. His wife was Sarah [—?—]. His elder children were born in Tennessee, placing him there between 1831 and 1832, but he was not listed as head of household there in 1830. There were, however, *plenty* named Adams. I could start searching all of them, but what would I find? Too many slash marks that wouldn't mean a thing.

So I had to go back to Missouri, where I knew who Greenberry was.

On the nonalphabetized tax list of Greene County, Greenberry was listed between James H.M. Smith and John T. Williams. *Smith, Adams, Williams.* Was this a conspiracy? I was beginning to feel persecuted by so many common names! Greenberry had moved from the county by 1856, leaving no clue as to his destination. I found only one county land record for Greenberry.

On 10 January 1843, Green B. Adams mortgaged to Jasper Ruyle, for $5, "land on which he then lived on an unsurveyed township and range," as well as one sorrel mare seven years old, one iron grey colt, three cows, and two calves, if Jasper Ruyle agreed to stand security on a promissory note given to Samuel Asher on 21 July 1831 for $43.75. Green B. was also indebted to Jasper Ruyle for $27.68 that he had borrowed 15 October 1841. There was no release on the mortgage, found in Greene County, Missouri, Deed Book C:104-105.

This land record has three significant clues for the genealogist.

1. Greenberry was not a rich man. He was mortgaging the home place and two horses. He was taxed for only two horses in 1835. He was desperate!
2. He had signed a note to Samuel Asher in 1831. That note almost certainly was signed in Tennessee, as Greenberry was probably present when his child was born there that year. If I could find Samuel Asher, I should find Greenberry.
3. Jasper Ruyle was a friend indeed. Jasper stood as security and he loaned Greenberry more money in 1841. (What a good guy!) How long had they been friends? I hoped they had been friends for years and years and years. If I could find Jasper, perhaps I could find Greenberry as well.

Jasper Ruyle was not a difficult man to find. He had come to Greene County with his parents and large extended family from Wilson County, Tennessee, and had descendents remaining in Missouri. I checked the records in Wilson County, Tennessee. Greenberry Adams had married Sarah Perriman there. Her family also had come to southwest Missouri. So, Greenberry had come with his wife's family. Once I knew which county to look in, I found that Greenberry had sold his land in Tennessee in October 1833, which beautifully coincided with his appearance on the tax list of Greene County, Missouri, in 1834.

FOLLOW THE TRAIL

When you can identify your ancestor's friends and associates, begin following the trail of clues that connects them to each other. Carefully analyze each record that you find. As I have demonstrated, sometimes the clues are obscure, so the trail may not be obvious—but I can almost guarantee that one exists.

Tenets for the Tenacious: Suggestions for discovering the origins of pioneer ancestors

1. Adopt a versatile approach when choosing research techniques. No one or two (or even five) methods will work in any given case. The method that was brilliantly successful for one problem may slam you into a brick wall for the next. Difficult cases usually require trial and error until a clear trail emerges.

2. Learn all you can about your ancestor and his community. Don't focus on just a name. Learn his age, the name of his wife (or wives), the names and ages of all his children, the names of the children's spouses, the names of his associates, his religion, his occupation, his economic and educational status, the exact time of his migration, and where his neighbors originated. Study county histories for the names and origins of other early pioneers in the community where your ancestor settled.

Research Tip

Isolate the first five years that your ancestor lived in the new community. Consider everyone with whom he had contact during that period as potential relatives. As people migrated, they often traveled in groups. Group members often intermarried and continued to associate with one another in the new community—particularly if they belonged to an ethnic group such as the Ulster Scots, who retained their clan system in the new country for generations.

3. Expect your ancestor to be normal. *Normal* is defined here as doing what most people do at a given period of their lives. Expect him to move with others; expect him to be married to one wife at a time; expect him to have come from a place similar to his new place of residence. Assume that he will form connections with other people, try to support his family, shoulder family responsibilities, strive to improve his conditions, and behave as others in his age group and socioeconomic bracket.

Look for the records normally created during the course of a life. The odds are good that you will find data pertaining to your ancestor. If that fails, move to more exotic possibilities such as bastardy bonds, criminal records, and penitentiary archives.

4. Focus on families, not surnames. Work with as many correlated surnames as possible. Success in tracking origins often depends on the number of surnames you can associate with the ancestral family search. Look for relationship webs, not straight lines.

5. Extensively study the family in the frontier community where you are sure you know who they are. Reconstruct the family within that community. Then, think about how that family would have been configured at a different time; for example, how would they have appeared in 1840, 1830, and 1820? Avoid moving your research into eastern communities where you find the surname appearing, even if it is a rare one. Such fishing expeditions are rarely successful. You might spend years tracking people who had no relation to your ancestor.

Because people rarely disregard their past and completely start over, your best clues to discovering the origin of your ancestor are likely to be found in the frontier community to which he migrated. He probably retained business relationships as well as personal ones from the old community. Personal property from his past—including slaves—may surface in the new community as well.

6. Respect your elders, because it's usually the younger people who are hardest to track. A man who appears to be twenty to thirty years old and who moved to a new community just before the census was taken will be very difficult to find ten years earlier. To trace him, the researcher must link him with an older person in his new home, because a more mature man is more likely to have created records in a previous community and to appear as head of household in earlier censuses. Remember that an unusual name is no guarantee of smooth sailing—clerks just may have become more imaginative when trying to spell it. When you're attempting to discover pioneer origins, age is a more important factor to consider than a name, because mature individuals generally have more extensive personal and business histories.

7. Think big as well as small. Explore federal as well as county and state records. What federal records may have been created in a new territory? What entitlements might people have applied for? Consider veteran's benefits, bounty land, preemption grants, territorial petitions, depredations claims, and so forth. People in past centuries were no more inclined to pass up benefits and opportunities than they are now.

8. Search surrounding areas—apples don't fall far from the tree. Before the Civil War, people tended to hopscotch across the west. Rather than relocate from North Carolina all the way to Missouri, or from Massachusetts to Illinois in a single move, people frequently established short lived interim homes as they migrated across the continent. People also were as likely to move within a state as from one state to another. Significant records would have been generated in the course of each migration. You can follow

the trail more successfully when you understand traditional migration patterns for the period you are studying.

For example, it was not unusual for a family from the upper South to live in southern Indiana or Illinois for a while before settling in Missouri, Arkansas, or Texas. A look at a map showing the Tennessee, Cumberland, Licking, and Ohio Rivers will show you why.

9. Every record has potential value. Because you never know which record will provide the key, a researcher must pursue them all. Certainly, some records are more likely to reveal significant secrets than others. Probate minutes are more likely to reveal notable connections than county court minutes. Land records are more likely to produce links than tax records. Nevertheless, when the obvious records do not reveal the necessary connections, the researcher must turn to the harder-to-search, more obscure records that might reveal valuable nuggets of information.

10. Compare, contrast, and correlate records from the old community with records from the new. **Here are my suggestions for doing this effectively.** (a) Follow the record, not just the individual and his name. (b) Search the record for *subtle* clues rather than boldface headlines. (c) Notice associates in your ancestor's old community and see if they turn up in the new. (d) Determine as accurately as possible when your family left the area where you know who they are. I once saw a query in which the researcher asked whether the man who died in Alabama in 1843 was the same man who bought land in Kentucky in 1807. Thirty-six years is far too large a gap to be very useful. Try to establish connections within a period of just a few years—or preferably, just a few months—of when your family arrived or left the area where their identity is clear.

Tip

11. Identify conditions that may have motivated your ancestor to leave a community, such as debt, an unhappy domestic life, poor or overworked soil, the inheritance of land by other siblings, or perhaps even harassment from local law enforcement officers.

Debt records can be found in various places: circuit court minutes, newspaper articles or published court dockets, sheriff's sales, and mortgages (both real and chattel). Don't forget criminal records, particularly for young men.

12. Study the history of the period so you can determine what opportunities and land opened up within the five years prior to your family's departure. What Indian titles had been cleared? Were there 1812 bounty lands available? How about Oregon Donation lands?

Examples: North Carolina's "land grab" act of 1783 resulted in a rush to enter warrants in Tennessee. Many of Kentucky's early settlers moved into Indiana between 1803 and 1810. In 1818, people from eastern Tennessee flooded into Cherokee Indian lands in what became Monroe and McMinn Counties. The rush to Missouri began after 1819, when the first federal land office opened.

13. After you discover the origin of your ancestor, notice who stayed behind. Too often our research moves when our ancestor does, so we fail to study the records created after our ancestor departed. We must remember, however, that important documents involving that individual may continue to be generated for a long time. These may include deeds, powers of attorney, wills, land partitions, or court suits relating to the death of the individual's parents.

For example, Kindred Rose was sixty-six years old and had been away from his old home for thirty-five years when he gave power of attorney to settle his part of his father's estate in Tennessee.

14. Try to connect records created in one place with records created by a man of the same name in another. Another query I read asked, "Was Richard Bray (Barren Co. 1813–1819 and Monroe Co. KY W1820–1847) the same Richard Bray in Chatham County, North Carolina in 1800 and Surry County, North Carolina in 1810?"

If this had been my research problem, I would have begun by examining the tax records for Barren County, Kentucky, to determine the date on which Richard Bray first appeared. Was he taxed there in 1813? What was he taxed for? Did he own land? Slaves? How many horses?

When the study moved to Chatham and Surry Counties, I would have tried to determine whether the man living in that area showed the same lifestyle, enjoyed the same economic status, and associated with the same people as the man in Barren County. Most importantly, I would have followed the records in Surry County after 1810. Too often we move our search because we either think or know that our ancestor moved. People often can be connected to significant documents that were not created or recorded until after they moved away. In order to determine whether the two men are the same, I would have to play devil's advocate to see if I can find records for the Richard Bray in North Carolina after the appearance of the Richard Bray in Kentucky. Of course, I would hope that I don't find him, but I would have to look. Are there any records in North Carolina that directly conflict with records created at the time the man was supposed to be in Kentucky?

Did the man in Chatham County appear to be selling out? When he sold land, was he selling all his land or just a small portion? Was he trying to raise capital for a move, or was he giving his new son-in-law a small parcel? If he didn't own land in North Carolina but did in Kentucky, how did he afford it? Was he entitled? Did he inherit? Answering these questions would help me determine whether both Richard Brays are the same man.

15. Finally, don't give up. Tracking the origins of ancestors who lived on the frontier is, frankly, fun—but it's not easy. Researching this period is challenging, but rewarding. Over a hundred of the people for whom I am searching still elude me. The work requires not only extensive study of primary records, but creativity and logic as well. But people *can* be found—and you can be the one to do it.

---

[1] The hardiness map was developed by Arnold Arboretum, Harvard University, Jamaica Plain, Massachusetts (used with permission).

Ten Mistakes *Not* to Make in Your Family Research

An old Spanish proverb tells us that he is always right who suspects that he makes mistakes. The ten mistakes that I will discuss in this chapter are those commonly made in genealogical research. For those of you who think these mistakes are too obvious to belong in an advanced methodology book, be aware that most good genealogists have made and will continue to make these mistakes. It is only by being wary and constantly on the lookout that we can avoid falling into these traps. The mistakes described below may make us laugh, not only because we may recognize ourselves and our colleagues in them, but because we are all human and humans do humorous things. **As we discuss common research errors, no one should feel singled out for doing something foolish.** We all follow the same patterns, and we've all committed the same types of errors. There is nothing wrong with making mistakes. The trick is to treat them as learning experiences so we can avoid doing the same thing again.

Reminder

Mistake Number One: Learn to use just one or maybe two good sources, and then stick with them.

The census is most often recommended as the initial source for beginning genealogists. It is readily available and is likely to contain good information about our ancestors. Problems may arise, however, if you begin to use the census exclusively, or depend on it as your sole source of information for establishing family connections. Remember that the census provides only a skeleton for our research; we will have to search other records for the muscle, tissue, and vessels we need to reconstruct our ancestors' lives.

In addition to the census, beginning genealogists usually rely on birth and death records—those wonderful registries of vital statistics that became readily available during the twentieth century. If you have found one of those informative death certificates that lists the birth date and place of the individual who died, the names of his parents and their birthplace, as well as his mother's maiden name, you know that great amounts of information may be contained on that one little piece of paper. Birth records may be just as rewarding—but beware of becoming too dependent on those vital certificates. They are useful as you begin to identify the families from which you descend; but what will happen when you need to trace an ancestor who was born in Kentucky around, say, 1880? You send for a birth certificate, only to be told that no vital records for that period exist. If you've come to depend on such documents for all of your information, you are stuck.

Probate records are another source that genealogists quickly learn to depend upon. After checking the census and determining that an elderly person moved into a particular region and then disappeared, we often assume that he died there, and the next thing we do is send for a will. If there is no will, research grinds to a halt. If we do find a will and the ancestor that we are looking for is named among the children of the decedent, we've got it. Parent, child—right? Must be the same guy!

Or was he? Individuals who left wills always seem to end up with many, many, many children that they never had in real life. It's too easy to assume that the man named in the will is one's ancestor. Lots of people from many branches of the family may assume the same thing. For example, Christian Newcomer of Manor Township, Lancaster County, Pennsylvania, left a will in 1805 in which he named his sons John, Christian, Peter, Abraham, and Jacob. His daughters were Ann, Barbara, Elizabeth, and Magdalene. Probably every person who ever had ancestors named Newcomer living in Lancaster County has tried to attach his own John, Christian, Peter, Abraham, Jacob, Ann, Barbara, Elizabeth or Magdalene to that will, because that particular Christian Newcomer has had at least seventy-two children assigned to him by different genealogists.

Some fundamental mistakes that may occur when we use census and probate records exclusively include confusing people of the same name, overlooking people who appeared and disappeared again between censuses, and assigning children to families to whom they do not belong. To avoid these errors, it's necessary to consult other documents such as circuit court minutes, other kinds of court records, tax records, deeds, veteran's benefits, guardianship records, and newspapers. Don't confine your research to just one source, even if it seems to be a very helpful one. Look at everything you can possibly find.

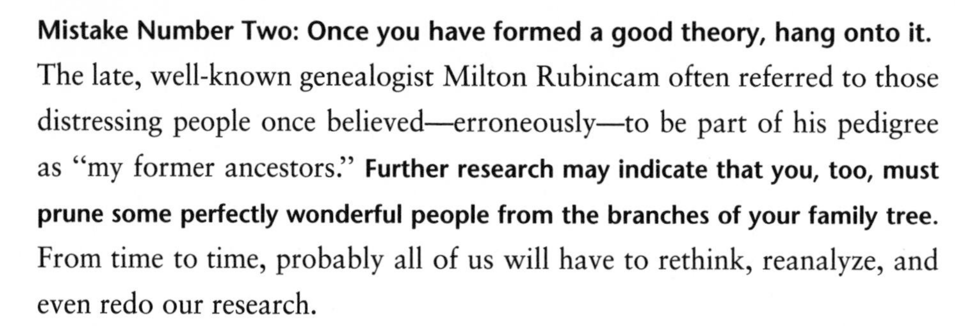

Mistake Number Two: Once you have formed a good theory, hang onto it. The late, well-known genealogist Milton Rubincam often referred to those distressing people once believed—erroneously—to be part of his pedigree as "my former ancestors." **Further research may indicate that you, too, must prune some perfectly wonderful people from the branches of your family tree.** From time to time, probably all of us will have to rethink, reanalyze, and even redo our research.

George Morgan of Wayne County, Pennsylvania, married a widow named Deborah Headley about 1802. I was trying to find her maiden name. Preliminary research indicated there were several *Hoadley* families living in the area, and since my information had come from a Daughters of the American Revolution application, I thought it possible that a mistake had been made with one letter and that I actually should be looking for *Hoadleys* instead of *Headleys*. The Wyoming Valley of Pennsylvania, where Wayne County was located, had been settled primarily by people from Connecticut. The Morgans, for instance, had come from Groton, Connecticut, so I checked some vital records from Connecticut to see if I could find any Hoadley families that might have migrated to Pennsylvania. I also checked several Hoadley genealogies and found that there was a group that had come from Branford, Connecticut, and settled in the Wyoming Valley. In Branford's vital records, I hoped to find a man named Hoadley who had married a Deborah ______; if I could find this, maybe I would have the right family. Sure enough: a Ralph Hoadley had married Deborah Frisbee on 5 May 1786—a possibility. Deborah had to have been young enough at the time of her marriage to Ralph in order to have had children after 1802, when she was married to George Morgan. Therefore, I looked for her birth record and found that she had been born in Branford on 8 July 1766, so she was just twenty when she married Ralph. Looking at more Hoadley vital record entries, I learned that Ralph Hoadley had been nice enough to die 8 July 1796, leaving Deborah free to marry George Morgan in 1802. That became my hypothesis: Deborah Frisbee had married first Ralph Hoadley, and then as Hoadley's widow, had married George Morgan.

I continued my search. Deborah Hoadley, widow of Ralph, died 18 May

1807. Oops! Back to the drawing board. It was difficult for me to abandon a hypothesis that had looked so promising. When you think you already have the answer, it's hard to keep looking for data that may disprove it, but, it's essential. Don't get too attached to a particular individual—as I was to Deborah Frisbee—or too excited about tracing a particular name. I had really begun to hope that *my* Deborah was part of the family that invented the round things you throw in the park to your Labrador retriever, but it was not to be.

Honest blunders are not serious errors. Serious errors occur when facts are manipulated, squeezed, and somehow molded to fit a favorite, preconceived hypothesis—even when those facts contradict each other. The temptation to manipulate the truth often occurs with the problem of identical names. So often we work diligently to gather enormous amounts of data on one family, only to learn that the person we've been pursuing was not our own ancestor but someone of the same name. It's awful to have to admit that all the work we've accomplished thus far has been for naught, and that it will never fit into any of our pedigree lines; but if we refuse to do so, we will perpetrate some serious errors.

John Tweedy was an early settler in St. Louis. Among his descendants was a grandson, Thomas D. Tweedy, who late in life joined the Grand Army of the Republic in Oregon. In his application papers, which his descendants had kept, Thomas stated that his grandfather, John Tweedy, had fought in the War of 1812. According to the War of 1812 service records, a man named John Tweedy served in Illinois. A John "Twitty" was listed in the Union County, Illinois, 1820 state census. How many men of the right age could there be named John Tweedy? After the War of 1812, many soldiers simply crossed the river from Illinois into Missouri. I was tempted to stop my work there, assuming that I had found Thomas Tweedy's grandfather, but I persisted.

Checking records in St. Louis County, Missouri, I found an 1829 deed in which John Tweedy had given a number of slaves to his children. He named those children as Joseph, Washington Walton, Adler, Calista, Mariah, Marshal, Watson, Robert, Elizabeth, Martha, John Alfred, and Landon.

There was a problem. The John "Twitty" household listed in the 1820 Union County, Illinois, census consisted of:

3 males under the age of 10   1 male 26-45   1 female over 45

The John Tweedy household in 1830 in St. Louis consisted of:

1 male under 5	
1 male 5-10	1 female 5-10
1 male 10-15	2 females 10-15
2 males 15-20	1 female 15-20
1 male 40-50	

The two households clearly didn't match. When I tracked John Tweedy's children to the 1850 census, two indicated that they had been born in the early 1820s and gave their birthplace as Virginia. Could the John Tweedy who served in Illinois have returned to Virginia? Was there a John Tweedy listed in the 1820 census in Virginia?

1820 Campbell County, Virginia, p. 147
John Tweedy

3 males under 10	2 females under 10
2 males 10-16	2 females 10-16
1 male 26-45	1 female over 45

Plainly, this family fit much better with the family in Missouri in 1830. Campbell County, Virginia, documents such as tax records, deeds, and probate records indicated that this was indeed the family who had moved to Missouri. John Tweedy had remained in Campbell County until about 1824, when he moved directly to Missouri. The man in Illinois shared his name, but he was not the same individual. Much of the work I had done on the John Tweedy in Illinois had to be discarded. No one likes to abandon work already done. It's so much easier and more enjoyable to continue pursuing avenues that seem to lead toward our destination—but if they're the wrong avenues, we'll inevitably have to turn around and go back. This brings us to the next mistake.

Mistake Number Three: If the records conflict, just come up with a good reason for the discrepancy.

Beginning genealogists have to be warned that records frequently contain errors. Ages found in the census cannot always be believed. The birthplace listed for an individual in one census may conflict with the birthplace shown for the same individual in a later decade. Names are not always what they seem, either. The census taker may not have accurately spelled the name of the person for whom you are looking. Some people didn't even spell their own names the same way all the time. (I've found instances where one name was spelled three ways on the same page.) Parents' names on death certificates may not be correct. Beginning genealogists have to be warned that family traditions are not necessarily facts, and that actual documentation is required to corroborate information.

Reminder

It is dangerous, however, to assume that the inconsistencies we find in old documents are simple errors that can safely be ignored. As I've worked in libraries and archives, I've noticed a disturbing trend. Many researchers who find information that conflicts with something they already believe tend to sweep away the inconsistencies with "good reasons"—or rather, with excuses and rationalizations. I hear people say, "The census taker must have missed him that year." Don't be tempted to sweep away missing entries or conflicting data as so much trash. If census takers missed as many people as some researchers claim, we wouldn't have much census material to work with. Considering the conditions under which counts were taken, the censuses are remarkably accurate. Although we know that they are incomplete, only a lazy genealogist would assume that "missing" data can never be found. Remember also that you must examine the actual census rather than just look in the index. If you can't find a listing for the family you seek, check to see if other neighbors also were missed. Determine whether boundary changes or family migrations could account for the omission. Check for all phonetic variations in spelling. Otherwise, you're neglecting necessary steps for finding the data you seek.

Ancestors who are missing from the expected tax rolls generate another excuse I often hear from some genealogists: "He must have been exempt from taxes that year." The researcher is *sure* the individual was in the county being searched. He was married there; his wife has been identified there. Why is there no trace of him on the tax rolls? "He must have been exempt." But was he?

Although Joseph Weaver's family were all in Maury County, Tennessee—which is where all his descendants thought he was as well—I could not find him on any tax roll there between 1815 and 1830. Wouldn't you like to know how to live in a county for fifteen years and never pay any taxes? Well, Joseph Weaver hadn't figured it out either. He was simply not in Tennessee; he was living in Pike County, Georgia.

Another popular excuse may be given when a researcher identifies a man believed to be an ancestor, but then finds a dower release showing that he was married to a different wife than expected. The genealogist then decides, "The first wife must have died, and he remarried." Don't be too quick to "knock off" a wife. There are several other possible explanations. You may not have the correct man, but rather one with the same name; or the wife may have used a middle or nickname; or perhaps a divorce, not a death, occurred.

One family assumed that when a wife married her second husband, her first husband, John Smathers, had died. The story had even progressed to the point where they believed that John had been killed in a hunting accident. Court records eventually revealed that the remarried woman had actually divorced John, who also had remarried and was living in Texas with his new wife and three children.

Consider the case of a will that doesn't name someone firmly believed by all descendants to be the decedent's child. The rationalizing researcher's argument? "He must have been mad at her, so he cut her off without a dime." Hannah Strain, supposedly the eldest daughter of Samuel Strain of Highland County, Ohio, married James P. Finley. According to a long-held family tradition, the reason that Hannah did not appear in Samuel Strain's will (although he named his other twenty-one children) was that she was cut out by her staunch Presbyterian father because he disapproved of her marriage to a Methodist. Onomastic evidence and chronology seemed to support the belief that she was Samuel's daughter. We know that fathers often omitted older children from wills if they had already received an advance on their inheritance. The problem in this case was that there was another man in the community, unrelated to Samuel Strain, who also could have been Hannah's father. Thomas Strain had been ignored by genealogists because he was much more difficult to track, but further research showed that he was indeed Hannah's father. She had not been named in Samuel Strain's will because she wasn't Samuel's child. Researchers had formed an excuse and kept her in the wrong family for nearly a hundred years.

When records conflict, creating a "good reason" for the discrepancy is easier than reviewing the inconsistencies and digging into the records for more details that might reveal the truth. It's also hard to admit that the theory you've believed for years might be wrong. If you keep an open mind and continue to evaluate those conflicting records, you can probably resolve the incongruity in some other logical way.

Important

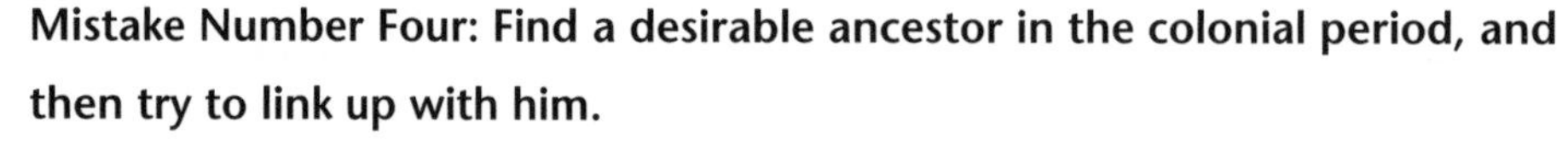

Mistake Number Four: Find a desirable ancestor in the colonial period, and then try to link up with him.

When the idea is phrased this way, most people would agree that it sounds ridiculous. **One of the first rules of genealogical research is to always move from**

the known to the unknown; yet many researchers violate that rule. They try to link themselves to a famous historical figure; to an accepted, proven pedigree; to a published genealogy; or to a person from an earlier time period who had the same name and was living in the same community where they think their ancestor should have been. These are particularly tempting methods for researchers who do not have easy access to records in the area where their family lived. People who take the easy way, however, usually have as much success as the drunk who looked for his lost coin under the lamppost where the light was better, instead of in the dark street where he dropped it.

How many times have you heard a genealogist say something like this: "Our ancestors came from England to Braintree, Massachusetts, about 1650. The only thing I have to do now is link them to my family in Hamilton County, Ohio, in 1833"? Or, how many of you have found a man of the same name as your ancestor—say, a fairly unusual name like Miles Cary—living in a location where you think your ancestor once resided, and then you tried to link them together even though one was recorded there in 1776 and the other in 1830. Haven't you done that? Be honest. I certainly have!

When I began my research, I found that Abraham Newcomer was a very unusual name in Warrensburg, Johnson County, Missouri. I tracked him back to 1850 in Cumberland County, Pennsylvania, without much difficulty. The family Bible said that Abraham Newcomer had married Mary Musselman in 1812 Lancaster County, Pennsylvania. There was an *Abram* Newcomer listed in Lancaster County in the 1810 census. Do you think that I ignored that and continued to work in Cumberland County, studying the Abraham Newcomer that I knew to be the right man, getting to know him by reconstructing his family and his associates? No way. I wanted to move backwards. I wanted to find the immigrant! So I immediately jumped to Lancaster County and started copying records that contained men named Newcomer. It seemed, however, that there were people named Newcomer by the thousands. There were at least five Abraham Newcomers living in Pennsylvania between 1750 and 1800—not to mention eighteen Newcomers named John and fourteen named Christian. After searching for twenty years, I still have not identified the father of Abraham Newcomer of Cumberland County, Pennsylvania.

Nothing will waste your time more than forgetting the crucial lesson of moving from the known to the unknown. For every success you have linking one name to another by working both ends of the chain, you will probably have ten failures.

Mistake Number Five: To avoid confusion, study only one piece of data at a time.

Too often we study documents as if they had no relationship to the people who created them. Don't put your documents in boxes—connect them, correlate them, look at other records that were produced at the same time, and analyze them in context. These records were produced by real human beings for specific reasons. Think about what those reasons were. Are they consistent with other things that your ancestor did? For instance, would a man who was shown on the tax roll as owning one cow and no other property in 1815 write a will the following year in which he bequeathed three horses, four cows, and 160 acres of real property? You must compare documents and correlate the information.

Important

Records do not exist in a vacuum; they belong to a set of events and documents that need to be examined.

The following case is an effort to identify and distinguish four men named John Franklin, all of whom lived in south-central Kentucky around 1800. The following tax listings come from a microfilmed copy of the Barren County, Kentucky, tax rolls, available through the Kentucky Historical Society. In 1807 John Franklin Sr. paid taxes on 150 acres on Beaver Creek, where he had lived since 1799.

> John Franklin, 150 acres 2nd rate land, Bvr Creek entered by Scot, 1 poll, 3 blacks over 16, 6 blacks under 16, five horses.

In 1808 there were three men named John Franklin on the tax roll, but no John Franklin Sr. What had happened to him?

> John Franklin, 170 acres of 3rd rate land on Barren's Creek entered by I. Lowe. 1 poll, 3 blacks over 16, 17 blacks under 16.
>
> John Franklin Jr. 100 acres of 3rd rate land on Barren's Creek entered by Thos. Bandy, 1 poll, 1 black under 16, 6 horses.
>
> John Franklin 100 acres of 3rd rate land on B.S. Crk entered by Goodwin; no polls, no horses, no blacks.

None of the above named men were designated by *Sr.*, although one man was using the designation of *Jr.* Who, if any, of those listed on the tax roll was the man for whom I was searching?

Perhaps John Franklin Sr. had died. If so, there should be probate records for a man with that much real and personal property, but I could find no probate and no sale for the 150 acres on Beaver Creek. Maybe John Franklin Sr. was the man who didn't pay a poll because he was overage. If that were the case, why did he sell all of his personal and real property?

He could have moved away, but he didn't. I could find no record that John Franklin had sold the land on Beaver Creek, nor that he had bought the land on Barren's Creek. The man living on Barren's Creek had almost the same personal property as the man who had lived on Beaver Creek—which tells us that we should keep looking at the records in this community. How can we determine how John Franklin acquired that land if we can't find a sale?

Is there anything else on this tax roll that might give us a clue where to look next? A man by the name of I. Lowe entered that piece of property on Barren's Creek. Isaac Lowe left a will. In it, he said:

> It is my will that my executors raise the money to pay the State price of the tract of land I exchanged to John Franklin, Senr. and to get a grant and have a conveyance made to the said Franklin when a patent is issued.

By correlating two clues from the tax roll with one from what appeared to be an unrelated record, we have solved the problem. John Franklin Sr. was still in Barren County, now living on Barren's Creek.

Don't confine your research by studying only one document at a time; if you do, you won't be able to reconcile conflicting data.

Some researchers believed that Rev. Elijah Williams of Polk County, Missouri, was the son of another Elijah Williams who lived in adjoining Dallas County. However, the records that the two men generated during their lifetimes point away from such a connection rather than toward it.

The first Elijah Williams (the elder man) arrived in Missouri in December 1833 and settled in what became Dallas County.	Rev. Elijah Williams arrived in Missouri in 1838. He moved directly into Polk County.
Elijah Williams of Dallas County associated with the Rice, Summers, and Marlin families.	Rev. Elijah Williams associated with the Oliver, Harper, and Devin families.

In the fall of 1838, Elijah Williams was an elderly man with five minor children and a young wife. Like many in those hard times, he was forced to mortgage both his property and his next year's grain crop.	In 1838, Rev. Elijah Williams bought 230 acres from the Springfield Land Office, paying cash.
In 1850, the mortality schedule reported that Elijah Williams Sr. died, age sixty. If he left an estate, the record was lost in the Dallas County courthouse fire. He was buried in a cemetery on the Dallas/Webster county border.	In 1857, Rev. Elijah Williams died, age fifty-six years. He left a considerable amount of property.

Even if the chronology didn't prove that the two men couldn't be father and son, their behavior did. I don't think most sons—particularly one who was a Christian minister—would callously ignore the economic troubles of their father and half-siblings. Although their names would suggest a relationship, their recorded behavior does not.

Mistake Number Six: Keep looking for those "magic" documents.

Genealogists love to tell about all the wonderful cases we have solved, and all the marvelous discoveries made possible by our brilliant research. If you listen to too many genealogy experts, you may begin to believe that we have these little magical document boxes. If we ever encounter a problem that we cannot solve, we simply leave the magic boxes at the archives, and they fill themselves with long-lost, detailed documents while we sleep.

Some families are able to locate magically detailed documents, such as land partitions that name all the heirs, or wills that identify specific relationships. For other families, however, such documents don't seem to exist. I have heard a genealogist say, "I have researched this family for years, and I just know Absalom's father is Meshach, but I can't find the proof." That tells me that she probably is searching for a magic document. If indeed she has studied Absalom for years, reading every document that he produced; if she has studied his children, siblings, nephews, and nieces, and all the records they produced; and if she then thoroughly investigated

Meshach, studying all the documents that he and his associates produced, this genealogist should be able to put together a beautiful argument for her case, producing circumstantial evidence for the relationship, and showing how the two men fit together. Even if those records do not provide "proof," they will show whether or not the two men were linked during their lives. I fear, however, that most genealogists merely skim all those records produced by Absalom, his children, brothers, and sisters, and then they skim the records produced by Meshach, looking only for that magical phrase, "my son." When they don't find it, they give up because they lack "proof."

The most effective strategy is not to keep looking for a magic document, but to gather as much information as possible. Carefully examine each record you find, correlate the data with that of other records, and look for circumstantial evidence that will establish relationships among them. For an example of this type of search, see my "Problematic Parents and Potential Offspring: The Example of Nathan Brown," published in the June 1991 issue of the *National Genealogical Society Quarterly*. This article, which describes my fruitless search for records that would conclusively prove a connection between the immigrant Nathan Brown and his children, will give you an idea of how to proceed in similar circumstances. I never found the magic document. But the case is so strong that no one but Nathan could possibly have been the father of those children.

Mistake Number Seven: Hopscotch across decades.

Because the census is so readily available, it is easy to make the mistake of just going from one decade to the next, searching for one nuclear family. When that family cannot be located in the expected census or index, or there are too many people of the same name to be able to distinguish them, the researcher hits a brick wall.

Chart 1 on page 206 is a typical census record for a family living in Greene County, Missouri. We'll use it to help us find Archibald C. Morris's parents, and his place of residence before he moved to Missouri.

Because we can deduce from the ages of the children listed in Chart 1 that the family must have been in Missouri at least since 1850, the next step is to check the 1850 Missouri census to verify their county of residence and perhaps obtain more helpful information.

Notice that the family in Chart 2 on page 206 includes two people with rather unusual names. Archibald had a son named Philander, and now we

Chart 1
United States 1860 Federal Census
Greene County, Missouri, Campbell Township

123-125						
Archibald C. Morris		41	Farmer	$500	$200	NC
Patsy Morris		40	Keeping house			VA
William	m	22				KY
Philander	m	20				KY
Winifred	f	18				TN
Susan	f	16				TN
Burwell	m	14				MO
Simon	m	12				MO
Mary	f	8				MO

find another household member who also is named Philander. Even though the census says that he was just a laborer or a hired hand, we know it's important to note those individuals as well. A name as unique as Philander is a revealing hint towards a relationship, but it pays to look into every individual in your household of interest.

Chart 2
United States 1850 Federal Census
Greene County, Missouri, Campbell Township

234-234					
Archibald C. Morris		32	Farmer	$300	NC
Patsy Morris		29	Keeping house		VA
William	m	12			KY
Philander	m	10			TN
Winifred	f	7			TN
Susan	f	6			TN
Burwell	m	4			MO
Simon	m	2			MO
Philander Davis	m	25	Laborer		VA

Again, data from the two censuses tell us that the family was apparently in Tennessee in 1840, so we check the census index:

1840 Tennessee Census Index		
Morris, Andrew	Morris, Henry	Morris, John
Morris, Benjamin	Morris, Isaac	Morris, Robert
Morris, Caleb W.	Morris, James	Morris, Samuel
Morris, Daniel	Morris, James	Morris, Seth
Morris, David	Morris, John Sr.	Morris, Simon
Morris, Edward	Morris, John	Morris, Thomas
Morris, Frederick	Morris, John	Morris, William
Morris, George	Morris, John	Morris, William
Morris, Henry	Morris, John	Morris, William
Morris, Henry	Morris, John	Morris, William
Morris, Henry	Morris, John	Morris, William

No Archibald Morris. Maybe the census taker in Missouri made a mistake when he wrote down the ages of the children, or perhaps he was given incorrect information and the family was actually in Kentucky by 1840.

1840 Kentucky Census Index		
Morris, Adam	Morris, Ishmael	Morris, Joshua
Morris, Allen	Morris, James	Morris, Randall
Morris, Conrad D.	Morris, James	Morris, Sarah
Morris, David	Morris, Jehu	Morris, Seaborn
Morris, David Jr.	Morris, John	Morris, St. Clair
Morris, Douglas	Morris, John	Morris, Timothy
Morris, Fielding	Morris, John	Morris, Washington
Morris, George	Morris, John	Morris, Wilbourn
Morris, Harmon	Morris, John	Morris, William
Morris, Isaac	Morris, John Sr.	Morris, William J.
Morris, Isaac W.R.	Morris, Josiah	

There were plenty of Morris families living in Kentucky too—but no Archibald. Leaping across the decades has brought us to a dead end, so we had better go back to the censuses of Greene County and this time not just concentrate on the nuclear family. Let's also look at the neighbors listed in that census and see if they can give us more information about Archibald.

Chart 3
United States 1860 Federal Census
Greene County, Missouri, Campbell Township

122-126						
William Cartwright	m	38	Farmer			NC
Susan	f	36				NC
Patsy	f	12				TN
Archibald	m	10				MO
Simon	m	8				MO
123-127						
Archibald C. Morris	m	42	Farmer	$500	$200	NC
Patsy	f	40				VA
William	m	22				KY
Philander	m	20				KY
Winifred	f	18				TN
Susan	f	16				TN
Burwell	m	14				MO
Simon	m	12				MO
Mary	f	8				MO
124-128						
Caleb W. Morris	m	47	Farmer	$700	$600	NC
Mary	f	45				KY
Susan	m	14				TN
David	m	11				MO
124-127						
Simon Morris	m	25	Farmer	——	$100	KY
Lucinda	f	20				MO
Caleb	m	8/12				MO

Archibald is a rather unusual name, so let's see if there were any others by that name in the neighborhood.

The family listed above Archibald Morris in Chart 3 had a child named Archibald, one named Patsy, and one named Simon. The ages and birthplaces given for the children living in that household follow a pattern similar to that of the Morris family. That should help us. Listed on the other side of Archibald Morris's household was a man named Caleb Morris. His age was given as forty-seven, so he was obviously not Archibald's father, but he could be a brother. Do you notice anything else from his listing that might give you any further clues? How about the naming patterns? Simon Morris was listed next to Caleb. Apparently, Simon lived with Caleb because he was not listed in a separate dwelling, even though he had a separate household. As a farmer, Caleb Morris owned real property. We can see from the second number after Simon's name that although he had personal property, he owned no real property. Simon was probably just starting out, so there is a good possibility that Simon was Caleb's son.

Have we overlooked anything in our census work? Shouldn't we look for Archibald Morris in North Carolina, where he was born? The answer is no. Moving census research to an individual's state of origin before later censuses listing him as head of household have been fully explored is a common mistake. If we couldn't find Archibald Morris in Tennessee or Kentucky, the last places he was thought to have lived before moving to Missouri, how could we hope to find him way back in North Carolina? Certainly no birth certificates for that time period are available there. Even if we did find an Archibald Morris in North Carolina, it is unlikely to be our man from Missouri because the gap between the two time periods is too wide to establish a definite connection. In this particular search, we have gone from the 1860 census to the 1850 and then to the 1840, and although we've learned a little more from checking some of the neighboring households, we're stuck. Instead of continuing to move backward in time, let's go forward and see what we might learn from a later census. I have heard so many genealogists protest, "But I know all about the family at that time period already." You'd be surprised what later censuses can reveal.

By 1870, there was an older man living with Archibald, probably his father. Simon was born in North Carolina, as was Archibald. This new household member may have generated some records of his own. This is what we are looking for: new people coming and going. Caleb Morris no longer appears in the immediate vicinity, so he probably moved some distance away—although he still could be in the same county. Archibald's neighbor in the 1870 census was Burwell Davis. We can't ignore him;

Chart 4
United States 1870 Federal Census
Greene County, Missouri, Campbell Township

452-454					
Archibald Morris	52	Farmer	$1000	$200	NC
Patsy	48				VA
Mary	28				MO
Simon Morris	82				NC
453-455					
Burwell Davis	70	Retired farmer			VA
Winifred Davis	68				VA

remember that Archibald had a son named Burwell. Also remember that another Davis—Philander—was living with Archibald in 1860.

We now have several possible avenues for further research: Simon Morris (possibly Archibald's father), Caleb Morris (possibly Archibald's older brother), Burwell Davis, and Philander Davis (both possible relatives). And of course, we are dying to get back in North Carolina, aren't we? Before we proceed there, however, we still need to discover where the family was in 1840, so let's go to the censuses for Tennessee and Kentucky.

1840 Tennessee Census Index

Morris, Andrew	Morris, Henry	Morris, John
Morris, Benjamin	Morris, Isaac	Morris, Robert
Morris, Caleb W.	Morris, James	Morris, Samuel
Morris, Daniel	Morris, James	Morris, Seth
Morris, David	Morris, John Sr.	**Morris, Simon**
Morris, Edward	Morris, John	Morris, Thomas
Morris, Frederick	Morris, John	Morris, William
Morris, George	Morris, John	Morris, William
Morris, Henry	Morris, John	Morris, William
Morris, Henry	Morris, John	Morris, William
Morris, Henry	Morris, John	Morris, William

Simon and Caleb Morris were listed in the 1840 census index and were in the same county. Archibald apparently was too young to be listed as a head of household. Now that we have a possible county of residence in which to search, we can focus our study to see if we can find corroborating records that indicate our Archibald Morris belongs in this family. As you can see, it is important to build a web of family relationships in the area where you can confirm individual identities, so that when you are ready to follow the trail into a new state, you have more people to look for. This example was a simple one, but the method also works for more complex problems if you examine enough records.

Remember that the best clues to origin lie in the community where your ancestor's place of residence already has been established, not in the county where you think he might have been earlier.

Mistake Number Eight: Go after those surnames.

Welcome all Name Gatherers! The contest is about to begin. How many records of people of the same surname can you find? Compete with your friends. Fill file drawers, stuff cabinets, and load databases. Cover the dining room table, cram closets, and shove records under the bed. Don't prejudice your search by looking only where your ancestor lived; look everywhere! Gather names from all over the country.

Seriously, no one would recommend that you stop looking for a particular surname, just don't confine your search only to people who bear that surname. To be a successful researcher, you must also seek and study the people who associated with your family. Broaden your horizons. When you hear of someone else who is researching a surname of your interest, learn what time period and geographical location they are working with so that you can determine whether or not that family might be connected with yours.

Some people (for example, Christine Rose, CG, CGL, FASG) focus on collecting information on particular surnames to disperse among a large group of people. That's fine. **But, if your goal is to find a link with one ancestral family, you probably will be more successful if you consider their migration pattern, their neighbors and associates, and the people who lived with, depended upon, and cared for your ancestor, even though those individuals may not have the same surname.** Otherwise, you are going to collect drawers full of information that you will never use, and study a lot of people who are not even remotely connected to you.

Reminder

Mistake Number Nine: If it looks old, it is probably a primary source.

Just because a record is old, you cannot assume that it is contemporary with your ancestor. A document describing your ancestor may be 150 years old, but if it was created 40 years after your ancestor died, how sure can you be that the information is accurate? If your children were to write today about something that you said or did in 1960, would they get it right? Three examples of old records that frequently contain questionable information are death certificates, family stories, and Bible records.

Death certificates are primary sources that provide direct evidence for two pieces of information about a death: date and location—but not cause. You cannot depend on a doctor from the nineteenth or early twentieth century to accurately determine what caused a death. I have also seen examples where a doctor fudged when reporting a suicide or a stigmatized disease in order to protect family members. Moreover, the primary cause of death is not necessarily the underlying cause. One doctor wrote on a death certificate that the primary cause of the man's death was a blow to the head. The secondary cause was another man's wife.

Other than the date and place of death, all information on a death certificate must be considered as hearsay. The decedent obviously could not have been the person who wrote the certificate, and the recorder may not have been the one who supplied the information or entered it on the original form. Someone could have made a mistake in spelling or interpretation. We often forget that individuals completing death certificates were likely to be under great emotional strain, and that stress might distort the accuracy of the information they supply. To someone who has just lost a loved one, it may not seem important to remember the deceased person's mother's maiden name.

Traditional family stories have their place and can provide good clues to follow up with research, but they often perpetuate erroneous information. Watch for these common mistakes:

a. Skipped generations.

b. Too-recent immigration dates. When there are several generations separating living family members from the family who immigrated, the former may believe that the latter arrived much later than they actually did.

c. Stories and records from one side of the family that have become confused with those from the other. The essence of the story may be true, but the names and details may not be correct.

d. Embellishment. The man said to be an Army officer actually may have been a private—or even a deserter.

e. Historical incongruities and impossibilities. For instance, a Civil War soldier could not have participated in both the Battle of Gettysburg and that of Vicksburg, Mississippi, as was the tradition on my husband's side of the family. The battles occurred at the same time.

f. Inconsistencies and contradictions. For example, one branch of the family believes great-grandfather came from Germany in 1870, while another has him being killed in the Mountain Meadow Massacre in Utah in 1857.

g. Omitted females.

h. Omitted children who died young.

i. Omitted unpleasant information, such as divorces, crimes, or illegitimate children.

j. Dubious connections with a famous family of the same name.

Bibles are an important source of family records, but unless the events were recorded as soon as they happened, these documents also may be subject to errors and distortions. Bible records may have been copied from an older Bible, or they may have been reconstructed in a new volume from memory. Consult the December 2002 issue of the *National Genealogical Society Quarterly* for an in-depth discussion of Bible records.

Mistake Number Ten: When it comes to assembling, organizing, and publishing your work, always plan to do that tomorrow.

More and more people are discovering the joy of finding their ancestors. More people are attending genealogical conferences, taking classes, and engaging in research. With so many now working in the field of family history, we have the potential to discover more connections and link more families than ever before. But are we sharing the information we have? Are we so busily engaged in our own exciting searches that we never take time to assemble, organize, and publish our discoveries so that others can benefit? What would happen to our research if something happened to us?

If, for some reason, you couldn't return to your office, would someone else be able to walk into it and know what material should be saved, what should be published, and what should be donated to a society? Will someone else take the time to organize your research if you don't? It isn't necessary to publish a book. Many genealogists have neither the interest nor the money for such an undertaking, but there are other ways to make the fruits of your hard work available to other researchers.

Idea Generator

To begin, keep your files, documents, family notebooks, and photographs carefully arranged. Remember that if you're reluctant to begin organizing your own computer files and the stacks of papers and notecards you've accumulated, no one else will want to do it either. Analyzing, arranging, and typing the material is as much a part of the research process as the actual investigations themselves. Your research is not done until you have properly organized it.

Once your research in a particular area is complete, donate photocopies of your work to your state historical society, or to historical or genealogical societies in the community where your ancestor lived. Submit articles to local, regional, and national genealogical journals so that other people can learn of your successes—and possibly help you further your own research. Please don't let your contributions be lost. That would be the biggest mistake of all.

Analysis of Evidence

Facts are stubborn things; and whatever may be our wishes, our inclinations, or the dictates of our passions, they cannot alter the state of facts and evidence.

—John Adams

Careful analysis of evidence is absolutely critical to the success of your genealogical research. It is probably the *most* important step. Seldom, if ever, can 100 percent proof be obtained in genealogical research. We must base our conclusions about relationships between individuals on the factual material and circumstantial evidence found in available records. Sometimes a string of circumstantial evidence may be superior to one single piece of material information. When carefully pieced together, reliable data will almost always form a pattern that points either *to* or *away from* the suspected relationship. By accumulating information and carefully analyzing the available records, we can reach valid genealogical conclusions.

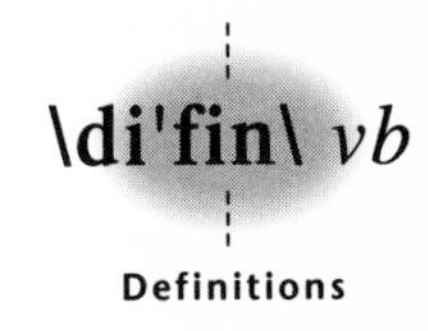

For this discussion, let's define *genealogical evidence* simply as anything that indicates that something is true. Evidence may include written records, oral testimony, or even recorded behavior. Genealogists often refer to two basic types of evidence: *direct* and *indirect.*

Direct evidence is that information provided by a witness who saw or heard the event, or evidence that in itself conclusively establishes a fact without inference or presumption. For instance, if we find a pension application in which Dr. Morris stated that he was at Mrs. Brown's bedside when she died, that is direct evidence. Other pension applications may include statements from individuals confirming that they attended a certain wedding or funeral. If, in a deed, the grantor stated that he was giving a piece of property to "his son" for love and affection, that statement is direct evidence of their relationship.

Indirect evidence is that which establishes proof by inference, based on a variety of supporting information, observed behaviors, and recorded data. From such evidence, you can logically conclude that a theory is likely to be true. The connection is proven because all the facts are consistent with one another.

A QUIZ

The following exercise will help you check your recognition of direct vs. indirect evidence. Place a *D* after each example that shows *direct* evidence, and an *I* after each example of *indirect* evidence.

1. An original receipt for the purchase of a coffin, as evidence for the death date.
2. A will that names a wife and children.
3. A land partition by the heirs and legal representatives of a deceased individual indicating that each heir will receive a one-seventh part, as evidence of the number of children.
4. A tombstone that reads: "Willie s/o Robert & Susan Clark" as evidence of a child/parent relationship.
5. A church baptismal record that reads: "Thomas bap. 2 February 1799, son of Samuel and Mary Smith."
6. A deed in which Henry Hickman sold land "in the right of his wife, Mahala, widow of Moses Foren" (no recorded marriage can be found for Mahala and Henry Hickman).

Answers (in the opinion of the author)

1. *Indirect.* A coffin *could* have been built before the death occurred; but we know that during the eighteenth and nineteenth centuries, coffins generally were not built until they were needed. If the receipt for payment is in the probate file of the deceased, we may logically conclude that the coffin was built at the time of death.
2. *It depends.* If the will says, "my wife Elizabeth, my son Arthur, and my daughter Jane," that is direct evidence. If bequests were made to "Elizabeth, Arthur, and Jane," you may have to look for additional evidence before determining the relationship of each of those individuals to the testator.

3. *Again, be careful.* You must evaluate exactly what the record says. If the deed says, "Sally Smith sold her 1/7 share of the land that she received from the will of her father, John Smith," that is direct evidence. If the deed says, "William Smith sold the 1/7 part of the land owned by John Smith in his lifetime," you don't know if William Smith obtained his share as a brother, son, or nephew, or by purchase from another heir. Analyze the evidence as given; don't jump to conclusions.
4. *Direct evidence.*
5. *Direct evidence.* Just be sure you know which "Thomas" and which "Samuel and Mary Smith" are identified.
6. *Direct evidence.* The law that gives a man the property that his wife inherited after their marriage can be used to establish proof of a marriage beyond a reasonable doubt, even without a record of the marriage itself. Such a record does not provide the date and place of the marriage, of course, but it does prove that the event occurred. In this case, it also establishes the identity of the wife.

Surely you have heard that primary sources are superior to secondary ones. While no one argues that point, there can be a great deal of argument over what constitutes a primary vs. a secondary source. **I believe that what truly matters is not so much whether the source is defined as primary or secondary, but how reliable that source is.** *Reliability* is defined by Webster as "proven dependability in producing consistent results." *Dependable and consistent.* This means that a specific source can be depended upon to produce nearly the same degree of accuracy over time.

Important

Contemporary Bible records are a reliable genealogical source. *Contemporary* means that the Bible entries were created at the time the event occurred. This does not mean that every Bible record is correct; rather, it means that genealogists recognize contemporary Bible records as more reliable sources for family information than many other documents. Why? Because people had a vested interest in making those records accurate, and had very little to gain by falsifying them. If a child's birth was recorded on the date it occurred, is the date likely to be wrong, or confused with the birth date of another child? For a person of deep religious faith, falsifying a Bible record might be seen as almost blasphemous.

On the other hand, if there *was* something to be gained by falsifying a record, you can be sure that someone did so at one time or another, perhaps when applying for a pension, or when trying to preserve a family's reputation by misstating the cause of death. It's important to consider *why* and *by whom* a record was created in order to evaluate the potential reliability of its contents.

Analysis of evidence is a complex subject. A discussion of this topic that included adequate examples and explanations could take us far afield from my objective, which is to provide explicit information to help you solve specific problems; therefore, I have prepared a short quiz to help you learn how to choose the most reliable source for a specific type of genealogical data. Circle the answer you believe is the best source for the information needed.

ANALYZING SOURCES OF EVIDENCE: A QUIZ

1. If you were searching for the birth date of Jasper Jabberwocky, would you rely primarily on: (a) the birth date engraved on the tombstone, (b) the birth date given in his obituary in the newspaper, or (c) the date given in his application for a Civil War pension?
2. If you were searching for all of the children of Josephine Crumberwombbie, would you rely primarily on: (a) the will of her husband, Abraham Crumberwombbie, (b) the family records in the Bible that belonged to Josephine Crumberwombbie, or (c) the final distribution of the estate of Josephine Crumberwombbie?
3. If you were trying to locate the death date of Zachariah Timberbottom, would you rely primarily on: (a) the death certificate from the state Bureau of Vital Records, (b) Zachariah's tombstone, or (c) the newspaper obituary column?
4. If you were trying to verify the marriage date of Susanna Elvira Busybee, would you rely primarily on: (a) abstracts of church records published in the *New York Genealogical and Biographical Record*, (b) Susanna's application for a widow's pension, or (c) a published genealogy entitled *The Busybee Family and Descendants of Their Hive*?
5. If you were looking for Philander Freelove's birthplace, would you rely primarily on: (a) an affidavit in his 1818 pension application, in which he described his service with Col. David Shephard's Virginia military company, and gave his birthplace as Virginia, (b) the 1850 census, which lists his age as eighty-eight and his birthplace as Pennsylvania, or (c) the 1880 census, in which one of his children stated that Philander was born in Maryland?

Answers

Again, these are *my* answers, with explanations as to why I made the choices I did. Analyzing evidence is rarely as simple as it may seem at first glance, which is why I chose to give the quiz at the beginning of the chapter rather than at the end. None of these questions was meant to be a "trick" one; rather, I wanted to show the complexity of the subject. When analyzing a record or piece of genealogical evidence, you must consider your past experiences as well as the logical reasons.

1. Birth dates were not all that important to many of our ancestors, and our forefathers were often perplexed when government officials persisted in asking for them. However, neither the date on the tombstone nor the one in the obituary could have been given by the individual himself, while the one in the pension application would have been; therefore, we would accept the pension application (c) as most likely to be accurate.
2. The mother's own Bible record (c) would most likely reflect the most complete list of her children, including those who died young. The final distribution of an estate would more likely list all of the heirs. A will is the least likely to list all the children. There is no rule that says a man must list all of his children in his will, and often he does not. Moreover, all of Abraham's children may not be Josephine's, and vice versa.
3. A death certificate (a) is an excellent source for two items (and two items only): the date and place of death. The obituary is the next best source because it would have been published near the date the event occurred. Even though the family would try to give the stone carver an accurate date of death for the departed loved one, the tombstone may have been made long after the death occurred. In addition, the intervention of another human being (the stone carver) in the process increases the likelihood of errors.
4. The widow's pension application (b) is probably the most reliable source here because she would have given the date herself, and her marriage was probably one of the most important and memorable events of her life. If, however, she had a reason to give an inaccurate date, such as in the case of Wayty Parks Couse Woodworth, described later in this chapter (see page 225), the published church records are likely to be the next most reliable.
5. While we would probably give more weight to the 1818 pension application because it was a sworn statement given by the individual himself, we would need to consider the issue of boundary disputes that took place between Pennsylvania, Maryland, and Virginia to determine where to look for a record of Philander's parents. We would probably need to check the records produced in all three states, so the answer is (a, b, and c).

BUILDING A SOLID WALL OF EVIDENCE

Now that we have some idea of what evidence is and why some records are more reliable than others, let's review the steps involved in building a strong foundation of evidence and discuss the terms used in analysis and evaluation.

Let's say that you have found a document, publication, or record that provides information on a family of your interest. It may be a published genealogy, a family group sheet sent to you in the mail, an Internet site or a family tree submitted to an online registry, or a manuscript deposited at a genealogical society. It may be a will—say, a will published in a book or journal, or a photocopy or microfilm of the original. Perhaps you have located a deed, a veteran's claim, a death certificate, or a marriage license. Whatever the source, you have found a piece of evidence. Now what?

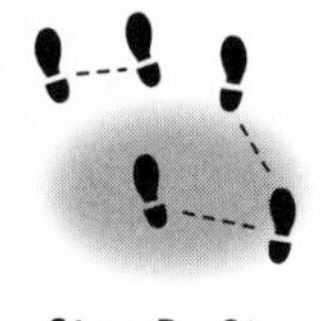

Follow these steps:

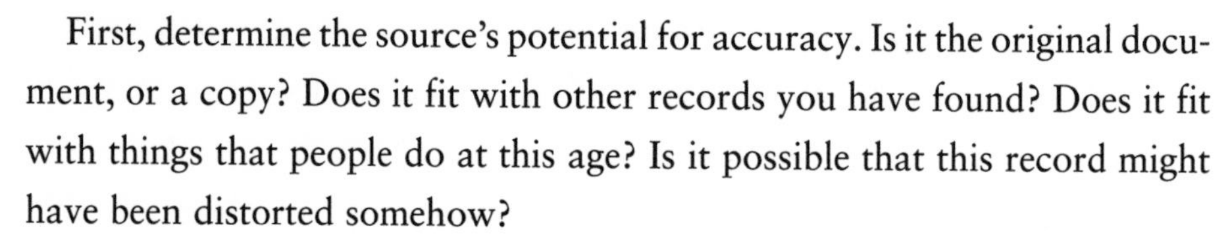

First, determine the source's potential for accuracy. Is it the original document, or a copy? Does it fit with other records you have found? Does it fit with things that people do at this age? Is it possible that this record might have been distorted somehow?

Second, determine whether the record provides enough evidence to support your hypothesis.

Third, compare the record with others you have located. Does it agree with them, or does it contradict other claims and raise doubts?

When you follow these steps, you are analyzing evidence. You pull from that record as much information as you can possibly glean, and then you look at it both as an independent source and as one of a number of related sources. When examining the record itself, ask whether the internal facts are consistent with one another, whether the chronology is correct (did that mother *really* give birth at age nine, or did you forget to do the math?), and whether any information within the document might have been falsified, misunderstood, or copied incorrectly.

Carefully look at the document itself, then compare and contrast its contents with what you have found in other records. This is called *correlation of evidence*. Much as you would place pieces in a jigsaw puzzle to correctly form a picture, you must fit your pieces of evidence together to correctly show your ancestor's life. The pieces must fit exactly, or your picture will be distorted.

ANOTHER QUIZ

How much value would you place on the reliability of each of these records?

1. The word-for-word transcription of a will published in a compiled genealogy
2. A Civil War diary describing the battle of Pittsburgh Landing
3. A microfilmed copy of a deed of gift from a father to his "beloved son"
4. The certified copy of a typed will made in South Carolina in 1798
5. A newspaper obituary published two days after the stated death
6. A tombstone inscribed with the death date

What were your answers? Following are my opinions.

1. As a rule, I would give more value to a transcribed will than an abstracted one. Not only is the complete document likely to include more than just the names of the wife and children, but we could expect that someone preparing a book on his own family for publication would be more careful than someone abstracting two hundred wills for a general-use publication. The reputation of the compiler and abstractor must also be considered.
2. A diary is always accepted as a good source because we assume that the individual made the entries soon after the events occurred. If the individual feels that these events are significant enough to record, he is likely to make an accurate record. In this case, the reference to the "battle of Pittsburg Landing" provides a clue to Civil War experts that the diary was a contemporary one. The battle is more commonly called "Shiloh," but the Confederates referred to it as "Pittsburg Landing."
3. As long as I am sure I have the right man of that name, phrases such as this are the jewels I love to find! As long as the microfilm is legible and I read it correctly, this is as good as the original deed in the courthouse.
4. I almost fell for this one until I realized that there were no typewriters in 1798. Moreover, a certified copy is only as good as the clerk who copies it. Many clerks could not care less about old records. I once watched a clerk incorrectly copy a marriage date and then stamp it certified! Needless to say, I asked her to do it again correctly.
5. Newspaper obituaries usually give accurate dates, places, and circumstances for the deaths they report. Just watch out for the assertions that "she never whispered a word about pain or despair," that "she was the best mother any child could have," or that "he never said a word of disparagement against any of his neighbors." Flowery death notices and obituaries are fun to read, but their validity must be questioned.

6. Death dates on tombstones must always be questioned. When was the stone made? How accurate was the information the stonecutter received? Did he write it down properly? Did he carve the stone with the same information he received? Can the stone be read accurately? Are you reading the actual stone, or a cemetery transcription? Despite their likelihood for errors, inscribed markers certainly are better than the disappointing, bare fieldstone that probably marks the grave of your long-sought ancestor.

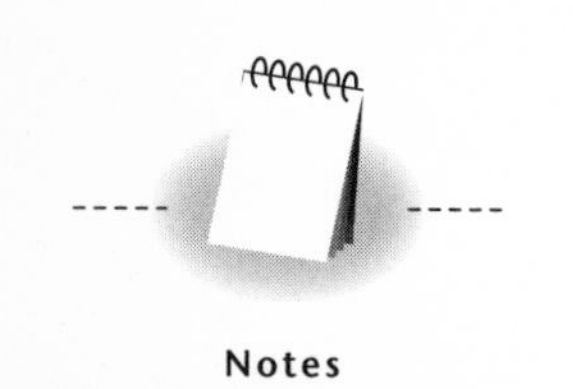

Notes

Cemeteries of Greene County, Missouri, Vol. II. Boone Township including Ash Grove Cemetery. (Springfield, Mo., Ozarks Genealogical Society, 1988.)

Let's consider three different examples of evidence for a death date. Say that you are compiling a family group sheet on the William Cawlfield family. You find a tombstone transcription from the Ozarks Genealogical Society that gives William's dates as 1803–1916 (see Figure 11-1 below). Is the source reliable enough so that you could enter the death date on the family group sheet? Most people would think so. Would they cite the source? Probably not.

Figure 11-1
Transcription from the Hamilton Cemetery, Greene County, Missouri.

Greene County, Missouri Cemeteries - Book II
Read by Ozarks Genealogical Society - 25 March 1986

HAMILTON (CAWLFIELD) CEMETERY

Location: Section 16 Township 30 Range 24 Boone Township
Directions: Just north of Ash Grove on west side of SR "V".
Read: Small cemetery read as one section. Rows read south to north and east to west.
Read By: Daniel Kelley. Compared By: Inabell Williams. Proofed By: Mary Cunningham and Inabell Williams. Typed By Daniel Kelley and Hazle Tyler.
Typing Proofed By: Mary Cunningham
Remarks: Farm fenced on three sides and open to the road. Found no recent burials, but it is cared for.

Row 1

CAWLFIELD	John T.	1847 - 1896	
ARWOOD,	baby	1907 - 1907	s/o Anna & Harold
HARPER	(Francis L.	13 July 1836 - 7 Aug 1905	
	(May Olive	17 Apr 1845 - 27 Jan 1907	
	Footstones placed on back of base of double stone: A.H.S., M.L.A., J.H.C., J.S.C., J.H.H.		
HARPER	William Frances	1790 - 1878	

Row 2

CAWLFIELD	Daniel B.	11 Apr 1841 - 2 Nov 1845	s/o Wm. and L.B.

Row 3

CAWLFIELD	Jas. H.	24 Mar 1853 - 25 Apr 1916	
CAWLFIELD	(William	20 Nov 1803 - 1 Dec 1916	
	(Levica B.	15 Jan 1818 - 24 July 1854	his wife
CAWLFIELD	Jane S.	20 July 1842 - Oct 1854	dau/o Wm. & L.B.
HARPER	W. Luvisa	1 Oct 1871 - 10 Sep 1872	dau/o F.L. & Mary O.
HARPER	Agnes	1876 - 1876	
HARPER	Mattie	1879 - 1879	
HARPER	Daniel B.	1884 - 1884	

Row 4

HAMILTON	(John H.	2 May 1847 - 20 June 1875	
	(Rebecca B.	6 Mar 1844 - (no date)	his wife
HAMILTON	Mary L.	29 Dec 1870 - 2 Feb 1890	dau/o J.H. & R.B.
SAYE	Annie H.	8 Feb 1873 - 5 Jul 1902	w/o Ed SAYE "At rest"
SAYE	W. E.	1868 - 1939	
SAYE	Laurie T.	1877 - 1908	

The second example of evidence for a death date is a photograph of William Cawlfield's actual tombstone (see Figure 11-2 on page 223).

The dates shown on Cawlfield's tombstone are 1803–1853. Have you changed your mind about the reliability of the previous record? (This example isn't really fair to the Ozarks Genealogical Society, which is very careful

Figure 11-2
Tombstone of William and Levica Cawlfield, Hamilton Cemetery, Greene County, Missouri.

in its compilations and has an excellent reputation for accuracy. But its compilers are all human, and occasionally an error does creep in. When we reexamine the compilation, it is easy to see how this mistake was made. The death year for James H. Cawlfield, 1916, was simply copied again.)

A visit to the cemetery might yield additional information. Most compiled cemetery transcriptions do not indicate whether the tombstone appears to be contemporary with the death. Too often, memorial stones erected by later generations show the wrong dates; but you usually can't tell when a tombstone was made unless you go to the cemetery. Assuming that you are familiar with the types of memorial stones used during various eras, you can usually determine whether the stone is old or modern. What about this one? Was the stone carved in 1854 at Levica's death? Probably not. It probably was set at the same time as the identical one behind it—that of James H. Cawlfield, who died in 1916. Nevertheless, we can supplement the tombstone inscription with additional information. The letters of administration for William Cawlfield's estate were issued on 5 December 1853. Therefore, the inscription on the tombstone is surely correct, even if the carving was not done at the time of the event.

To get an idea of the kinds of stones that are appropriate or not yet available in certain time periods, see Sharon DeBartolo Carmack's *Your Guide to Cemetery Research*, p. 97-102 (Cincinnati: Betterway Books, 2002).

The third example is Joseph Porter's tombstone, which reads: Born May 13 1782; Died Dec 18 1852.

Is this tombstone a reliable source for the death of Joseph Porter? Does the tombstone appear contemporary with the death date? What other records could we seek to corroborate this date? Joseph Porter left a number of documents that we can examine. His will was probated 22 December 1852. Even better, the probate packet contained a bill from the physician. Thos. G. White charged the estate for medication and visits, the last dated 18 December 1852.

To summarize, for each record you find, ask:

- Who made the record?
- For what purpose?
- How could errors have crept in?
- Is there any reason to believe this record is wrong?
- Is this record supported by other documents?
- Does the information make sense in light of data you have already gathered?

Reminder

Genealogical researchers quickly discover that no matter what record we analyze, there is a chance that it might be wrong. We have learned that there is no record on which we can rely absolutely. Once you acknowledge that no record can be counted upon 100 percent, you see why expert genealogists tell you that you cannot prove a relationship by one record alone. If you have three reliable sources that independently support one another, your case of proof is much stronger. When I say that the records must be *independent* of one another, I mean that they should have been created by different individuals for different reasons, and they should come from different sources.

The birth date on a death certificate, on a tombstone, and in a newspaper obituary might have been supplied by a single individual, one who was close to the person when he died. Thus these three records are not independent sources and should not be used to corroborate one another. If you're looking for a birth date, it would be ideal to find the same date (or close) in a church record, in a census taken when the individual was thirty years of age, and in a pension application made when his widow was sixty years of age.

Once you recognize that no one document can absolutely prove a relationship, you find yourself always searching for more evidence. As you do this, contradictions will arise. Genealogical lectures are full of examples where primary records—reliable, original sources—give incorrect information. So, good researchers learn to question every record they examine. Experience will help you develop a "feel" for the records that are likely to be accurate and those that are likely to be in error.

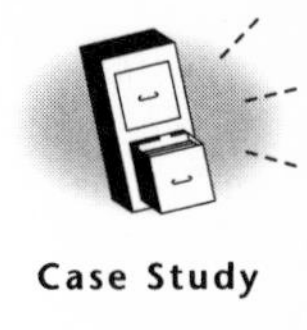

Case Study

CASE EXAMPLES

My ancestress Wayty Parks Couse Woodworth applied for a widow's pension for the Revolutionary War service of her deceased husband, Joseph Woodworth. She gave her marriage date as 8 February 1799. Because New York did not keep civil marriage records for that period, I accepted the date as accurate. Then I found a published church record that gave her marriage as 9 February 1800. I wondered which to accept until I learned about one of the government's requirements for receiving a widow's pension: the marriage had to have taken place before 1800. I had caught my ancestress in a lie! My guess is that she knew her husband had been a soldier; he was the father of her ten children, and she felt that she deserved the pension. She probably thought that silly rule about being married before 1800 was just government red tape! Besides, who would ever know? The point is that when you're working with a record produced by someone likely to gain from the information given, it is important to look for possible intentional errors.

To summarize, we genealogists gather evidence and analyze it. We ask questions about its reliability. We ask whether the record is contemporary with the event. We then seek other records. After we find a group of related records, we ask whether they support or contradict the information we already have. We almost always find conflicting information, so then we have to decide which record is more likely to be correct.

I mentioned earlier that genealogists place great value on Bible records. But Bible records, too, must be critically evaluated. Figure 11-3 on page 226 is an entry from Cornelia Croak's Bible records. The compiler of this genealogy was kind enough to provide us with an actual copy of the entry.

The genealogist should recognize two very important factors in this entry. First, all of the entries appear to be in the same hand. Second, notice the entry for "grandfather." No one calls a child "grandfather" at birth! The entries in this Bible cannot possibly be contemporary with the events they describe.

When a genealogist sees a page of entries like this, what should they do? Turn to the title page to learn when the Bible was published.

In this case, the Bible in question was published after the date of every single entry! The careful researcher should look for another valuable clue on the page next to the front piece: Does the handwriting of the Bible's

Figure 11-3
Cornelia Croak's Bible.

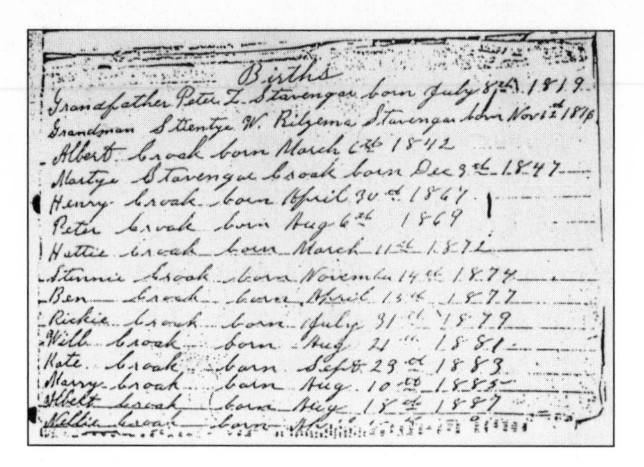

Births
Grandfather Peter Z. Stavenga born July 8th 1819
Grandman Stientye W. Ritzema Stavenga born Nov 1st 1816
Albert Croak born March 6th 1842
Martye Stavenga Croak born Dec 3rd 1847
Henry Croak born April 30th 1867
Peter Croak born Aug 6th 1869
Hettie Croak born March 11th 1872
Stinnie Croak born November 14th 1874
Ben Croak born April 15th 1877
Rickie Croak born July 31st 1879
Will Croak born Aug 21st 1881
Kate Croak born Sept 23rd 1883
Marry Croak born Aug 10th 1885
Albert Croak born Aug 18th 1887
Nellie Croak born [illegible]

owner match that of the family entries? If not, as in Cornelia Croak's Bible, who, then, made those entries? We haven't a clue. So, how reliable is the information? Not very. This Bible record is no more reliable than a compiled family genealogy, because one person entered all the information long after the births occurred, and that person probably was not the original owner of the Bible.

Review Rising's Reminders (see page 228) when you evaluate your genealogical evidence. Look for subtle clues in your records, not just the obvious statements. How likely is it that a given assertion is true? One of the biggest errors you can make is to accept a genealogical record at face value. You must find support from other records, as I did in the case of Joseph Porter's tombstone and the corroborating medical receipt.

Keep the chronology in mind when examining records. Don't separate people and records from their proper time and place. Chronological tools can be used effectively to both support and refute hypotheses about genealogical relationships.

Warning

What does it take to prove a relationship? How much is enough? **Technically, there is absolutely *no* way we can be 100 percent sure of any familial relationship from the past.** There are simply too many human variables. You can, however, strive to improve the probability that your conclusions are accurate by using as many records as you can find. Ideally, these will include original sources, and you will use the most reliable records to build your case. To analyze the information you have, you will stand outside of it—or ask another genealogist to review it—and see how many other explanations there might be for the conclusion you have drawn. If, after a thorough examination, you feel you have the best and least convoluted answer to the problem, you have probably done "enough"—but accept the idea that new evidence might someday change your conclusion.

Genealogists often see their task as one of accumulating as much information as possible about the ancestor and his family. The critical task of evaluating and then perhaps discarding data is either ignored or superficially performed. Ascertaining the reliability and validity of genealogical evidence requires astute and critical thinking. The genealogist must be able to recognize possibilities, study the evidence carefully, and rule out unlikely or impossible conclusions.

Don't expect one record to prove a relationship. *Do* assemble many records and weigh and analyze each cautiously and carefully. If you respect these two essentials of genealogical research, you are most likely to reap the reward of an accurate and complete family history.

ANALYSIS AND CORRELATION TERMS

Assumption A notion that one is inclined to believe without complete evidence.

Direct evidence Testimony provided by someone who witnessed the event (*this does not necessarily make it true*); evidence that conclusively establishes a fact without inference or presumption.

Evidence An indication that something is true.

Indirect evidence Evidence that establishes proof by means of the correlation of various facts, and that can be inferred by logical reasoning. Also called *circumstantial evidence.*

Inference The process involved in drawing a reasonable conclusion or making a logical judgment on the basis of circumstantial evidence and prior conclusions rather than on the basis of direct observation.

Primary source A source with first-hand knowledge of a contemporary event; or an official document that records first-hand knowledge of an event soon after it occurs.

Reliability Proven dependability in producing consistent results. Characteristic of specific sources that produce the same degree of accuracy over time. For example, contemporary Bible records are considered *reliable* genealogical sources.

Secondary source Information recorded on the basis of what someone was told about an event; secondhand knowledge.

Validity The extent to which a statement reflects the truth; sound, grounded on principles of evidence, facts, and logic. For example, a deed naming the "heirs and legal representatives" of a deceased individual is considered a *valid* document on which to base descent.

RISING'S REMINDERS

1. Examine each document in your possession that pertains to the family or problem at hand. Look not only for the obvious, but for the subtle clues.
2. Ask of each document, "Does this document actually say what I *think* it says? Does it appear to be sound and logical? (Is it valid?) Can I depend on *this type* of document or source to usually reflect the truth? (Is it reliable?) How close was the document or source to the actual event?"
3. If an event cannot be proved, how likely is it to be true? (a) Impossible. (b) Possible, but highly unlikely. (c) Possible, but not probable. (d) Possible. (e) Probable, but not definite. (f) Very likely true.
4. Consider the source. What parts are probably true? Likely to be true? May not be true? Are probably incorrect? Learn about standard genealogical sources and their reliability. For instance, it is accepted that Frederick Virkus's *Compendium of American Genealogy* is incorrect about 30 percent of the time. Computerized census indexes have an estimated 10 to 20 percent omission rate, and a 30 to 40 percent inaccuracy rate.
5. Differentiate between good research and good conclusions. Some genealogists may be competent in finding and exploring records, but cannot adequately analyze or interpret what they find.
6. Follow the "Occam's Razor" principle: If more than one explanation fits a situation, choose the simplest. Use the fewest assumptions needed to explain a circumstance.
7. Consider the chronology when examining records. Don't separate people and records from their proper time and place. Chronology can be used effectively to both support and refute hypotheses about genealogical relationships.
8. "The proof lies upon him who affirms, not upon him who denies." *Legal Maxim.* If you assert that a genealogical connection is accurate, *the burden of proof lies with you*; not upon the person who disputes it.
9. Be reasonable. *Think* about the records and the individuals who created them. Exercise good judgment. Use common sense.

Common Errors In The Analysis Of Records

1. Confusing or mistaking the identity of individuals or families.
2. Assuming relationships due to a common surname.

3. Not sufficiently considering name changes, boundary changes, geographic locations, etc.
4. Relying on printed or published compilations rather than original records.
5. Assuming records (particularly old ones) are contemporary with the event.
6. Misinterpreting terminology.
7. Reaching premature conclusions.
8. Not testing conclusions thoroughly.
9. Neglecting to check documentation and references.
10. Not considering the social/historical context.

Common Sources of Errors Found in Genealogical Records

1. Human mistakes in recording and copying.
2. Gaps in the time between the event and the recording of it.
3. Self-serving documents that require certain information. (Read the Wayty Parks Couse Woodworth example on page 225.)
4. Improper custody during their lifetime: Public records that fall into private hands; Bible records found at garage sales; records stored somewhere other than where they were created.
5. The recording of irrelevant information that does not fit the purpose of the document.
6. A recorder with no personal knowledge of the event.
7. An incompetent recorder.
8. The desire to protect or enhance the reputation of a family or individual.
9. Deceit and fraud (although this is not common).
10. Variations in spelling.
11. Destruction, damage, or changes to the original record.

Common Errors Found in Genealogical Evidence

Type of Evidence *(order approximate)*	Types of Errors *(see list above)*	Reliability
1. Personal knowledge/ eyewitness account	2, 3, 8	Excellent
2. Official records: vital, land, probate	1, 7, 8, 10, 11	Excellent
3. Testimony of evidence	1, 2, 3, 8	Excellent
4. Private records: church, business	1, 4, 7, 10, 11	Varies

5. Beneficiary records: pension, bounty land, insurance, etc.	1, 2, 3, 7, 8, 9, 11	Generally good
6. Personal diaries, journals, family Bibles, etc.	1, 2, 3, 4, 7, 8, 11	Excellent to poor
7. Newspaper accounts		
a. contemporary events	1, 6, 7, 11	Generally good
b. past or feature articles	1, 2, 3, 5, 6, 8, 11	Poor
8. Compiled family genealogies	1, 2, 3, 6, 7, 8, 9, 11	Very good to poor
9. General printed works: local history	1, 2, 6, 7, 8, 9, 10, 11	Good to fair
10. Oral family traditions	1, 2, 3, 6, 7, 8, 9	Poor
11. Folklore, legends, stories	All the above!	Poor

Do you now want to go back to the file cabinets or to the old files on your computer and begin again on some of those "lost" families? If so, my goal in writing this book was reached. Perhaps some genealogy will always be "lost," but how will you know which lines will remain forever blocked and which can be solved unless you apply some of the techniques just learned? Good luck with your research and remember, "No one's genealogy is ever finished."

ANALYSIS AND CORRELATION OF INFORMATION: BIBLIOGRAPHY

Bamman, Gale Williams. "The Origins of Robert and Elizabeth (Cochran) Black of Smith County, Tennessee: Using Names of Slaves to Trace White Ancestry." *The American Genealogist* 69 (October 1994): 219-223.

Devine, Donn. "Do We Really Decide Relationships by a Preponderance of the Evidence?" *National Genealogical Society Newsletter* 18 (September-October 1992): 131-133.

Jacobus, Donald Lines. "On the Nature of Genealogical Evidence." *The New England Historical and Genealogical Register* 92 (July 1938): 213-220.

———. "Confessions of a Genealogical Heretic: Society Regulations and Hearsay Evidence." *The New England Historical and Genealogical Register* 112 (April 1958): 81-87.

Johnson, Louise F. "Testing Popular Lore: Marmaduke Swearingen aka

Blue Jacket." *National Genealogical Society Quarterly* 82 (September 1994): 165-178.

Mills, Elizabeth Shown. "The Search for Margaret Ball." *National Genealogical Society Quarterly* 77 (March 1989): 43-65.

———. "In Search of Mr. Ball: An Exercise in Finding Fathers." *National Genealogical Society Quarterly* 80 (June 1992): 115-133.

Rising, Marsha Hoffman. "Problematic Parents and Potential Offspring: The Example of Nathan Brown." *National Genealogical Society Quarterly* 79 (June 1991): 85-99.

Rubincam, Milton. "Pitfalls in Genealogical Research." *National Genealogical Society Quarterly* 43 (June 1955): 41-45.

Sheppard, Walter Lee. "What Proves a Lineage? Acceptable Standards of Evidence." *National Genealogical Society Quarterly* 75 (June 1987): 125.

Stevenson, Noel C. *Genealogical Evidence: A Guide to the Standard of Proof Relating to Pedigrees, Ancestry, Heirship and Family History.* (Laguna Hills, Calif.: Aegean Park Press, 1979.)

Straney, Shirley Garton, CG. "The Kallikak Family: A Genealogical Examination of a Classic in Psychology." *The American Genealogist* 69 (April 1994): 65-80.

Stratton, Eugene A. "Analyzing Evidence." *Applied Genealogy.* (Salt Lake City: Ancestry, 1988.)

Thorndale, William. "The Parents of Colonel Richard Lee of Virginia." *National Genealogical Society Quarterly* 76 (December 1988): 253-267.

Index